GUIDE TO FOOD STORAGE

Follow this guide for food storage, and you can be sure that what's in your freezer, refrigerator, and pantry is fresh-tasting and ready to use in recipes.

in the freezer *(at -10° to 0° F)*

DAIRY

Cheese, hard	6 months
Cheese, soft	6 months
Egg substitute, unopened	1 year
Egg whites	1 year
Egg yolks	1 year
Ice cream, sherbet	1 month

FRUITS AND VEGETABLES

Commercially frozen fruits	1 year
Commercially frozen vegetables	8 to 12 months

MEATS, POULTRY, AND SEAFOOD

Beef, Lamb, Pork, and Veal

Chops, uncooked	4 to 6 months
Ground and stew meat, uncooked	3 to 4 months
Ham, fully cooked, half	1 to 2 months
Roasts, uncooked	4 to 12 months
Steaks, uncooked	6 to 12 months

Poultry

All cuts, cooked	4 months
Boneless or bone-in pieces, uncooked	9 months

Seafood

Fish, fatty, uncooked	2 to 3 months
Fish, lean, uncooked	6 months

in the refrigerator *(at 34° to 40° F)*

DAIRY

Butter	1 to 3 months
Buttermilk	1 to 2 weeks
Cheese, block, opened	3 to 4 weeks
Cheese, commercial grated Parmesan	1 year
Cream cheese, fat-free, light, and ⅓-less-fat	2 weeks
Egg substitute, opened	3 days
Fresh eggs in shell	3 to 5 weeks

MEATS, POULTRY, AND SEAFOOD

Beef, Lamb, Pork, and Veal

Ground and stew meat, uncooked	1 to 2 days
Roasts, uncooked	3 to 5 days
Steaks and chops, uncooked	3 to 5 days

Chicken, Turkey, and Seafood

All cuts, uncooked	1 to 2 days

FRUITS AND VEGETABLES

Apples, beets, cabbage, carrots, celery, citrus fruits, eggplant, and parsnips	2 to 3 weeks
Apricots, asparagus, berries, cauliflower, cucumbers, mushrooms, okra, peaches, pears, peas, peppers, plums, salad greens, and summer squash	2 to 4 days
Corn, husked	1 day

in the pantry *(keep these at room temperature for 6 to 12 months)*

BAKING AND COOKING STAPLES

Baking powder
Biscuit and baking mixes
Broth, canned
Cooking spray
Honey
Mayonnaise, fat-free, low-fat, and light (unopened)
Milk, canned evaporated fat-free
Milk, nonfat dry powder

Mustard, prepared (unopened)
Oils, olive and vegetable
Pasta, dried
Peanut butter
Rice, instant and regular
Salad dressings, bottled (unopened)
Seasoning sauces, bottled
Tuna, canned

FRUITS, LEGUMES, AND VEGETABLES

Fruits, canned
Legumes (beans, lentils, peas), dried or canned
Tomato products, canned
Vegetables, canned

WeightWatchers®
ANNUAL RECIPES *for* SUCCESS
2008

Oxmoor
House®

©2007 by Oxmoor House, Inc.

Book Division of Southern Progress Corporation

P.O. Box 2262, Birmingham, Alabama 35201-2262

ISBN-13: 978-0-8487-3154-0

ISBN-10: 0-8487-3154-9

ISSN: 1526-1565

Printed in the United States of America

First Printing 2007

Be sure to check with your health-care provider before making any changes in your diet.

Weight Watchers, **POINTS**, and the Core Plan are registered trademarks of *Weight Watchers* International, Inc., and are used under license by Healthy Living, Inc.

OXMOOR HOUSE, INC.

Editor in Chief: Nancy Fitzpatrick Wyatt

Executive Editor: Katherine M. Eakin

Art Director: Keith McPherson

Managing Editor: Allison Long Lowery

WEIGHT WATCHERS® ANNUAL RECIPES *for* SUCCESS 2008

Editor: Terri Laschober Robertson

Development Editor: Anne C. Cain, M.P.H., M.S., R.D.

Copy Editor: Diane Rose

Editorial Assistants: Rachel Quinlivan, R.D.; Vanessa Rusch Thomas

Photography Director: Jim Bathie

Senior Photo Stylist: Kay E. Clarke

Associate Photo Stylist: Katherine G. Eckert

Director, Test Kitchens: Elizabeth Tyler Austin

Assistant Director, Test Kitchens: Julie Christopher

Test Kitchens Professionals: Kathleen Royal Phillips; Catherine Crowell Steele; Ashley T. Strickland; Kate Wheeler, R.D.

Director of Production: Laura Lockhart

Production Manager: Theresa Beste-Farley

Production Assistant: Faye Porter Bonner

CONTRIBUTORS

Designer: Carol O. Loria

Indexer: Mary Ann Laurens

Copy Editor: Dolores Hydock

Menu Planner Editor: Carolyn Land Williams, M.Ed., R.D.

Recipe Development: Gretchen Feldtman Brown, R.D.; Katherine Cobbs; Jennifer Cofield; Georgia Downard; Caroline Grant, M.S., R.D.; Nancy Hughes; Ana Kelly; Alison Lewis; Debby Maugans; Jackie Mills, R.D.

Editorial Interns: Tracey Apperson, Cory L. Bordonaro, Amy Edgerton

Test Kitchens Intern: Carol Corbin

Test Kitchens Professional: Jane Chambliss

Photo Stylists: Ana Kelly, Debby Maugans

COVER: Frozen Banana Split Squares, *page 39*

To order additional publications, call 1-800-765-6400.

For more books to enrich your life, visit **oxmoorhouse.com**

contents

recipes

special-occasion menus

7-day menu planners

indexes

Cranberry-Glazed Salmon,
page 69

Double-Chocolate Bundt Cake,
page 45

Hunter's-Style Beef Pie,
page 90

Moroccan Butternut Soup, *page 157*

Weight Watchers® Annual Recipes *for* Success 2008

empowers you to make the right food choices every day. There's never been a better time to make a positive change for your health, and you can do it while still enjoying the foods you love.

Here's how:

- An introduction to the Weight Watchers Experience
- Nine truly inspiring weight-loss Success Stories from people just like you
- 300 great-tasting recipes that bring pleasure back to mealtime
- A **POINTS**® value for every recipe
- Core Plan® recipes marked with ☑
- Complete nutritional analysis with every recipe (see "About Our Recipes" on page 192 for more information)
- More than 40 color photographs of delicious recipes
- Step-by-step recipe instructions, how-to photography, prep and cook times, and Test Kitchen secrets
- Five Special-Occasion Menus with a game plan for preparing each meal to help you celebrate in style
- Four weeks of 7-Day Menu Planners that incorporate many recipes from the cookbook plus some new ones, too

our favorite recipes ▶▶

All of our recipes are rigorously tested to ensure ease of preparation, excellent taste, and good nutrition. But some are a cut above the rest. These recipes are so outstanding that they've each earned a place as one of our favorites. We hope you'll enjoy them just as much.

▲ Steak Crostini with Avocado-Horseradish Mayonnaise, **POINTS** value: 2 *(page 22)*. Party guests will love these crostini topped with tender steak and a gourmet mayonnaise.

◀ Ginger-Apple Salad, **POINTS** value: 2 *(page 112)*. Crystallized ginger adds a peppery-sweet note to this apple salad, which garnered high praise in our Test Kitchens.

◀ Pecan Pie Squares, **POINTS** value: 5 *(page 48)*. This bar-cookie version of classic pecan pie has a rich, buttery crust and a sweet nutty filling that will earn these squares a place on your holiday buffet.

◀ Grilled Rosemary Flatbreads, **POINTS** value: 3 *(page 32)*. Simply seasoned with olive oil and rosemary, these rustic grilled flatbreads received our Test Kitchens' highest rating.

▲ Thai Turkey Burgers with Mango Mayonnaise, **POINTS** value: 9 *(page 128)*. Our secret ingredient gives these sophisticated burgers an exotic kick. When served with the special sauce, they're sure to get rave reviews.

◀ Chile-Rubbed Pork Tenderloin with Quick Mole Sauce, **POINTS** value: 4 *(page 96)*. Our tender, juicy pork with a quick-and-easy mole sauce is a surefire winner.

◀ Fennel, Feta, and Kalamata Coleslaw, **POINTS** value: 1 *(page 113)*. This fennel slaw gets its amazing flavor not from mayonnaise but from feta cheese, olives, and white balsamic vinegar.

◀ Chilled Tomatillo-Avocado Soup with Tomato Salsa, ✓ **POINTS** value: 3 *(page 156)*. This summertime soup boasts a rich, bold flavor, a smooth texture, and a refreshing salsa garnish.

◀ Orange-Sesame Snow Peas, **POINTS** value: 1 *(page 148)*. This crunchy side dish gets a boost of flavor from citrus, smoky sesame seeds and oil, and a dash of red pepper.

◀ Pear-Date Upside-Down Cake, **POINTS** value: 5 *(page 45)*. A spice cake studded with chopped dates forms the base for syrup-coated pears in this old-fashioned skillet dessert.

◀ Greek Isle Chicken, ✓ **POINTS** value: 7 *(page 104)*. Seared chicken, fresh tomatoes, olives, and just a few other ingredients come together for a fabulous meal in just about half an hour.

◀ Crab Cakes over Mixed Greens with Lemon Dressing, **POINTS** value: 6 *(page 73)*. These tender crab cakes are mouthwatering when served on a bed of crisp greens and topped with a tangy dressing.

Weight Watchers has been a recognized leader in weight management for over 40 years, with a history of helping people successfully lose weight.

At Weight Watchers, weight management is a partnership that combines our knowledge with your efforts. We help you on your journey to make the positive changes required to lose weight. We guide you to make positive behavioral changes in your life, inspiring you with our belief in your power to succeed and motivating you every step of the way.

THE MEETINGS ARE THE MAGIC

Weight Watchers provides information, knowledge, tools, and motivation to help you make the decisions about nutrition and exercise that are right for you. We help you make healthy eating decisions, and we encourage you to enjoy yourself by becoming more active. To provide motivation, mutual support, encouragement, and instruction from our Leaders, Weight Watchers organizes group meetings around the world. Meeting Leaders, who were all once meeting members, share their inspiring stories of personal success with others.

The weekly meeting has continued to be at the core of the Weight Watchers program throughout its 40-year history. In fact, research shows that people who attend Weight Watchers meetings lose three times more weight than those who go it alone.[1] The meetings promote weight loss through education and group support in conjunction with a flexible, healthy diet that does not require the purchase of specific foods.

Each week, approximately 1.5 million members attend approximately 50,000 Weight Watchers meetings around the world, which are run by more than 15,000 leaders.

[1]Heshka S et al. Weight loss with self-help compared with a structured commercial program: a randomized trial. JAMA 289(14):1792, 2003.

THE WEIGHT WATCHERS PHILOSOPHY

Weight Watchers provides for healthy weight loss. Weight loss of up to two pounds per week is encouraged through food choices that lower daily calories and through physical activities that burn calories. Food choices meet scientific recommendations for satisfying nutrition needs and for lessening the risk of developing long-term diseases. Activities include a broad range of options that boost both weight loss and overall health. Weight Watchers recognizes that these same strategies are vital for keeping weight off.

> Weight Watchers is realistic, practical, livable, and flexible.

Weight Watchers is realistic, practical, livable, and flexible. Weight Watchers encourages members to set realistic weight-loss goals. An initial loss of 10% of body weight—for example, a 200-pound person losing 20 pounds—is a smart milestone that has important health benefits. A practical, livable, and flexible approach is easier to follow because it can fit easily into different lifestyles.

Our Leaders help set a member's weight goal within a healthy range based on body mass index. When members reach their weight goal and maintain it for six weeks, they achieve Lifetime Member status. This gives them the privilege to attend our meetings free of charge as long as they maintain their weight within a certain range.

Weight Watchers believes in imparting knowledge in a way that enables members to learn the what, how, and why of weight loss. Smart choices are easier to make when a person understands the principles of weight loss.

FLEXIBLE FOOD PLANS

The Weight Watchers approach recognizes that each person has unique preferences for particular foods that are satisfying to eat and that fit into their own weight-management routine and busy lifestyle. Some people prefer tracking and controlling what they eat. Others prefer focusing on a group of wholesome foods without counting or tracking. **Weight Watchers Turnaround**® offers both types of food plans and allows you to switch back and forth between plans for maximum flexibility and lasting weight loss.

THE FLEX PLAN is based on the Weight Watchers *POINTS*® Weight-Loss System.

■ Every food has a *POINTS* value that is based on calories, fat grams, fiber grams, and portion size.

■ Members who use the Flex Plan keep track of *POINTS* values and maintain their daily *POINTS* values within a set range called the *POINTS* Target.

■ You can enjoy a full range of food options at home, on the go, or when dining out.

THE CORE PLAN® offers foods from a list of wholesome, nutritious foods from all food groups—fruits and vegetables; grains and starches; lean meats, fish, and poultry; eggs; and dairy products.

■ No measuring or counting is required, as Core Foods provide eating satisfaction and fullness without empty calories.

■ For the occasional treat, you can also eat foods outside of this list in a controlled amount.

Weight Watchers backs up its weight-management plans with a strong commitment to the science of weight loss. The research and conclusions of experts and health organizations worldwide, including the World Health Organization and the National Institutes of Health, are incorporated into the Weight Watchers offerings. Weight Watchers also conducts its own research on weight-loss methods. As scientific findings change, the Weight Watchers plans evolve.

The Weight Watchers food plans empower you to make food choices in a way that suits your preferences and lifestyle.

TESTIMONY TO SUCCESS

At Weight Watchers, we celebrate the success and triumphs of all of our members in their weight-loss journeys because they are a testament to the effectiveness of our weight-loss plans. When our customers successfully lose weight, people notice. Family members, friends, colleagues, and acquaintances inquire about how they achieved such amazing results. The pages that follow will take you through a sample of those success stories.

For more information about the Weight Watchers program and a meeting nearest you, call 1-800-651-6000 or visit online at **www.weightwatchers.com**

"Now I don't stand in the back for every family photo. I'm proud to step up beside my kids and husband!"

I started to gradually gain weight after I got married about 15 years ago. I hit my heaviest when I became pregnant with our daughter, who is now 10. For the next nine years, my life was all about having children and taking care of them as babies and toddlers. Through those "overweight" years of my life, I constantly made excuses for why I didn't get my weight under control.

A FATEFUL TRIP In the summer of 2005, we took a family trip to Europe. When I came home and looked at the vacation photos, I was shocked. I had convinced myself that even though I needed to "lose a few pounds" I still looked good. When I could barely recognize my own image, I knew I had to stop making excuses and stop settling for less than I could be.

FINDING THE TIME I'm a very busy mom, and I also work full time. I honestly didn't believe I had time to attend meetings, so I subscribed to Weight Watchers Online.

stop making excuses

You *can* do it! I am very busy with a full-time job, two active children, an active church life, and a wonderful marriage. If I can find the time for myself, anyone can!

christine

Age **38**   Height **5'7"**

Was **181 lbs**   Lost **50 lbs***

Weight **131 lbs**

As of **1/8/2007**

*Results Not Typical

THE HARDEST PARTS The most difficult challenge was learning portion control. I always felt that I was eating pretty healthfully, which I generally was, but I was also eating way too much.

As soon as I started tracking **POINTS**® values, I saw immediate results: I lost one to two pounds per week and started on my path to improve the way I looked.*

BRING IN THE NEW My overall theme is "My time is now!" because I always said that "someday" I would lose weight. I had to realize that my life *now* is important, and I had to make weight loss a priority in my life. Now I don't stand in the back for every family photo. I'm proud to step up beside my kids and husband!

"I feel sexier and more fit today at 49 years young than I did at 25 years old."

On the day that Donna's doctor recommended gastric bypass surgery, she made a decision that changed her life.

A LIFELONG STRUGGLE   It seems I have always struggled with my weight. In fact, at my nine-month-old checkup, my doctor told my mother that I was "an overweight baby"! By the time I was 45, I weighed over 300 pounds. My doctor, with true concern, recommended gastric bypass surgery.

I was totally humiliated, hopeless, and in excruciating pain. I knew that gastric bypass was not for me. Two friends of mine had gone that route and died from complications. I felt that I needed to get to the root of my problems with food, change my behavior, and conquer the issue once and for all.

AT WORK   A Weight Watchers At Work meeting had been thriving in my office for some time. After my doctor's visit, I decided it was time to join the Weight Watchers meetings and start following the **POINTS**® Weight-Loss System. During the first few weeks, I was so overwhelmed that I didn't allow the staff to weigh me. I was not prepared to look at the numbers. After a few weeks of following the program, I gained the confidence and courage I needed to confront my true weight.

IN THE GYM   One of the greatest struggles was getting into the gym. When you are big, people stare and judge you in a gym setting. That makes it difficult to be there, stay there, or get anything done.

I hired a personal trainer once a week to teach me how to move my body. Today, I believe completely in the power of movement.

Weight Watchers has changed my life forever. I feel that those of us who lose large amounts of weight without surgery prove that it can be done. We prove that a healthy lifestyle is possible no matter what the "statistics" may indicate. I feel sexier and more fit today at 49 years young than I did at 25 years old.

donna

Age **49**   Height **5'8"**
Was **334 lbs**   Lost **161 lbs***
Weight **173 lbs**
As of **2/22/2007**

*Results Not Typical

it can be done!

I believe that to change your life, you must combine fitness and nutrition. Find a way to bring both components together into your life in a manner that's realistic and sustainable.

"I've run a marathon, skydived, and done two triathlons. I call myself a converted couch potato!"

Tory used to only dream of a life filled with action, adventure, and self-confidence. Today, she's lost over 100 pounds* and is doing more than she ever imagined.

CONFESSIONS OF A CONVERTED COUCH POTATO   Several years ago, I was looking through scrapbooks at a relative's home. I noticed that she had digitally altered all the pictures of me to either make me look thinner or to place something in front of me. Incredibly hurt, I e-mailed her to say that I expected my family to accept me as I was because I was a fat woman and always would be—after all, I had worked hard to love myself at 222 pounds! It was only later that I thought, "If I love myself, why am I abusing my body with overeating and lack of exercise?" I also had a nagging feeling that my weight was keeping me from doing all kinds of things. That was my year of self-discovery, and it culminated with my subscribing to Weight Watchers Online to change my lifestyle.

FORGETTING ABOUT "AMNESIA EATING"   I used to tell my kids I was an amnesia eater. I didn't binge or stress eat; I just ate because the food was there. Three minutes after having a brownie, I'd forget and take another! Following the **POINTS**® Weight-Loss System and keeping track of everything I ate—a healthier diet—helped keep me in check. I also started exercising. I'm an adventurer at heart, and I used to wish I could do the simplest things, like bike through Seattle. Today, I've run a marathon, skydived, and done two triathlons. I call myself a converted couch potato!

SURPRISE—I'M SKINNY!   One of the best parts of this journey was surprising my family, whom I hadn't told about my weight loss, when I visited for the holidays. At the airport, I watched in amusement as my brother walked past me four times! My mom didn't recognize me either; she nearly started to cry when she realized who it was!

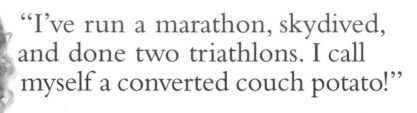

tory

Age **37**   Height **5'3"**

Was **222 lbs**   Lost **101.4 lbs***

Weight **120.6 lbs**

As of **3/14/2007**

*Results Not Typical

✿staying on track

• Eat lots of little meals to keep from getting ravenous and out of control.

• Keep a drawer filled with snacks low in **POINTS** values—like granola bars and raisins—to grab without worrying about straying from the plan.

• Make your own chips by sprinkling chili powder on corn-tortilla wedges and baking them.

"The Flex Plan has been a good structured way for me to change my habits."

I knew I had to change my lifestyle when I realized I had become a foodaholic. I hid food around my house, and if I had something in my mouth when my husband walked into the room, I'd pretend I wasn't eating. I would also reward myself with food for doing mundane things. After a load of laundry, for example, I would give myself a treat.

sharon

Age **49**   Height **5'2"**

Was **196.4 lbs**   Lost **78.1 lbs***

Weight **118.3 lbs**

As of **3/9/2007**

GAME OVER?   My husband and I are avid players of an online game, and we joined a guild with other enthusiasts. My husband was going to send in a picture of us from about 30 years ago, when I was slimmer. That's when I realized he was embarrassed by how we looked. I had become humongous; I was a size 24! I looked at him and said, "I've got to quit." He said, "Just log off the game." And I said, "No, I have to stop eating the way I'm eating."

*Results Not Typical

DOCTOR KNOWS BEST   I went to the doctor looking for a magic weight-loss pill. I saw the "w" form on his lips, and I knew he was going to say, "Weight Watchers." I stopped him and told him I couldn't go to meetings. Then he told me about Weight Watchers Online. I registered that day.

SHARON LEARNED...
• Eating right does get easier. For the first six months, it was hard work, and I had to be careful about when and what I was eating, but now, eating right is a daily routine that I don't have to think about.
• My husband used to look at me more like his mother because I took care of him and fed him. Now when he comes home, I get a hug and a kiss and we spend time together. It's nice to have the marriage back.

turned on to weight loss

• Fruits and vegetables can be better than sweets. If I really need something, I eat a handful of cherry tomatoes because they're like candy.

• Snacks are not off-limits. I plan my **POINTS**® values for breakfast and lunch so that I usually have 2 to 4 **POINTS** values left for afternoon snacks.

11

"Knowing that I have complete control over my body and my health is the best feeling of all."

When Lauren joined Weight Watchers, she thought she might lose a little weight. Little did she know that by dropping pounds she'd gain "physical strength, confidence, energy, and knowledge about being healthy."

lauren

Age **38**   Height **5'8"**

Was **164.6 lbs**   Lost **30.2 lbs***

Weight **134.4 lbs**

As of **2/16/2007**

*Results Not Typical

NO MORE EXCUSES   I never worried about my weight growing up—I ate as much as I wanted and never packed on a pound. But when I was pregnant with my second child, I gained around 40 pounds and had a lot of trouble slimming down. When my daughter went off to kindergarten, I knew I could no longer use her birth as an excuse for not shedding those last 20 pounds.

FOR A FRIEND   One summer afternoon at the beach (with me in my large cover-up, as usual), my friend Jill mentioned that she was going to join Weight Watchers meetings in the fall. I couldn't let her down when she asked me to join the meetings with her. I figured I might lose 10 pounds and that would be awesome.

As soon as I started following the **POINTS**® Weight-Loss System, I began to lose weight. Soon, I was getting compliments from everyone I knew, and shopping for clothes became a big treat—every month I was a new size. By the time I hit my goal, I had gone from a size 12 to a size 4!*

BUILDING STRENGTH   Before joining Weight Watchers, I had no fitness routine, but something clicked once I started losing weight. I joined a women-only gym with a circuit training program and started going three days a week. I met tons of women who were doing Weight Watchers, and we had plenty to talk about, so workouts seemed to go fast. I gradually became strong enough to do real military-style push-ups (something I couldn't even do in my 20s!). I began to feel more athletic, and I've come to love Spinning class. I even ran my husband's Corporate Challenge 5K last summer!

♣lauren lightens up

• When you start the plan, do a large grocery-shopping trip immediately and buy lots of fresh fruits and veggies plus some desserts that are low in **POINTS** values for a treat.

• After 9 p.m., I watch TV in the bedroom instead of the family room so I'm not as tempted to walk over to the fridge and search for something to eat while sitting on the couch.

I'M IN CHARGE   I feel a tremendous sense of confidence these days. I changed my hairstyle and got a brand new wardrobe—I look years younger! Knowing that I have complete control over my body and my health is the best feeling of all.

valerie

Age **30**   Height **5'6"**

Was **219.4 lbs**   Lost **77 lbs***

Weight **142.4 lbs**

As of **7/7/2007**

*Results Not Typical

"For the first time, the person staring back in the mirror and the person I envision in my head are one and the same."

Even a cross-country move in the midst of her weight loss couldn't deter this motivated meetings member. Valerie picked up her plan and took it right along with her. Seventy-seven pounds lighter* and holding, Valerie shares her discoveries.

"ABOVE NORMAL"   I've been overweight my entire life. Every year, I went to the doctor for my physical and was told I was "above normal." Unlike in school, where being "above normal" was a good thing, that quality applied to weight was not. My classmates' teasing reminded me of that fact every day.

I grew up in a household where we had to be members of the "clean-plate club." Bad habits started young and grew into worse. Dorm food and the belief that fast food was "real food" packed on more pounds.

FACING THE TRUTH   I tried fad diet after fad diet. I could survive for about two weeks before deprivation set in and I fell off the wagon. The pounds came back and then some.

I became a sports physical therapist and athletic trainer but got the feeling my clients weren't listening to me. They had a 219-pound trainer telling them to exercise and get in shape. Ironic. When my 15 extra pounds became 70, I didn't even recognize myself anymore. That was the day I decided to join Weight Watchers.

THE BIG MOVE   Just shy of four months on the plan, I had to move across the country. The amazing thing about Weight Watchers is that I was able to find a new meeting with a great Leader and an inspiring group. I felt at home immediately. I'm so glad I didn't give up.

MAKING NEW FRIENDS   For the first time in my life, I feel that the person staring back in the mirror and the person I envision in my head are one and the same. Often I tell people that I am actually a shy person at heart. They just laugh at me. I guess I really have changed!

a move to confidence

• Don't be embarrassed about your weight-loss journey. You're taking care of yourself.

• Don't do it alone. If you aren't joining with somebody, make a friend at the meeting or tell a coworker; just find somebody to help you.

13

"Spend time now—save time later. I divide my dry food into portion sizes and put them into resealable bags right after I get home from the grocery store."

Before signing up for Weight Watchers Online, Taysha would hover in the background at parties, watching other people having fun. Now that she's 72 pounds* lighter than she used to be, she's the first one to hit the dance floor.

DANCE—A LOT My fat wardrobe was depressing—big shirts and loose-fitting jeans. Now I live in tight jeans, skirts, and tank tops. When my girlfriends and I go out, I'm no longer alone in the corner feeling self-conscious. My confidence shows. I get asked to dance—a lot!

taysha

Age **24**   Height **5'5"**

Was **223 lbs**   Lost **72 lbs***

Weight **151 lbs**

As of **3/18/2007**

*Results Not Typical

SHE LOST IT ONLINE All my life I was big. You name the fad diet—I tried it. I decided to sign up for Weight Watchers Online and start following the **POINTS**® Weight-Loss System after a doctor told me that I was actually obese. The remark hurt my feelings, but it was the catalyst I needed to get serious about getting healthy.

I'm a computer nerd, so doing the plan online suited my personality. I boot up both at home and at work, so I have access to WeightWatchers.com 24-7. Despite the hours and hours I've spent on the site, I still haven't hit *half* the wealth of information that's available. There are great articles about exercise, body-fat percentage, and innovative ways to work out.

I adore the **POINTS** Tracker. It helps me figure out my daily food and activity **POINTS** values. For a smorgasbord of food choices, I check out the Recipe Builder. And the Community section is a great place to bounce ideas off other dieters. I get fabulous tips on things like spreading low-fat sour cream on a baked potato instead of butter.

PRAISE AND FEEDBACK It's important to have feedback. Whenever I achieved a mini-goal, my computer screen would flash, "Congrats, you've lost 5 lbs." I'd feel proud and do something to pamper myself, such as getting a manicure. I had both my computer buddies and those in real life egging me on. But my biggest motivator was myself. Without the help of my own willpower and ability to turn on a computer, I wouldn't have made it through!

❁staying positive

• Weigh yourself just once a week. If you constantly step on the scale, you'll be discouraged by fluctuations that may be only water weight.

• Be positive. Say "*when*" not "*if* I lose 5 pounds."

"I made small goals like trying to get all my fruits and veggies in on any particular day."

As Stacey's husband left for a year's deployment in Iraq, she decided it was time to fight her own battle—with weight—for the last time.

STACEY'S INVESTING IN HER HEALTH   Weight had been a never-ending battle in my life. I spent years yo-yo dieting. I would deprive myself and starve the weight off and inevitably gain it all back, plus "interest." As I neared my 40th birthday, I discovered that my cholesterol was 250, and my doctor was threatening to put me on medication.

Around that time, I also learned that my husband was being deployed to Iraq for a year. Everything seemed to be coming at me at once. As I looked at my life, I felt a sense of sadness. Due to the weight gain, I was not able to do many of the things I wanted to do or keep up with my four children. My health was in jeopardy, and I felt that my husband deserved more.

ATTITUDE ADJUSTMENT   It was time for a change. As I looked at the year ahead, I felt that it would be a good time to concentrate on myself. One day, I was checking the weather online and saw an ad for Weight Watchers Online.

ACCEPTING HELP   Once I opened my mind, the unending resources I found through Weight Watchers Online helped me change my life. I began realizing that this was not a race.

RODEO MAMA   When I started following the plan, I was so heavy that I couldn't run. I knew I wanted to incorporate some activity into my life again, so I started walking. Little by little, I worked my way back to being able to run again. As the weight came off, I realized that my active dreams were bigger than I first thought. I always wanted to take

stacey

Age **39**   Height **5'2"**

Was **165 lbs**   Lost **44 lbs***

Weight **121 lbs**

As of **3/12/2007**

*Results Not Typical

up horseback riding. I started lessons immediately and recently rode in my first rodeo!

Now I feel beautiful for the first time in my life. My husband thinks I am more attractive than ever—after four kids and 19 years of marriage.

invest in your health

• Eat as many **POINTS**® values as you can while still losing, rather than trying to eat as little as possible without starving. Eating more allows you greater flexibility, which makes this easier to do over the long haul.

• Realize that the plan doesn't require perfection; it takes persistence.

"When you're in front of an audience night after night, you're asking a lot of yourself physically. You need energy, and you need to be healthy."

It's no fun moving around and feeling that spare tire, especially when your job requires nimbleness. New York actor Bryan chose to unload it by signing up for Weight Watchers Online.

bryan

Age **39**   Height **5'8"**

Was **188.5 lbs**   Lost **29.5 lbs***

Weight **159 lbs**

As of **7/2/2007**

*Results Not Typical

"THE MADNESS MUST STOP" When my wife and I first started dating, we were going out pretty much every night. We never stopped to think about how much we were eating because we were having so much fun, but it all caught up with me. "The madness must stop," I said.

I was in the process of pursuing my dream of professional acting. I knew that I had to lose weight because I needed to redo my headshots, and I wanted to make sure that I looked good. Plus, having just gotten engaged, I wanted to make sure I fit into my tux.

My fiancée was doing Weight Watchers Online, so I knew how easy it was. I figured, why not give it a try?

KEEPING THE FOOD It takes determination to get to a healthy weight and be happy. I love to eat, and I won't stop eating the things that I love. Following the **POINTS®** Weight-Loss System, I don't feel like I'm on a diet that tells me that I can't have this and I can't have that. I can have whatever I want as long as I make sure it's within my **POINTS** balance.

The funniest thing is that I'm still eating all of the same foods I was before—just not as much.

WEIGHT-LOSS TAG TEAM Since I'm following the plan along with my wife, I feel like we're our own support system. Naturally, we're completely open about how much weight we lose each week. Doing it that way, we sort of keep each other in check.

STAYING ON THE PLAN I like the way I look. I look in the mirror now, and I see a healthier person. I feel happier. Feeling healthy is one thing, but feeling happy is another, and I definitely feel happy.

staying healthy *and happy*

• You don't have to give up the foods you love. I'm still eating all of the same foods I was before—just not as much.

• Following the plan with my wife gives us our own support system to help keep each other in check.

appetizers & beverages

SWEET AND SPICY SNACK MIX

POINTS value: 2

prep: 7 minutes • cook: 17 minutes

This mix cures your sweet and salty craving in one bite. We tested with a 10-ounce package of low-fat microwave popcorn and used about half the bag in this recipe.

5   cups popped low-fat
    microwave popcorn
2   cups multigrain cereal squares
    (such as Cascadian Farms)
2   cups multigrain toasted oat
    cereal (such as Cheerios)
1   cup butter-flavored pretzels
    (such as Snyder's of Hanover
    Butter Snaps)
½   cup raisins
2   tablespoons unsalted butter,
    melted
2   tablespoons honey
1   tablespoon chili powder
Dash of ground red pepper
    (optional)

1. Preheat oven to 350°.
2. Combine first 5 ingredients in a large bowl. Combine melted butter, honey, chili powder, and, if desired, ground red pepper, stirring well. Pour butter mixture over popcorn mixture, and stir to combine.
3. Spread mixture on a baking sheet lined with foil. Bake at 350° for 15 minutes. Cool and store in an airtight container. YIELD: 11 servings (serving size: 1 cup).

Per serving: CAL 120 (20% from fat); FAT 2.7g (sat 1.4g); PRO 2g; CARB 24.1g; FIB 1.7g; CHOL 5mg; IRON 4.8mg; SOD 200mg; CALC 22mg

☑ HERB-ROASTED CHICKPEAS

POINTS value: 2

prep: 6 minutes • cook: 50 minutes

Keep these crunchy chickpeas on hand for munching or to add crunch to salads. They're a lower-fat alternative to packaged nuts and seeds (see our "Crunchy Comparison" below).

2   (19-ounce) cans chickpeas
    (garbanzo beans), rinsed and
    drained
2   teaspoons olive oil
2   teaspoons dried oregano
1   teaspoon garlic powder
¼   teaspoon salt
¼   teaspoon black pepper

1. Preheat oven to 400°.
2. Pat chickpeas dry with paper towels. Combine chickpeas, olive oil, and remaining ingredients in a medium bowl; toss well.
3. Arrange chickpeas in a single layer on a jelly-roll pan. Bake at 400° for 50 minutes, stirring twice. Cool completely. Store in an airtight container. YIELD: 8 servings (serving size: ¼ cup).

Per serving: CAL 112 (17% from fat); FAT 2.1g (sat 0.3g); PRO 4.2g; CARB 19.4g; FIB 3.9g; CHOL 0mg; IRON 1.3mg; SOD 223mg; CALC 33mg

☑ ROASTED CAJUN-SPICED EDAMAME

POINTS value: 2

prep: 3 minutes
cook: 1 hour and 45 minutes

These roasted soybeans have 20 percent less fat than packaged flavored soy nuts. For a reduced-sodium version, use salt-free Cajun seasoning.

1   (16-ounce) package frozen
    shelled edamame, thawed
Olive oil–flavored cooking spray
1   tablespoon Cajun seasoning
1   teaspoon onion powder
¼   teaspoon kosher salt

1. Preheat oven to 300°.
2. Arrange edamame in a single layer on a baking sheet; lightly coat with cooking spray.
3. Combine Cajun seasoning, onion powder, and salt; sprinkle over edamame, and toss to coat. Bake at 300° for 1 hour and 45 minutes, stirring every 30 minutes. Cool completely. Store in an airtight container. YIELD: 6 servings (serving size: ¼ cup).

Per serving: CAL 103 (28% from fat); FAT 3.2g (sat 0g); PRO 8.1g; CARB 9.4g; FIB 4.1g; CHOL 0mg; IRON 1.6mg; SOD 379mg; CALC 52mg

crunchy comparison

per ¼ cup	fat	fiber	POINTS value
Herb-Roasted Chickpeas	2.1g	3.9g	2
Peanuts, salted	18.3g	2.9g	5
Roasted Cajun-Spiced Edamame	3.2g	4.1g	2
Roasted soy nuts, salted	4.0g	5.0g	2
Roasted pumpkin seeds, salted	16.0g	5.0g	5
Sunflower seed kernels, salted	17.3g	3.5g	5

ROASTED RED PEPPER DIP

POINTS value: 0

prep: 10 minutes • other: 5 minutes

*The combination of sun-dried tomatoes and roasted red bell peppers creates a wonderfully rich, savory flavor. Serve this dip with breadsticks or fresh raw veggies. One serving of this dip has a **POINTS** value of 0; ¼ cup has a **POINTS** value of 1.*

1   ounce sun-dried tomatoes packed without oil (about 8 tomatoes)
¾   cup boiling water
1   (12-ounce) jar roasted red bell peppers, drained and chopped
½   cup (4 ounces) ⅓-less-fat cream cheese, softened
½   cup light sour cream
2   tablespoons chopped fresh parsley
1   tablespoon lemon juice
¼   teaspoon salt
¼   teaspoon black pepper
2   teaspoons bottled minced garlic

1. Combine sun-dried tomatoes and boiling water in a small bowl; let stand 5 minutes. Drain.
2. Combine tomatoes, chopped red bell peppers, and remaining ingredients in a food processor. Process 15 seconds; scrape sides of bowl once. Process an additional 20 seconds or until smooth. Transfer to a bowl; cover and chill. YIELD: 2½ cups (serving size: 1 tablespoon).

Per serving: CAL 15 (54% from fat); FAT 0.9g (sat 0.6g); PRO 0.5g; CARB 1.3g; FIB 0.1g; CHOL 3mg; IRON 0.1mg; SOD 69mg; CALC 3mg

LAYERED BEAN DIP

POINTS value: 1

prep: 7 minutes

We used refrigerated fresh salsa (found in the deli department or produce section of the supermarket) because it has less than half the sodium of bottled salsa. However, if you can't find a container of fresh, the bottled version will work in the recipe. Serve with light tortilla chips.

1   (16-ounce) can fat-free spicy refried beans
¼   cup fat-free sour cream
1   (8-ounce) container refrigerated guacamole
1   cup refrigerated fresh salsa
1   cup (4 ounces) preshredded reduced-fat 4-cheese Mexican blend cheese
½   cup diced tomato
2   tablespoons chopped green onions

1. Combine beans and sour cream in a small bowl, stirring until blended. Spread mixture into bottom of a shallow 1-quart serving dish. Spread guacamole over bean mixture. Top with salsa; sprinkle with cheese, tomato, and green onions. Cover and chill. YIELD: 4 cups (serving size: ¼ cup).

Per serving: CAL 81 (44% from fat); FAT 4g (sat 1g); PRO 4.2g; CARB 7.1g; FIB 3g; CHOL 3mg; IRON 1.1mg; SOD 215mg; CALC 59mg

delightful dippers

- Assorted fresh veggie slices, ½ cup, **POINTS** value: 0
- Light tortilla chips, 1 ounce (8 to 12 chips), **POINTS** value: 3
- Whole wheat pita, 1 (6-inch) round, **POINTS** value: 2
- French bread slices, 1 ounce, **POINTS** value: 1
- Melba toast rounds, 5, **POINTS** value: 1
- 7-grain crackers, 15, **POINTS** value: 2
- Baked whole wheat crackers, 4, **POINTS** value: 1

CHICKEN DIP WITH TARRAGON

POINTS value: 1

prep: 4 minutes

Serve this with whole-grain crackers, pita wedges, or fresh veggies, or use it as a sandwich spread.

½   cup (4 ounces) ⅓-less-fat cream cheese
1   (4.5-ounce) can chunk chicken breast in water, drained and pressed dry
½   teaspoon dried tarragon
⅛   teaspoon salt
⅛   teaspoon freshly ground black pepper

1. Combine all ingredients in a medium bowl; stir until well blended. YIELD: ¾ cup (serving size: 1 tablespoon).

Per serving: CAL 41 (64% from fat); FAT 2.9g (sat 1.6g); PRO 3.4g; CARB 0.4g; FIB 0g; CHOL 13mg; IRON 0.2mg; SOD 120mg; CALC 9mg

HOT CRABMEAT DIP

POINTS value: 1

prep: 4 minutes • cook: 5 minutes

Fresh crabmeat makes this an extra-special dip that's great for entertaining. Fresh crabmeat usually comes in a 1-pound container, but you can keep the remaining crabmeat in the refrigerator 2 to 3 days. Serve the dip with whole-grain crackers or Melba toast.

1   (8-ounce) package ⅓-less-fat
    cream cheese
2   tablespoons light mayonnaise
1   tablespoon fresh lemon juice
¼   teaspoon garlic powder
¼   teaspoon freshly ground black
    pepper
⅛   teaspoon salt
8   ounces lump crabmeat
2   tablespoons chopped fresh
    chives
2   teaspoons chopped fresh
    parsley

1. Combine first 6 ingredients in a medium saucepan; cook over medium heat, stirring constantly, until cheese melts.
2. Stir in crabmeat, chives, and parsley; cook over medium heat, stirring constantly, until thoroughly heated. YIELD: 2 cups (serving size: 1 tablespoon).

Per serving: CAL 27 (63% from fat); FAT 1.9g (sat 1.1g); PRO 2.1g; CARB 0.4g; FIB 0g; CHOL 11mg; IRON 0mg; SOD 69mg; CALC 12mg

EDAMAME HUMMUS

POINTS value: 1

prep: 7 minutes • cook: 8 minutes

Instead of chickpeas, this hummus features edamame (green soybeans). Serve with pita wedges or fresh vegetables.

1½ cups frozen shelled edamame
    (green soybeans)
3   garlic cloves, peeled
1   tablespoon olive oil
½   teaspoon ground cumin
¼   teaspoon kosher salt
¼   teaspoon freshly ground black
    pepper
½   cup chopped fresh cilantro
¼   cup fresh lemon juice
3   tablespoons tahini (sesame-seed
    paste)
2   tablespoons water

1. Cook edamame in boiling water 5 to 7 minutes or until tender. Drain.
2. Place garlic and next 4 ingredients in a food processor, and pulse 3 times or until chopped. Add edamame, cilantro, and remaining ingredients; process until smooth. YIELD: 1½ cups (serving size: 1 tablespoon).

Per serving: CAL 30 (63% from fat); FAT 2.1g (sat 0.2g); PRO 1.4g; CARB 1.8g; FIB 0.7g; CHOL 0mg; IRON 0.3mg; SOD 24mg; CALC 10mg

edamame

Edamame (soybeans that are harvested before maturity) contribute health benefits as well as fresh green color to **Edamame Hummus.** Soybeans are a source of complete protein and fiber; they contain no cholesterol and are a good source of monounsaturated and polyunsaturated fats (heart-healthy fats).

☑ WHITE BEAN SPREAD WITH SAGE AND LEMON

POINTS value: 0

prep: 5 minutes

*This spread is similar to hummus, but the predominant flavor is sage instead of garlic. Serve with pita wedges or French bread. A 2-tablespoon serving of the spread has a **POINTS** value of 1.*

1   (15.5-ounce) can Great Northern
    beans, rinsed and drained
1   tablespoon extravirgin olive oil
1   tablespoon water
1   tablespoon fresh lemon juice
¾   teaspoon dried rubbed sage
¼   teaspoon kosher salt
⅛   teaspoon freshly ground black
    pepper

1. Combine all ingredients in a food processor; process until smooth. Serve immediately, or cover and chill until ready to serve. YIELD: 1¼ cups (serving size: 1 tablespoon).

Per serving: CAL 18 (40% from fat); FAT 0.8g (sat 0.1g); PRO 0.7g; CARB 2g; FIB 0.8g; CHOL 0mg; IRON 0.2mg; SOD 65mg; CALC 5mg

ROASTED EGGPLANT SPREAD

POINTS value: 0

prep: 4 minutes • cook: 20 minutes
other: 20 minutes

Fresh vegetables or low-fat pita chips are great with this flavorful spread. Make this the day before your party, and bring it to room temperature before serving. You can enjoy up to ¼ cup of the spread without having to count a POINTS value.

1   (1-pound) eggplant, peeled and cut into ½-inch-thick slices
Olive oil–flavored cooking spray
½   teaspoon kosher salt, divided
½   cup plain low-fat yogurt
1   garlic clove, crushed
1   tablespoon tahini (sesame-seed paste)
2   teaspoons lemon juice
½   teaspoon hot sauce

1. Preheat oven to 400°.
2. Place eggplant slices on a baking sheet coated with cooking spray. Coat both sides of eggplant with cooking spray, and sprinkle evenly with ¼ teaspoon salt. Bake at 400° for 20 minutes or until browned, turning once. Place cooked slices on a cutting board, and let stand until cool.
3. Finely dice eggplant, and place in a medium bowl. Stir in remaining ¼ teaspoon salt, yogurt, and remaining ingredients. Serve immediately, or cover and chill until ready to serve. Bring to room temperature before serving. YIELD: 2 cups (serving size: 1 tablespoon).

Per serving: CAL 8 (45% from fat); FAT 0.4g (sat 0.1g); PRO 0.4g; CARB 1.1g; FIB 0.4g; CHOL 0mg; IRON 0.1mg; SOD 33mg; CALC 9mg

TOMATO-BASIL BRUSCHETTA

POINTS value: 1

prep: 7 minutes • cook: 5 minutes

Bruschetta is an appetizer of toasted bread that is usually topped with some type of cheese, vegetable, or herb. Here, fresh basil leaves add beauty and an extra punch of flavor.

18   (¼-inch-thick) slices diagonally cut whole-grain French baguette
Cooking spray
⅓   cup light mayonnaise
⅓   cup tub-style light cream cheese
1   tablespoon chopped fresh basil
18   (¼-inch-thick) diagonal slices plum tomato (about 5 large plum tomatoes)
¼   teaspoon freshly ground black pepper
18   basil leaves

1. Preheat oven to 400°.
2. Place baguette slices on a baking sheet; coat slices with cooking spray. Bake at 400° for 5 minutes or until bread is toasted; set aside.
3. Combine mayonnaise, cream cheese, and basil in a small bowl, and stir well.
4. Spread 1 teaspoon cheese mixture on each bread slice; top with tomato slices, and sprinkle with pepper. Top each tomato slice with a basil leaf. YIELD: 18 servings (serving size: 1 bruschetta).

Per serving: CAL 61 (41% from fat); FAT 2.8g (sat 0.9g); PRO 1.9g; CARB 7.3g; FIB 1g; CHOL 4mg; IRON 0.5mg; SOD 121mg; CALC 20mg

CROSTINI WITH BLUE CHEESE AND TOMATO

POINTS value: 1

prep: 12 minutes
cook: 5 minutes and 15 seconds

This tasty appetizer is especially good in the summer when tomatoes are at their ripest. Use mild or strong blue cheese according to personal preference.

24   (¼-inch-thick) slices diagonally cut French baguette
Cooking spray
⅓   cup tub-style light cream cheese
6   tablespoons (1 ounce) crumbled blue cheese
½   teaspoon minced garlic
⅛   teaspoon coarsely ground black pepper
1   cup finely chopped tomato
2   tablespoons chopped fresh basil
⅛   teaspoon salt

1. Preheat oven to 400°.
2. Place baguette slices on a baking sheet; coat slices with cooking spray. Bake at 400° for 5 minutes or until bread is toasted; set aside.
3. While bread bakes, combine cream cheese and blue cheese in a small microwave-safe bowl. Microwave at HIGH 15 seconds or until softened. Add garlic and pepper; stir until combined.
4. Combine tomato, basil, and salt in a small bowl. Spread about 1 teaspoon cheese mixture on each bread slice; top with 2 teaspoons tomato mixture. YIELD: 24 servings (serving size: 1 crostino).

Per serving: CAL 42 (26% from fat); FAT 1.2g (sat 0.7g); PRO 1.6g; CARB 5.9g; FIB 0.4g; CHOL 3mg; IRON 0.3mg; SOD 108mg; CALC 20mg

GOAT CHEESE–GREEN OLIVE TAPENADE CROSTINI

POINTS value: 1

prep: 5 minutes • cook: 5 minutes

Green olives and fresh orange rind give this tapenade a decidedly fresh twist that earned a top rating in our Test Kitchens.

1   cup pitted green olives
2   tablespoons fresh flat-leaf parsley leaves
1   tablespoon capers, drained
1   teaspoon grated fresh orange rind
¼   teaspoon freshly ground black pepper
1   tablespoon olive oil
8   ounces goat cheese, softened
32 (¼-inch-thick) slices French bread baguette, toasted

1. Combine first 5 ingredients in a food processor; pulse 4 times or until coarsely chopped. Add olive oil, and pulse 5 times or until finely chopped.
2. Spread about 1½ teaspoons goat cheese over each baguette slice, and top each with about 1½ teaspoons tapenade. YIELD: 32 servings (serving size: 1 crostino).

Per serving: CAL 62 (51% from fat); FAT 3.5g (sat 1.6g); PRO 2.4g; CARB 5.4g; FIB 0.3g; CHOL 5.6mg; IRON 0.4mg; SOD 172mg; CALC 29mg

STEAK CROSTINI WITH AVOCADO-HORSERADISH MAYONNAISE

POINTS value: 2

(pictured on page 61)

prep: 12 minutes • cook: 13 minutes
other: 35 minutes

½   teaspoon dried oregano
¾   teaspoon kosher salt, divided
½   teaspoon freshly ground black pepper
½   pound flank steak
1   ripe peeled avocado, seeded
¾   teaspoon wasabi (Japanese horseradish)
1   teaspoon lime juice
1   garlic clove, crushed
3   tablespoons fat-free mayonnaise
Cooking spray
12 (½-inch-thick) slices diagonally cut French baguette, toasted
Oregano sprigs (optional)

1. Combine dried oregano, ½ teaspoon salt, and pepper in a small bowl; rub evenly over flank steak. Let stand 30 minutes.
2. Combine avocado and next 3 ingredients in a food processor; process until smooth. Add remaining ¼ teaspoon salt and mayonnaise; pulse until blended.
3. Prepare grill.
4. Place steak on grill rack coated with cooking spray; cover and grill 8 to 10 minutes or until desired degree of doneness, turning occasionally. Remove steak from grill, and let stand 5 minutes. Cut steak diagonally across grain into thin slices.
5. Place steak slices on toasted baguette pieces; top each with 2 teaspoons avocado spread. Reserve remaining spread for another use. Garnish with oregano sprigs, if desired. YIELD: 12 servings (serving size: 1 baguette slice, about 2 thin slices steak, and 2 teaspoons spread).

Per serving: CAL 79 (49% from fat); FAT 4.3g (sat 0.9g); PRO 5.2g; CARB 6.2g; FIB 0.8g; CHOL 7mg; IRON 0.6mg; SOD 216mg; CALC 13mg

☑ CITRUS AND SOY MUSHROOMS

POINTS value: 1

prep: 17 minutes • cook: 5 minutes
other: 2 hours

These Thai-flavored mushrooms are a refreshing addition to an appetizer buffet. Plus, you can make the dish a day ahead—ideal for entertaining.

1   pound whole mushrooms, cleaned
¼   cup finely chopped green onions (white part only)
2   tablespoons chopped fresh parsley
3   tablespoons low-sodium soy sauce
¼   teaspoon grated fresh lime rind
1½   tablespoons lime juice
1   tablespoon extravirgin olive oil
1   tablespoon Dijon mustard
½   teaspoon freshly ground black pepper
½   teaspoon minced garlic
Cooking spray

1. Combine first 10 ingredients in a large zip-top plastic bag; seal tightly. Toss gently to coat mushrooms well. Refrigerate at least 2 hours or overnight, turning occasionally.

2. Preheat broiler.

3. Drain mushrooms, reserving marinade. Arrange mushrooms on a broiler pan coated with cooking spray. Broil 5 minutes or until tender.

4. While mushrooms broil, place reserved marinade in a small saucepan and bring to a boil over medium-high heat. Cook 2 minutes or until reduced to 2 tablespoons. Toss mushrooms gently with reduced marinade. Serve warm or at room temperature with wooden picks. YIELD: 6 servings (serving size: ½ cup).

Per serving: CAL 45 (52% from fat); FAT 2.6g (sat 0.4g); PRO 2.8g; CARB 4.1g; FIB 1.1g; CHOL 0mg; IRON 0.7mg; SOD 305mg; CALC 10mg

easy entertaining

An appetizer party is one of the simplest ways to entertain. Prepare a few of our appetizers—no one will guess they're light—and round out your buffet with these tips.

Wine: Bring your recipes to the wine store and ask for assistance in selecting wines that complement the menu. Choose a mixture of reds and whites.

Fresh fruit and vegetables: A colorful platter of fresh fruits and vegetables serves as an elegant decoration and provides healthful dippers for your dips and spreads.

Fresh bread: Purchase specialty breads from your local bakery.

Cheeses: To fill out the menu with no fuss, offer a sampling of cheeses to your guests. Brie, goat cheese logs, Gorgonzola or another blue cheese, Parmigiano-Reggiano, Cheddar, colby, and Monterey Jack are good options.

ASIAN-STYLE LETTUCE WRAPS

POINTS value: 1

(pictured on page 60)

prep: 15 minutes • other: 5 minutes

You can use rotisserie chicken from your grocery store's deli department in this recipe to save time. For added crunch, stir chopped cucumber or diced water chestnuts into the chicken mixture. Serve with an Asian dipping sauce or peanut sauce, if desired.

2   garlic cloves, finely minced
¼   cup fresh lime juice
3   tablespoons low-sodium soy sauce
2   teaspoons sugar
1   teaspoon sesame oil
¼   teaspoon crushed red pepper
2   cups shredded cooked chicken breast
¼   cup chopped fresh cilantro
2   tablespoons chopped fresh mint
12   small, tender Bibb or iceberg lettuce leaves, rinsed, drained, and dried

1. Combine first 6 ingredients in a large bowl, stirring well with a whisk. Add shredded chicken and herbs, and toss to combine. Let stand 5 minutes.

2. Spoon about 2½ tablespoons chicken mixture in center of each lettuce leaf. YIELD: 12 servings (serving size: 1 chicken-filled lettuce wrap).

Per serving: CAL 50 (23% from fat); FAT 1.3g (sat 0.3g); PRO 7.6g; CARB 1.9g; FIB 0.2g; CHOL 20mg; IRON 0.5mg; SOD 151mg; CALC 10mg

TACO CUPS

POINTS value: 1

prep: 13 minutes • cook: 20 minutes

A 2.1-ounce package of mini phyllo shells contains 15 shells, so you'll need to buy two packages. Store the remaining shells in an airtight container in the refrigerator or freezer for another use.

½   pound ground sirloin
2   tablespoons 40%-less-sodium taco seasoning
½   cup bottled salsa
2   tablespoons canned chopped green chiles
24   mini phyllo shells
½   cup (2 ounces) reduced-fat shredded Monterey Jack cheese
¼   cup bottled salsa
¼   cup fat-free sour cream

1. Preheat oven to 350°.

2. Cook beef and taco seasoning in a large skillet over medium-high heat until beef is browned, stirring to crumble. Drain, if necessary; return to pan. Add ½ cup salsa and chiles, and stir.

3. Fill phyllo shells evenly with meat mixture. Top evenly with cheese. Bake at 350° for 10 minutes or until thoroughly heated and cheese melts. Remove from oven, and top each taco cup with ½ teaspoon each of salsa and sour cream. YIELD: 2 dozen (serving size: 1 taco cup).

Per serving: CAL 48 (45% from fat); FAT 2.4g (sat 0.6g); PRO 2.8g; CARB 3g; FIB 0.1g; CHOL 8mg; IRON 0.4mg; SOD 128mg; CALC 30mg

CRISP CITRUS COOLER

POINTS value: 1

prep: 6 minutes • other: 30 minutes

This citrusy spritzer resembles a mojito—a popular Cuban cocktail made with lime juice, powdered sugar, mint, rum, and club soda.

1   medium lemon
1   large lime
1   (1-ounce) package fresh mint leaves, divided
3   tablespoons "measures-like-sugar" calorie-free sweetener (such as Splenda)
1   (6-ounce) can pineapple juice
1½   cups diet tonic water

1. Cut lemon and lime in half crosswise, and squeeze 3 tablespoons juice from each into a large zip-top plastic bag, reserving rinds. Add reserved rinds, half of mint leaves, sweetener, and pineapple juice to bag; seal tightly. Squeeze mixture 15 to 20 seconds or until oils from rinds are released and mint leaves are bruised. Refrigerate 30 minutes.
2. Strain mixture through a fine sieve over a pitcher, squeezing rinds to extract remaining juice. Discard fruit and mint; gently stir in tonic water.
3. Fill 5 tall glasses three-quarters full with crushed ice. Top ice evenly with remaining mint leaves, and pour mixture into glasses. Serve immediately. YIELD: 5 servings (serving size: about ½ cup).

Per serving: CAL 29 (3% from fat); FAT 0.1g (sat 0g); PRO 0.3g; CARB 7.4g; FIB 0.2g; CHOL 0mg; IRON 0.3mg; SOD 12mg; CALC 9mg

POMEGRANATE FIZZER

POINTS value: 2

(pictured on page 60)

prep: 5 minutes • other: 30 minutes

The jewel-tone colors of the pomegranate and berry juices make this sparkly beverage perfect for the holidays. It's easily doubled or tripled if you're serving a crowd.

1   (16-ounce) bottle pomegranate juice (such as POM Wonderful)
1   cup mixed berry juice (such as Dole's Berry Blend)
2   tablespoons lime juice
1   cup diet ginger ale
Lime wedges (optional)

1. Combine first 3 ingredients in a pitcher; cover and chill, if desired.
2. Stir in ginger ale just before serving. Serve immediately over ice. Garnish with lime wedges, if desired. YIELD: 4 servings (serving size: 1 cup).

Per serving: CAL 99 (0% from fat); FAT 0g (sat 0g); PRO 0.5g; CARB 24.9g; FIB 0g; CHOL 0mg; IRON 0.2mg; SOD 35mg; CALC 21mg

PINEAPPLE-GINGER PUNCH

POINTS value: 2

prep: 2 minutes • cook: 5 minutes

This refreshing beverage features sweet pineapple juice with a kick of mint and peppery ginger.

4   (6-ounce) cans pineapple juice
2   large mint sprigs
2   (12-ounce) cans diet ginger ale

1. Combine pineapple juice and mint sprigs in a medium saucepan. Bring to a boil; remove from heat, and cool to room temperature. Discard mint sprigs.
2. Transfer pineapple juice to a pitcher, and gently stir in ginger ale. Serve immediately over ice. YIELD: 4 servings (serving size: about 1⅓ cups).

Per serving: CAL 99 (2% from fat); FAT 0.2g (sat 0g); PRO 0.7g; CARB 24.1g; FIB 0.4g; CHOL 0mg; IRON 0.6mg; SOD 26mg; CALC 24mg

ICED GREEN TEA–CITRUS PUNCH

POINTS value: 2

prep: 2 minutes • cook: 6 minutes
other: 1 hour and 35 minutes

*Antioxidant-rich green tea offers a number of health benefits, such as reducing the risk of cancer, rheumatoid arthritis, and heart disease. If you prefer to make this punch with a calorie-free sweetener, the **POINTS** value will be 1.*

6   cups water, divided
1   cup sugar
16   green tea bags
1¾   cups fresh orange juice
¼   cup fresh lemon juice
Orange slices (optional)

1. Bring 3 cups water and sugar to a boil in a large saucepan, stirring until sugar dissolves. Remove pan from heat; add tea bags, and steep 5 minutes. Remove tea bags with a slotted spoon (do not squeeze).
2. Cool tea to room temperature; stir in orange juice, lemon juice, and remaining 3 cups water. Cover and

chill at least 1 hour. Serve over ice; garnish with orange slices, if desired. YIELD: 8 servings (serving size: 1 cup).

Per serving: CAL 123 (0% from fat); FAT 0g (sat 0g); PRO 0.4g; CARB 31.3g; FIB 0.1g; CHOL 0mg; IRON 0.1mg; SOD 1mg; CALC 7mg

COFFEE-ICE CREAM PUNCH

POINTS value: 3

(pictured on page 55)

prep: 7 minutes • cook: 2 minutes

Serve this coffee punch at a brunch gathering or for dessert.

2   cups strong brewed coffee or espresso
½   cup 2% reduced-fat milk
¼   teaspoon almond extract
2   cups light, no-sugar-added vanilla ice cream
2   cups light, no-sugar-added chocolate ice cream
6   tablespoons frozen fat-free whipped topping, thawed
Ground nutmeg (optional)

1. Combine first 3 ingredients in a small pitcher.
2. Place ice cream in a punch bowl. Add coffee mixture, stirring gently until ice cream slightly melts. Spoon into coffee cups, and top each serving with whipped topping. Sprinkle with nutmeg, if desired. YIELD: 6 servings (serving size: about ¾ cup punch and 1 tablespoon whipped topping).

Per serving: CAL 146 (35% from fat); FAT 5.6g (sat 2g); PRO 4.5g; CARB 20.4g; FIB 2.3g; CHOL 13mg; IRON 0.1mg; SOD 86mg; CALC 85mg

TRIPLE-FRUIT SOY SMOOTHIES

POINTS value: 2

prep: 4 minutes • other: 30 minutes

If you're in a hurry, you can skip the first step of freezing the fruit. The smoothies won't be quite as thick and frosty, but the flavor will still be great.

3   cups strawberries, halved
2   medium bananas, sliced into 1-inch pieces
½   cup orange juice
1   cup vanilla soy milk (such as Silk)
⅓   cup "measures-like-sugar" calorie-free sweetener (such as Splenda)

1. Place strawberries and banana slices on a foil-lined jelly-roll pan. Freeze 30 minutes.
2. Place frozen fruit, orange juice, soy milk, and sweetener in a blender; process until smooth. YIELD: 4 servings (serving size: 1 cup).

Per serving: CAL 154 (8% from fat); FAT 1.4g (sat 0.2g); PRO 3.3g; CARB 34.7g; FIB 4.6g; CHOL 0mg; IRON 1.2mg; SOD 36mg; CALC 97mg

EASY SANGRÍA SLUSH

POINTS value: 4

prep: 5 minutes • other: 8 hours

Sangría is always great for entertaining because you can make it ahead and then transfer it to a pitcher for serving. This recipe is easily doubled or tripled if you're preparing it for a party. Garnish this refreshing wine beverage with fresh fruit kebabs or slices.

3   cups zinfandel or other fruity dry red wine
½   cup orange juice
½   cup pineapple juice
⅓   cup thawed lemonade concentrate
1   cup sparkling water or club soda

1. Combine first 3 ingredients in a 4-cup glass measure. Pour evenly into ice cube trays. Freeze overnight or until firm.
2. Add frozen juice cubes to food processor; process 30 seconds or until coarsely chopped. Add lemonade concentrate and sparkling water; process 1 minute or until smooth. Pour into a pitcher to serve. YIELD: 5 servings (serving size: 1 cup).

Per serving: CAL 185 (0% from fat); FAT 0.1g (sat 0g); PRO 0.4g; CARB 19g; FIB 0.1g; CHOL 0mg; IRON 0.3mg; SOD 11mg; CALC 10mg

CHAI-SPICED HOT CHOCOLATE

POINTS value: 4

prep: 5 minutes • cook: 10 minutes
other: 15 minutes

Indian chai is a spiced milk tea made with black tea, milk, sweetener, and spices—usually cardamom, cinnamon, ginger, and peppercorns. For this soothing beverage, we combined the traditional chai spices with milk and cocoa instead of tea.

6   whole cloves
4   whole cardamom pods
2   (3-inch) cinnamon sticks
½   teaspoon whole black peppercorns
3¾   cups 1% low-fat milk
½   cup packed light brown sugar
4   (¼-inch) slices fresh ginger
⅓   cup unsweetened cocoa
Additional cinnamon sticks (optional)

1. Place first 4 ingredients in a zip-top plastic bag. Seal bag, and crush spices into small pieces using a rolling pin or meat mallet.
2. Combine crushed spices, milk, brown sugar, and ginger in a medium saucepan. Cook over medium heat 8 minutes, stirring until sugar dissolves and tiny bubbles form at edge of saucepan (do not boil). Remove from heat; cover and let stand 15 minutes.
3. Add cocoa to milk mixture, and stir. Cook mixture over medium heat 2 minutes, stirring constantly until blended. Strain mixture through a sieve, and serve immediately. Garnish with cinnamon sticks, if desired. YIELD: 5 servings (serving size: ¾ cup).

Per serving: CAL 186 (15% from fat); FAT 3g (sat 1.8g); PRO 8.4g; CARB 35.1g; FIB 1.9g; CHOL 7mg; IRON 1.3mg; SOD 117mg; CALC 288mg

SPICED MOCHA LATTE

POINTS value: 2

prep: 2 minutes • cook: 2 minutes

The drinks at the local coffee shop can be loaded with calories. This homemade version is not, and you can prepare it in 5 minutes. It's just the thing to perk you up in the afternoon, and it's a good source of calcium.

1   (0.55-ounce) envelope no-sugar-added instant cocoa mix
⅔   cup hot strong brewed coffee
⅓   cup fat-free milk
¼   teaspoon "measures-like-sugar" calorie-free sweetener (such as Splenda)
⅛   teaspoon ground cinnamon
1   tablespoon frozen fat-free whipped topping, thawed
Unsweetened cocoa (optional)

1. Combine cocoa mix and coffee in a large mug, stirring until blended.
2. Microwave milk at HIGH 30 seconds or until hot; stir into cocoa mixture. Add sweetener and cinnamon; stir until blended. Top with whipped topping. Dust with cocoa, if desired. Serve immediately. YIELD: 1 serving (serving size: 1 cup).

Per serving: CAL 95 (6% from fat); FAT 0.6g (sat 0.3g); PRO 7.4g; CARB 14.7g; FIB 0.9g; CHOL 5mg; IRON 0.6mg; SOD 188mg; CALC 237mg

MEXICAN MARSHMALLOW MOCHA

POINTS value: 3

prep: 4 minutes • cook: 7 minutes
other: 30 minutes

*We added marshmallow creme to make this exotic mocha drink especially rich. For an even lighter version, substitute a calorie-free sweetener, such as Splenda, in place of regular granulated sugar; the **POINTS** value will be 2.*

2   cups 1% low-fat milk
1   (3-inch) cinnamon stick
¼   cup unsweetened cocoa
3   tablespoons sugar
2½   teaspoons instant coffee granules
½   cup marshmallow creme
½   teaspoon vanilla extract

1. Combine milk and cinnamon stick in a medium saucepan over medium heat; bring to a simmer (do not boil). Remove from heat, and cool to room temperature. Discard cinnamon stick.
2. Combine cocoa, sugar, and coffee granules in a small bowl; stir well. Add cocoa mixture to milk mixture in pan, stirring with a whisk until smooth. Stir in marshmallow creme. Cook mixture over medium heat 3 minutes or until thoroughly heated, stirring constantly with a whisk. Reduce heat to low, and simmer 1 minute, stirring vigorously with a whisk to froth mixture. Remove from heat; stir in vanilla. Pour into mugs. YIELD: 3 servings (serving size: about ¾ cup).

Per serving: CAL 170 (14% from fat); FAT 2.7g sat 1.7g); PRO 6.9g; CARB 44.6g; FIB 2.4g; CHOL 7mg; IRON 1.1mg; SOD 97mg; CALC 211mg

breads ▶▶

THREE-SEED BREADSTICKS

POINTS value: 1

prep: 10 minutes • cook: 8 minutes

Serve these crunchy breadsticks instead of crackers with a bowl of soup or a mixed green salad. Store in an airtight container to keep them crisp.

1 (7.5-ounce) can refrigerated buttermilk biscuits
¾ cup oven-toasted rice cereal, coarsely crushed
1 tablespoon caraway seeds
1 tablespoon sesame seeds
1 tablespoon poppy seeds
1 large egg white, beaten
Cooking spray
1 teaspoon kosher salt

1. Preheat oven to 450°.
2. Cut each biscuit in half, and roll each half into a pencil-thin stick. Combine cereal and seeds in a shallow pan, stirring well. Brush biscuit sticks with egg white; roll in cereal mixture. Place breadsticks 2 inches apart on a large baking sheet coated with cooking spray, and sprinkle with salt.
3. Bake at 450° for 8 to 10 minutes or until lightly browned. YIELD: 10 servings (serving size: 2 breadsticks).

Per serving: CAL 73 (17% from fat); FAT 1.4g (sat 0.2g); PRO 2.6g; CARB 12.6g; FIB 0.4g; CHOL 0mg; IRON 0.9mg; SOD 376mg; CALC 26mg

COCONUT-BANANA FRENCH TOAST

POINTS value: 4

prep: 6 minutes
cook: 4 minutes per batch

Coconut milk and banana lend a tropical flavor to this filling one-dish breakfast meal. To lower the fat content, we've reduced the number of whole eggs and replaced them with egg substitute.

¾ cup light coconut milk
¾ cup egg substitute
1 large egg, lightly beaten
¼ cup sugar
½ teaspoon vanilla extract
⅛ teaspoon salt
Cooking spray
8 slices double-fiber whole wheat bread (such as Nature's Own)
1 medium banana, thinly sliced
Light maple-flavored syrup (optional)

1. Combine first 6 ingredients in a large bowl, stirring well with a whisk.
2. Heat a large nonstick skillet or griddle over medium heat. Coat pan with cooking spray. Dip 4 bread slices (twice on each side) in egg mixture. Cook 2 minutes on each side or until browned. Set aside, and keep warm. Repeat procedure with remaining bread and egg mixture. Serve with banana slices and, if desired, syrup. YIELD: 4 servings (serving size: 2 slices toast and ¼ banana).

Per serving: CAL 231 (23% from fat); FAT 5.8g (sat 2.5g); PRO 15.3g; CARB 43.3g; FIB 11g; CHOL 54mg; IRON 3.9mg; SOD 494mg; CALC 321mg

BANANA–MACADAMIA NUT PANCAKES

POINTS value: 3

prep: 6 minutes
cook: 3 minutes plus 2 minutes per batch

*Chopped macadamia nuts add a bit of crunch to these sweet banana pancakes. Serve with light maple syrup, if desired. One tablespoon of light syrup has a **POINTS** value of 1.*

1¼ cups all-purpose flour
1½ teaspoons baking powder
½ teaspoon baking soda
½ teaspoon salt
1 cup chopped ripe banana (about 2 small)
1 cup low-fat buttermilk
3 tablespoons light brown sugar
1 large egg
1 tablespoon butter, softened
1 teaspoon vanilla extract
⅓ cup chopped macadamia nuts, toasted
Cooking spray

1. Lightly spoon flour into dry measuring cups; level with a knife. Combine flour and next 3 ingredients in a large bowl; stir with a whisk. Combine banana and next 5 ingredients in a medium bowl; stir with a whisk until smooth. Add buttermilk mixture to flour mixture; stir just until combined. Stir in macadamia nuts.
2. Pour about ¼ cup batter per pancake onto a hot nonstick griddle or nonstick skillet coated with cooking spray. Cook 1 to 2 minutes or until tops are covered with bubbles and edges look cooked. Carefully turn pancakes over, and cook 1 to 2 minutes or

until bottoms are lightly browned.
YIELD: 11 pancakes (serving size: 1 pancake).

Per serving: CAL 133 (34% from fat); FAT 5g (sat 1.4g); PRO 3.3g; CARB 19.1g; FIB 1.2g; CHOL 23mg; IRON 1mg; SOD 258mg; CALC 69mg

PARMESAN-BASIL BISCUITS

POINTS value: 3

(pictured on page 59)

prep: 12 minutes • cook: 10 minutes

These quick and easy biscuits received rave reviews in our Test Kitchens. We preferred the appearance of finely shredded fresh Parmesan cheese on top of the biscuits, even though grated Parmesan is used in the biscuit dough. If you don't have fresh Parmesan, it's fine to top the biscuits with grated cheese.

1   cup all-purpose flour
1   teaspoon baking powder
¼   teaspoon baking soda
¼   teaspoon salt
3   tablespoons chilled butter, cut into small pieces
¼   cup grated Parmesan cheese
2   tablespoons chopped fresh basil
½   cup low-fat buttermilk
Cooking spray
1   tablespoon finely shredded fresh Parmesan cheese

1. Preheat oven to 425°.
2. Lightly spoon flour into a dry measuring cup; level with a knife. Combine flour and next 3 ingredients in a bowl. Cut in butter with a pastry blender or 2 knives until mixture resembles coarse meal. Stir in grated

Parmesan cheese and basil. Add buttermilk, stirring just until moist.
3. Spoon dough evenly into 8 mounds on a baking sheet coated with cooking spray. Lightly coat tops of biscuits with cooking spray, and sprinkle with finely shredded Parmesan cheese.
4. Bake at 425° for 10 to 12 minutes or until golden. Serve immediately.
YIELD: 8 biscuits (serving size: 1 biscuit).

Per serving: CAL 114 (43% from fat); FAT 5.4g (sat 3.4g); PRO 3.4g; CARB 12.8g; FIB 0.5g; CHOL 15mg; IRON 0.8mg; SOD 259mg; CALC 88mg

NECTARINE-OATMEAL SCONES

POINTS value: 4

prep: 14 minutes • cook: 20 minutes

Adding oats to the scones gives them a hearty, nutty flavor and also increases the fiber. We chose nectarines over peaches for this recipe because although the two fruits are similar in flavor, nectarines release less juice when baked. We tried substituting peaches, but the scones were too wet and gummy.

1¼   cups all-purpose flour
⅓   cup granulated sugar
2   teaspoons baking powder
½   teaspoon baking soda
¼   teaspoon salt
⅓   cup cold butter, cut into small pieces
1   cup regular oats
½   cup low-fat buttermilk
1½   cups chopped nectarines (about 3 small)
Cooking spray
1   tablespoon turbinado sugar

1. Preheat oven to 425°.
2. Lightly spoon flour into dry measuring cups; level with a knife. Combine flour and next 4 ingredients in a large bowl. Cut in butter with a pastry blender or 2 knives until mixture resembles coarse meal. Stir in oats. Add buttermilk to flour mixture, stirring just until moist. Gently fold in nectarines.
3. Turn dough out onto a lightly floured surface; knead lightly 3 or 4 times with floured hands. Pat dough into a 7-inch circle on a baking sheet coated with cooking spray. Cut dough into 10 wedges, cutting into but not through dough (do not separate wedges). Lightly coat tops of scones with cooking spray; sprinkle with turbinado sugar. Bake at 425° for 20 minutes or until lightly browned. YIELD: 10 servings (serving size: 1 wedge).

Per serving: CAL 193 (33% from fat); FAT 7g (sat 4g); PRO 3.8g; CARB 30g; FIB 2g; CHOL 17mg; IRON 1.3mg; SOD 276mg; CALC 79mg

buying nectarines

Nectarines are available during the spring and summer months, but the best-quality nectarines are found during July and August. Choose those that are golden yellow with generous blushes of red. Try to avoid green, bruised, or blemished nectarines.

PEANUT BUTTER–
CHOCOLATE CHIP SCONES

POINTS value: 4

prep: 16 minutes • cook: 14 minutes

Combine peanut butter and chocolate for a rich breakfast treat. Natural peanut butter—with no added sugars—boasts the best peanut flavor and contains no trans fats.

1¾ cups all-purpose flour
⅓ cup packed light brown sugar
2½ teaspoons baking powder
¼ teaspoon salt
2 tablespoons chilled butter, cut into small pieces
½ cup natural-style chunky peanut butter
½ cup fat-free milk
1 large egg, lightly beaten
1 teaspoon vanilla extract
¼ cup semisweet chocolate minichips
Cooking spray

1. Preheat oven to 425°.
2. Lightly spoon flour into dry measuring cups; level with a knife. Combine flour and next 3 ingredients in a large bowl; cut in butter with a pastry blender or 2 knives until mixture resembles coarse meal.
3. Combine peanut butter and next 3 ingredients, stirring with a whisk. Add to flour mixture, stirring just until moist. Stir in chocolate chips. Knead dough 4 times in bowl.
4. Pat dough into a 7-inch circle on a baking sheet coated with cooking spray. Cut dough into 12 wedges, cutting into but not through dough (do not separate wedges). Lightly coat with cooking spray.

5. Bake at 425° for 14 minutes or until lightly browned. YIELD: 12 servings (serving size: 1 scone).

Per serving: CAL 201 (40% from fat); FAT 8.9g (sat 2.7g); PRO 5.3g; CARB 25.1g; FIB 1.4g; CHOL 23mg; IRON 1.4mg; SOD 159mg; CALC 75mg

IRISH SODA BREAD
WITH RAISINS

POINTS value: 3

(pictured on page 56)

prep: 7 minutes • cook: 30 minutes
other: 10 minutes

Classic soda bread is leavened with baking soda and some type of acidic ingredient, usually buttermilk. Raisins add sweetness to this hearty bread.

2¼ cups all-purpose flour
¼ cup sugar
1½ teaspoons baking powder
½ teaspoon baking soda
1 teaspoon salt
3 tablespoons butter, chilled and cut into small pieces
¾ cup raisins
1 cup low-fat buttermilk
Cooking spray

1. Preheat oven to 350°.
2. Lightly spoon flour into dry measuring cups; level with a knife. Combine flour and next 4 ingredients in a large bowl; cut in butter with a pastry blender or 2 knives until mixture resembles coarse meal. Stir in raisins. Add buttermilk; stir with a fork just until moist.
3. Turn dough out onto a lightly floured surface; knead 3 or 4 times.

4. Press dough into an 8-inch round pan coated with cooking spray.
5. Bake at 350° for 30 minutes or until lightly browned. Cool in pan 10 minutes. Cut into 12 wedges. YIELD: 12 servings (serving size: 1 wedge).

Per serving: CAL 162 (18% from fat); FAT 3.3g (sat 2g); PRO 3.4g; CARB 30.2g; FIB 1g; CHOL 8mg; IRON 1.3mg; SOD 342mg; CALC 63mg

BANANA-OAT MUFFINS

POINTS value: 4

prep: 10 minutes • cook: 21 minutes

If you have overripe bananas, place them in the freezer to keep on hand for these muffins.

1 cup all-purpose flour
1 cup regular oats
½ cup sugar
¼ cup wheat germ
2 teaspoons baking powder
¼ teaspoon baking soda
¼ teaspoon salt
⅔ cup mashed very ripe banana (about 2 small)
⅓ cup reduced-fat sour cream
1 large egg
¼ cup canola oil
1 teaspoon vanilla extract
Cooking spray

1. Preheat oven to 375°.
2. Lightly spoon flour into a dry measuring cup; level with a knife. Combine flour and next 6 ingredients in a large bowl; make a well in center of mixture.
3. Combine banana and next 4 ingredients in a small bowl; add to dry ingredients, stirring just until moist.

Spoon batter evenly into 12 muffin cups coated with cooking spray.

4. Bake at 375° for 21 minutes or until a wooden pick inserted in center muffin comes out clean. Remove muffins from pans immediately; place on a wire rack. Serve warm. YIELD: 1 dozen (serving size: 1 muffin).

Per serving: CAL 169 (35% from fat); FAT 6.6g (sat 1.1g); PRO 3.3g; CARB 25.3g; FIB 1.5g; CHOL 20mg; IRON 1.2mg; SOD 166mg; CALC 62mg

PUMPKIN STREUSEL MUFFINS

POINTS value: 4

prep: 18 minutes • cook: 22 minutes
other: 5 minutes

A crunchy streusel tops these moist spiced muffins.

⅓ cup quick-cooking oats
2 tablespoons light brown sugar
2 tablespoons all-purpose flour
1½ tablespoons light stick butter, melted
2 cups self-rising flour
1 cup quick-cooking oats
¾ cup packed light brown sugar
2 teaspoons pumpkin-pie spice
¼ teaspoon salt
1 (15-ounce) can pumpkin
½ cup 1% low-fat milk
¼ cup canola oil
1 large egg, lightly beaten
Cooking spray

1. Preheat oven to 400°.
2. Combine first 4 ingredients, stirring until dry ingredients are moistened and mixture holds together; set aside.

3. Lightly spoon self-rising flour into dry measuring cups; level with a knife. Combine 2 cups flour and next 4 ingredients in a large bowl; make a well in center of mixture. Combine pumpkin and next 3 ingredients; stir with a whisk. Add to flour mixture, stirring just until moist.
4. Spoon batter evenly into 16 muffin cups coated with cooking spray. Sprinkle evenly with oat mixture.
5. Bake at 400° for 22 to 25 minutes or until golden. Cool muffins in pan on a wire rack 5 minutes; remove from pans, and place on wire rack. Serve warm. YIELD: 16 muffins (serving size: 1 muffin).

Per serving: CAL 181 (26% from fat); FAT 5.2g (sat 0.9g); PRO 3.6g; CARB 30.9g; FIB 1.9g; CHOL 15mg; IRON 1.8mg; SOD 259mg; CALC 87mg

CORN AND ZUCCHINI MUFFINS

POINTS value: 3

prep: 15 minutes • cook: 15 minutes

1 cup whole wheat flour
1 cup self-rising cornmeal mix
2 tablespoons sugar
¼ teaspoon baking soda
¼ teaspoon salt
1 (6-ounce) carton plain fat-free yogurt
⅓ cup 1% low-fat milk
3 tablespoons canola oil
1 large egg
1 cup shredded zucchini
¾ cup fresh corn kernels (3 small ears)
2 tablespoons minced onion
Cooking spray

1. Preheat oven to 425°.
2. Lightly spoon flour and cornmeal mix into dry measuring cups; level with a knife. Combine flour, cornmeal mix, sugar, baking soda, and salt in a large bowl; stir with a whisk. Make a well in center of mixture. Combine yogurt and next 3 ingredients in a small bowl; stir with a whisk. Add zucchini, corn, and onion; stir. Add vegetable mixture to flour mixture, stirring just until moist.
3. Spoon batter evenly into 12 muffin cups coated with cooking spray; coat batter with cooking spray. Bake at 425° for 15 minutes or until muffins spring back when touched lightly in center. YIELD: 1 dozen (serving size: 1 muffin).

Per serving: CAL 149 (29% from fat); FAT 4.8g (sat 0.5g); PRO 4.6g; CARB 23.2g; FIB 2.1g; CHOL 18mg; IRON 1.2mg; SOD 292mg; CALC 53mg

reheating tip

Corn and Zucchini Muffins freeze well and taste almost as good reheated as they do when fresh. To reheat frozen muffins, thaw them in the microwave oven until warm. Finish heating in a 350° regular or toaster oven until hot.

JALAPEÑO-CHEDDAR CORN BREAD

POINTS value: 3

prep: 11 minutes • cook: 25 minutes

If you want a little less heat in your corn bread, simply decrease the amount of pickled jalapeño peppers or use 2 tablespoons of fresh jalapeño peppers instead.

3	tablespoons canola oil
1	cup all-purpose flour
1	cup yellow cornmeal
1	tablespoon sugar
2	teaspoons baking powder
1	teaspoon salt
2	large eggs
1	cup low-fat buttermilk
2	tablespoons minced pickled jalapeño peppers
½	cup (2 ounces) reduced-fat shredded sharp Cheddar cheese

1. Preheat oven to 425°.
2. Place oil in 9-inch cast-iron skillet; place pan in oven for 5 minutes.
3. While pan heats in oven, lightly spoon flour into a dry measuring cup; level with a knife. Combine flour, cornmeal, and next 3 ingredients. Combine eggs and buttermilk, stirring with a whisk. Add to flour mixture, stirring just until moist. Stir in jalapeño peppers and cheese. Pour batter into preheated pan.
4. Bake at 425° for 20 to 23 minutes or until golden. Cut into 12 wedges. YIELD: 12 servings (serving size: 1 wedge).

Per serving: CAL 151 (35% from fat); FAT 5.8g (sat 1.4g); PRO 4.9g; CARB 20.3g; FIB 1g; CHOL 39mg; IRON 1.2mg; SOD 379mg; CALC 109mg

GRILLED ROSEMARY FLATBREADS

POINTS value: 3
(pictured on page 58)

prep: 25 minutes
cook: 6 minutes per batch
other: 1 hour and 15 minutes

Simply seasoned with olive oil and rosemary, these rustic grilled flatbreads received our Test Kitchens' highest rating. Place leftover grilled flatbreads in an airtight container and freeze up to 1 month.

1	package quick-rise yeast (about 2¼ teaspoons)
1½	cups warm water (100° to 110°)
3¾	cups all-purpose flour, divided
1	tablespoon kosher salt, divided
2	tablespoons chopped fresh rosemary, divided
	Cooking spray
2	tablespoons olive oil

1. Dissolve yeast in warm water in a large bowl; let stand 5 minutes.
2. Lightly spoon flour into dry measuring cups, and level with a knife. Stir 1 cup flour into yeast mixture. Cover and let stand 30 minutes.
3. Add remaining 2¾ cups flour, 1 teaspoon salt, and 1 tablespoon rosemary to yeast mixture; stir until a soft dough forms. Turn dough out onto a lightly floured surface, and knead until smooth and elastic (about 6 minutes). Place dough in a large bowl coated with cooking spray, turning to coat top. Cover and let rise in a warm place (85°), free from drafts, 40 minutes or until doubled in size. (Gently press two fingers into dough. If indentation remains, dough has risen enough.)
4. Prepare grill.
5. Punch dough down; divide into 12 equal portions. Roll each portion into a 4½- to 5-inch circle on a lightly floured surface. Brush dough rounds with olive oil; sprinkle rounds evenly with remaining 2 teaspoons salt and 1 tablespoon rosemary.
6. Place dough rounds on grill rack coated with cooking spray; grill 3 to 4 minutes on each side or until puffed and golden. YIELD: 1 dozen (serving size: 1 round).

Per serving: CAL 165 (15% from fat); FAT 2.8g (sat 0.4g); PRO 4.3g; CARB 30.2g; FIB 1.2g; CHOL 0mg; IRON 1.9mg; SOD 472mg; CALC 10mg

a warm place

When letting dough rise, anywhere in your house that's warm and free from drafts will do, but we've discovered that an oven is an ideal place. To warm the oven up a bit, turn it on for about 10 seconds, and then turn it off. Or place a cup of hot water in the oven. That provides about all the warmth that the dough requires.

You can also let your dough rise in a microwave oven. Just make sure that there is enough room above the bowl or pan for the dough to rise. To warm the inside of the microwave, bring 1 cup of water to a boil and remove it from the microwave before placing the dough inside to rise.

Regardless of where your dough rises, be sure to cover it with a slightly damp lightweight dish towel to keep the dough from drying and forming a thin crust.

CARAMELIZED ONION, GORGONZOLA, AND WALNUT FOCACCIA

POINTS value: 3

prep: 17 minutes • cook: 1 hour
other: 1 hour and 20 minutes

The sweetness of the caramelized onions is a great flavor contrast to the sharp blue cheese.

2   packages dry yeast (about 4½ teaspoons)
1   teaspoon sugar
1   cup warm water (100° to 110°)
1   teaspoon salt
2¾ cups all-purpose flour, divided
Cooking spray
1   tablespoon olive oil
5   cups thinly sliced onion (about 2 large)
⅓   cup chopped walnuts
½   cup (2 ounces) crumbled Gorgonzola or other blue cheese

1. Dissolve yeast and sugar in warm water in a large bowl; let stand 5 minutes. Add salt; stir to dissolve.
2. Lightly spoon flour into dry measuring cups; level with a knife. Add 2½ cups flour to yeast mixture, stirring until a soft dough forms. Turn dough out onto a floured surface. Knead until smooth and elastic (about 8 minutes). Add enough of remaining ¼ cup flour, 1 tablespoon at a time, to prevent dough from sticking to hands.
3. Place dough in a large bowl coated with cooking spray, turning to coat top. Cover and let rise in a warm place (85°), free from drafts, about 45 minutes or until doubled

yeast bread basics

1. Proof the yeast. It should swell and foam a few minutes after it's stirred into the warm liquid.

2. Knead the dough until it's noticeably smooth and elastic but still slightly tacky to the touch.

3. To tell when the dough has risen enough, gently press two fingers into it. If an indention remains, the dough is ready.

4. Punch the dough down to deflate it. Then turn the dough out onto a floured surface for rolling or shaping.

in size. (Gently press two fingers into dough. If indention remains, dough has risen enough.)
4. While dough rises, heat oil in a large nonstick skillet over medium-low heat. Add onion; cover and cook 30 minutes or until onion is tender, stirring occasionally. Uncover and cook 5 to 10 minutes or until onion is golden brown and most of liquid evaporates, stirring often.
5. Punch dough down. Pat dough into a jelly-roll pan coated with cooking spray. (If dough resists

stretching, let rest 5 minutes before proceeding.) Spread onion evenly over dough. Sprinkle walnuts and Gorgonzola evenly over top; cover and let rise in a warm place 30 minutes or until doubled in size.
6. Preheat oven to 400°.
7. Bake at 400° for 25 to 30 minutes or until lightly browned. Cut into 15 pieces. YIELD: 15 servings (serving size: 1 piece).

Per serving: CAL 135 (26% from fat); FAT 3.9g (sat 1.1g); PRO 4.5g; CARB 20.7g; FIB 1.4g; CHOL 3mg; IRON 1.4mg; SOD 210mg; CALC 30mg

OATMEAL-GRAHAM BREAD

POINTS value: 3

prep: 27 minutes • cook: 33 minutes
other: 1 hour and 20 minutes

1   package dry yeast (about 2¼
    teaspoons)
1   teaspoon sugar
1   cup warm water (100° to 110°)
2   cups bread flour
1   cup regular oats
½   cup graham cracker crumbs
1½ teaspoons salt
3   tablespoons honey
2   tablespoons butter, melted
Cooking spray
1   large egg white
1   tablespoon water
1   tablespoon regular oats

1. Dissolve yeast and sugar in warm water in a large bowl; let stand 5 minutes. Lightly spoon flour into dry measuring cups; level with a knife. Combine flour and next 3 ingredients. Add flour mixture, honey, and butter to yeast mixture, stirring until a soft dough forms.
2. Turn dough out onto a lightly floured surface, and knead until smooth and elastic (about 5 minutes). Place dough in a large bowl coated with cooking spray, turning to coat top. Cover and let rise in a warm place (85°), free from drafts, 40 minutes or until doubled in size. (Press two fingers into dough. If indentation remains, dough has risen enough).
3. Punch dough down; turn out onto a floured surface. Roll into a 12 x 7–inch rectangle. Starting with a short edge, roll up tightly, jelly-roll fashion, pressing firmly to eliminate air pockets; pinch seam and ends to seal. Place roll, seam side down, in an 8 x 4–inch loaf pan coated with cooking spray. Combine egg white and water, stirring with a whisk; brush evenly over loaf. Sprinkle loaf with 1 tablespoon oats. Cover and let rise 35 minutes or until doubled in size.
4. Preheat oven to 375°.
5. Bake at 375° for 33 minutes or until top is golden and loaf sounds hollow when tapped. Remove from pan; cool completely on a wire rack.
YIELD: 12 servings (serving size: 1 slice).

Per serving: CAL 161 (17% from fat); FAT 3.2g (sat 1.2g); PRO 4.6g; CARB 28.9g; FIB 1.4g; CHOL 5mg; IRON 1.6mg; SOD 335mg; CALC 10mg

CHOCOLATE-FILLED BRIOCHE

POINTS value: 4

prep: 36 minutes • cook: 15 minutes
other: 2 hours and 25 minutes

Brioche is a classic French yeast bread made rich with butter and eggs. We've used less butter and fewer eggs than a traditional brioche without sacrificing the rich tenderness.

1   package dry yeast (about 2¼
    teaspoons)
3   tablespoons sugar, divided
½   cup warm fat-free milk (100°
    to 110°)
2¾ cups all-purpose flour, divided
1   teaspoon vanilla extract
2   large eggs, divided
1   large egg yolk
1   teaspoon salt
⅓   cup butter, cut into small pieces
Cooking spray
⅓   cup dark chocolate chips

1. Dissolve yeast and ¼ teaspoon sugar in milk. Let stand 5 minutes.
2. Lightly spoon flour into dry measuring cups; level with a knife. Place 2½ cups flour and remaining sugar in a large bowl; make a well in center of mixture. Add vanilla to milk mixture. Pour milk mixture into well. Beat at medium speed with a mixer just until combined. Add 1 egg, egg yolk, and salt; beat just until combined. Gradually beat in butter. Turn dough out onto a work surface. Knead until smooth (about 8 minutes), adding enough of remaining flour, 1 tablespoon at a time, to prevent dough from sticking to hands.
3. Place dough in a large bowl coated with cooking spray, turning to coat top. Cover and let rise in a warm place (85°), free from drafts, 1½ hours or until doubled in size. (Gently press two fingers into dough. If indentation remains, dough has risen enough.) Punch dough down; cover and let rest 5 minutes.
4. Divide dough into 16 equal portions; shape portions into balls. Make an indentation in each ball, and tuck about 10 chocolate chips in each indentation. Pull dough over chips, and pinch to enclose chocolate in center of each ball. Place rolls, seam sides down, in muffin cups coated with cooking spray. Cover and let rise 45 minutes or until doubled in size.
5. Preheat oven to 350°.
6. Lightly beat remaining egg; brush tops of rolls with egg. Bake at 350° for 15 minutes or until golden. YIELD: 16 servings (serving size: 1 roll).

Per serving: CAL 165 (35% from fat); FAT 6.4g (sat 3.6g); PRO 3.9g; CARB 22.5g; FIB 0.7g; CHOL 49mg; IRON 1.2mg; SOD 188mg; CALC 19mg

desserts ▶▶

WINTER FRUIT WITH HONEY-YOGURT SAUCE

POINTS value: 2

prep: 8 minutes

For a superquick dessert or a satisfying snack, stir up a simple yogurt sauce to spoon over fruit.

⅔ cup vanilla low-fat yogurt
1   tablespoon honey
1   cup chopped pear
1   cup chopped red apple
1   cup seedless green grape halves
Ground nutmeg (optional)

1. Combine yogurt and honey in a small bowl; stir with a whisk.
2. Combine pear and next 2 ingredients in a large bowl. Spoon fruit evenly into dessert dishes. Spoon yogurt sauce evenly over fruit. Sprinkle lightly with nutmeg, if desired. YIELD: 4 servings (serving size: ¾ cup fruit and 2½ tablespoons yogurt sauce).

Per serving: CAL 119 (5% from fat); FAT 0.7g (sat 0.4g); PRO 2.6g; CARB 27.9g; FIB 2.4g; CHOL 2mg; IRON 0.3mg; SOD 29mg; CALC 80mg

BLUEBERRY FOOL

POINTS value: 2

prep: 6 minutes

A fool is a traditional English dessert made of cooked pureed fruit that's chilled and folded into whipped cream. This low-fat shortcut version uses fat-free whipped topping and a canned pie filling.

1   cup frozen fat-free whipped topping, thawed
½   cup vanilla low-fat yogurt
½   cup blueberry pie filling
2   gingersnaps, crushed

1. Combine first 3 ingredients in a large bowl; fold together with a rubber spatula.
2. Spoon mixture into stemmed glasses or custard cups, and sprinkle with gingersnap crumbs. YIELD: 4 servings (serving size: ½ cup blueberry mixture and 1 teaspoon crumbs).

Per serving: CAL 130 (6% from fat); FAT 0.8g (sat 0.3g); PRO 1.8g; CARB 27.5g; FIB 0.9g; CHOL 2mg; IRON 0.5mg; SOD 57mg; CALC 64mg

TROPICAL COCONUT CREAM PHYLLO NESTS

POINTS value: 2

prep: 17 minutes • cook: 9 minutes

Try using seasonal berries in place of the mango and pineapple for a twist on this tropical treat. You can also substitute canned pineapple and bottled mango slices for the fresh fruit. The phyllo nests can be made ahead and stored in an airtight container.

1   cup light coconut milk, divided
1   tablespoon cornstarch
¼   cup plus 2 teaspoons powdered sugar, divided
½   teaspoon vanilla extract
8   (12 x 8–inch) sheets frozen phyllo dough, thawed
Cooking spray
1   cup diced peeled ripe mango (about 1 medium)
1   cup diced pineapple

1. Preheat oven to 350°.
2. Combine ¼ cup coconut milk and cornstarch in a small saucepan; stir with a whisk until cornstarch is completely dissolved. Add remaining ¾ cup coconut milk, stirring until smooth. Bring to a boil over medium heat, and cook 1 minute, stirring frequently. Remove from heat, and cool completely. Add ¼ cup powdered sugar and vanilla, stirring with whisk.
3. Place 1 phyllo sheet on a large cutting board or work surface (cover remaining dough to keep it from drying); lightly coat with cooking spray. Cut sheet into 4 squares, and layer squares in a muffin cup, 1 square at a time, pressing down in the center

---

fresh fruits

Sweet, juicy fruits enliven desserts with fresh flavors and contribute valuable nutrients to your diet as well. Each serving size below has a **POINTS** value of 1.

fruit	serving size	major nutrients
Apples, sliced with peel	1¾ cups	fiber, vitamin C
Banana	½ large	fiber, potassium, vitamin C
Blueberries	1¼ cups	fiber, antioxidants
Grapes	½ cup	vitamin C, antioxidants
Mangos, sliced	¾ cup	vitamins A and C
Pears, sliced with peel	1 cup	fiber, vitamins C and K
Pineapple, diced	1¼ cups	vitamin C, thiamin
Strawberries, halved	2¼ cups	fiber, vitamin C, antioxidants

after each addition so dough takes the shape of the cup. Ruffle edges to create the appearance of a nest. Repeat with remaining phyllo sheets to make 8 nests. Bake at 350° for 5 minutes or until golden. Remove from oven, and cool completely.

4. Combine mango and pineapple in a medium bowl. Spoon 2 tablespoons coconut milk mixture into each phyllo nest; top each with ¼ cup fruit mixture. Dust evenly with remaining 2 teaspoons powdered sugar. YIELD: 8 servings (serving size: 1 filled phyllo nest).

Per serving: CAL 118 (21% from fat); FAT 2.7g (sat 1.7g); PRO 1.9g; CARB 22.4g; FIB 1g; CHOL 0mg; IRON 0.8mg; SOD 100mg; CALC 7mg

CARAMEL-BANANA POCKETS

POINTS value: 4

prep: 12 minutes • cook: 14 minutes

Bearing a slight resemblance to deep-fried sopaipillas, a favorite dessert in the southwestern U.S., these pillowlike pastries are made with wonton wrappers, filled with banana and caramel, and cooked in a skillet with a small amount of oil.

1½ teaspoons cornstarch
1 tablespoon water
2 small bananas, finely chopped (about 1 cup)
4 tablespoons fat-free caramel topping (such as Smucker's), divided
¼ teaspoon ground cinnamon
12 wonton wrappers
8 teaspoons canola oil, divided
2 teaspoons powdered sugar

1. Combine cornstarch and water in a small bowl, stirring well.

2. Combine banana, 1 tablespoon caramel topping, and cinnamon in a small bowl, stirring well. Working with 1 wonton wrapper at a time (cover remaining wrappers with a damp towel to keep from drying), moisten edges of each wonton wrapper with cornstarch mixture. Place about 2 teaspoons banana mixture in center of each wrapper; fold in half to close, forming a rectangle. Press edges to seal.

3. Heat 4 teaspoons oil in a large nonstick skillet over medium–high heat. Place 6 pockets in pan; cook 3 to 4 minutes on each side or until golden. Remove from pan, and cool on a wire rack. Repeat procedure with remaining oil and pockets. Dust with powdered sugar; serve with remaining 3 tablespoons caramel topping. YIELD: 6 servings (serving size: 2 pockets and 1½ teaspoons caramel topping).

Per serving: CAL 181 (33% from fat); FAT 6.6g (sat 0.5g); PRO 1.9g; CARB 28.8g; FIB 1.2g; CHOL 1mg; IRON 0.6mg; SOD 129mg; CALC 10mg

wonton wrappers

Look for wonton wrappers in the refrigerated case of your supermarket's produce section. Though Chinese in origin, these handy squares of pre-made dough can be used to wrap anything from pot stickers to Italian ravioli to our sweet **Caramel-Banana Pockets.**

STRAWBERRY-MANGO SORBET SUNDAES

POINTS value: 2

prep: 9 minutes

Try experimenting with other flavored sorbets for a variation on this refreshing dessert. The POINTS value will remain the same.

1 (16-ounce) jar sliced peeled mango (such as Del Monte SunFresh)
1 cup diced strawberries
1 teaspoon finely chopped fresh mint
1 pint strawberry sorbet

1. Remove 1 cup mango and ⅓ cup juice from jar. Reserve remaining mango for another use. Dice mango, and combine with reserved juice, strawberries, and mint in a medium bowl, stirring gently.

2. Place a ¼-cup scoop sorbet in each of 8 stemmed glasses or bowls, and top with ¼ cup fruit mixture. YIELD: 8 servings (serving size: ¼ cup sorbet and ¼ cup fruit mixture).

Per serving: CAL 98 (0% from fat); FAT 0.1g (sat 0g); PRO 0.3g; CARB 24.2g; FIB 1.4g; CHOL 0mg; IRON 0.2mg; SOD 4mg; CALC 8mg

PEANUT BUTTER–CHOCOLATE ICE CREAM

POINTS value: 6

prep: 6 minutes • cook: 16 minutes
other: 3 hours and 30 minutes

You'll love this creamy frozen rendition of chocolate–peanut butter cups. Compare it to a ½-cup serving of traditional peanut butter–chocolate ice cream, which can have a POINTS value that ranges from 7 to 9.

1⅓ cups sugar
⅓ cup cocoa
2½ cups 2% reduced-fat milk, divided
3 large egg yolks, lightly beaten
½ cup fat-free half-and-half
½ cup reduced-fat creamy peanut butter

1. Combine sugar and cocoa in a medium saucepan; add 1 cup milk, stirring with a whisk. Cook over medium heat 4 minutes or until hot. Gradually add about one-fourth hot milk mixture to eggs, stirring constantly with whisk. Add to remaining hot milk mixture, stirring constantly.
2. Add remaining 1½ cups milk, half-and-half, and peanut butter, stirring with whisk until smooth. Cook 12 minutes over medium heat or until mixture reaches 160°, stirring constantly with whisk. Transfer mixture to a bowl. Cover and chill at least 1 hour, stirring occasionally.
3. Pour mixture into the freezer can of a 4-quart ice-cream freezer, and freeze according to manufacturer's instructions. Spoon ice cream into a freezer-safe container. Cover and freeze 2 hours or until firm. YIELD: 9 servings (serving size: ½ cup).

Per serving: CAL 268 (30% from fat); FAT 8.8g (sat 2.9g); PRO 7.7g; CARB 42.4g; FIB 2g; CHOL 74mg; IRON 1mg; SOD 147mg; CALC 122mg

CHAI TEA LATTE ICE CREAM

POINTS value: 4
(pictured on page 53)

prep: 2 minutes • cook: 17 minutes
other: 1 hour and 40 minutes

If you're a fan of the chai lattes at your local coffeehouse, you're going to love this ice cream. It's ultracreamy and fragrantly spiced and is the perfect ending to a spicy Indian- or Thai-style meal.

2 cups 2% reduced-fat milk
8 chai tea bags (such as Bigelow Vanilla Chai)
1 (3-inch) piece vanilla bean, split lengthwise
1 (12-ounce) can evaporated fat-free milk
⅔ cup sugar
2 tablespoons cornstarch
¼ teaspoon ground ginger
¼ teaspoon ground cinnamon
⅛ teaspoon salt
⅛ teaspoon ground cardamom
⅛ teaspoon ground nutmeg
⅛ teaspoon ground cloves
Dash of black pepper
2 large egg yolks

1. Cook 2% milk over medium-high heat in a heavy saucepan to 180° or until tiny bubbles form around edge (do not boil). Remove from heat. Add tea bags and vanilla bean; let stand 15 minutes. Remove and discard tea bags, pressing liquid out of bags. Remove vanilla bean; scrape seeds from bean into milk mixture, and discard bean. Add evaporated milk, stirring with a whisk.
2. Combine sugar and next 9 ingredients in a medium bowl. Gradually add milk mixture to sugar mixture, stirring constantly with whisk. Return milk mixture to pan. Cook over medium heat until mixture thickens and coats the back of a wooden spoon, stirring constantly. Transfer mixture to a bowl. Place over an ice bath and cool completely, stirring occasionally.
3. Pour milk mixture into the freezer can of a 2- to 3-quart ice-cream freezer, and freeze according to manufacturer's instructions. Spoon ice cream into a freezer-safe container. Cover and freeze 1 hour or until firm. YIELD: 7 servings (serving size: about ½ cup).

Per serving: CAL 174 (13% from fat); FAT 2.6g (sat 1.3g); PRO 6.3g; CARB 31.3g; FIB 0.1g; CHOL 68mg; IRON 0.2mg; SOD 144mg; CALC 222mg

tempering eggs

When combining eggs and a hot liquid, such as milk, it's important to acclimate the eggs to the temperature of the hot liquid in stages so they don't curdle. The traditional way to "temper" your egg mixture is to whisk one-fourth of the hot milk into the egg mixture in a slow, steady stream. Then whisk your egg-and-milk mixture back into the pan of hot milk, and cook as directed.

S'MORES ICE CREAM MIXER

POINTS value: 5

prep: 8 minutes • cook: 3 minutes

Toasting marshmallows doesn't always require a campfire. You can use a baking sheet to get the toasty taste without the mess. Be sure to spread the marshmallows out as much as possible on the pan.

1   cup miniature marshmallows
Cooking spray
1   (1.75-quart) container chocolate light ice cream (such as Edy's), softened
1   cup coarsely chopped graham crackers (about 5 sheets)
½   cup fat-free hot fudge topping

1. Preheat oven to 400°.
2. Spread marshmallows in a single layer on a jelly-roll pan coated with cooking spray. Lightly coat marshmallows with cooking spray. Bake at 400° for 3 minutes or until golden brown.
3. Spoon ice cream into a large freezer-safe container. Add marshmallows, graham crackers, and fudge topping. Gently stir until well blended. Cover and freeze until firm. YIELD: 10 servings (serving size: ½ cup).

Per serving: CAL 240 (21% from fat); FAT 5.6g (sat 2.9g); PRO 5.2g; CARB 41g; FIB 1.6g; CHOL 28mg; IRON 0.3mg; SOD 163mg; CALC 86mg

FROZEN BANANA SPLIT SQUARES

POINTS value: 5
(pictured on cover)

prep: 14 minutes
other: 10 hours and 10 minutes

¾   cup graham cracker crumbs
2   tablespoons light brown sugar
2   tablespoons butter, melted
Cooking spray
4   cups strawberry fat-free frozen yogurt (such as Edy's), softened
½   cup fat-free hot fudge topping
1   medium banana, thinly sliced
1   (8-ounce) container frozen fat-free whipped topping, thawed
15   chocolate-covered almonds, coarsely chopped (such as Dove)

1. Combine first 3 ingredients in a small bowl. Press into bottom of an 8-inch square baking pan coated with cooking spray. Spread yogurt evenly over crumbs. Cover and freeze 2 hours or until firm.
2. Melt fudge topping in microwave at HIGH 20 seconds. Drizzle fudge topping over yogurt, and spread evenly. Top evenly with sliced banana. Spread whipped topping over banana, spreading to edge of pan. Sprinkle with almonds. Cover and freeze 8 hours or until firm.
3. Let stand at room temperature 10 minutes before cutting into 2½ x 2–inch pieces. YIELD: 12 servings (serving size: 1 piece).

Per serving: CAL 232 (15% from fat); FAT 3.9g (sat 1.9g); PRO 4.4g; CARB 44.4g; FIB 0.8g; CHOL 8mg; IRON 0.3mg; SOD 129mg; CALC 107mg

PUMPKIN CUSTARDS WITH BRITTLE TOPPING

POINTS value: 6
(pictured on page 57)

prep: 7 minutes • cook: 45 minutes
other: 9 hours

Crunchy peanut brittle and a smooth and creamy pumpkin mixture create a perfect marriage of textures in these heavenly custards.

1   (15-ounce) can pumpkin
1   (14-ounce) can fat-free sweetened condensed milk
4   large eggs
1   teaspoon pumpkin-pie spice
2   teaspoons vanilla extract
⅛   teaspoon salt
Cooking spray
¼   cup chopped peanut brittle

1. Preheat oven to 325°.
2. Place first 6 ingredients in a blender; process just until smooth. Pour custard mixture evenly into 6 (6-ounce) ramekins or custard cups coated with cooking spray. Place ramekins in a 13 x 9–inch baking pan; add hot water to pan to a depth of 1 inch.
3. Bake at 325° for 45 minutes or until center of custard barely moves when ramekin is touched. Remove ramekins from pan; cool completely on a wire rack. Cover and chill at least 8 hours. Sprinkle each custard with 2 teaspoons peanut brittle before serving. YIELD: 6 servings (serving size: 1 custard).

Per serving: CAL 288 (13% from fat); FAT 4.2g (sat 1.3g); PRO 10.5g; CARB 51g; FIB 2.2g; CHOL 149mg; IRON 1.7mg; SOD 210mg; CALC 208mg

CARAMEL-COCONUT BANANA PUDDING

POINTS value: 4

prep: 9 minutes • other: 8 hours

We've added coconut milk, caramel topping, and sweetened coconut to a simple banana pudding recipe to create a make-ahead tropical dessert.

¾ cup 1% low-fat milk
¾ cup light coconut milk
¼ teaspoon vanilla extract
1 (3.4-ounce) package banana cream instant pudding mix
16 reduced-fat vanilla wafers
3 medium-size ripe bananas
2 cups frozen fat-free whipped topping, thawed
¼ cup fat-free caramel topping
2 tablespoons flaked sweetened coconut, toasted

1. Combine first 4 ingredients in a medium bowl. Beat with a mixer at medium speed for 2 minutes or until mixture begins to thicken.
2. Arrange wafers on bottom of an 8-inch square baking dish. Peel and slice bananas. Arrange half of banana slices over wafers. Spread half of pudding mixture over banana slices, and top with remaining banana slices. Spread remaining pudding over banana slices. Spread whipped topping over pudding. Cover and refrigerate 8 hours.
3. Drizzle caramel topping over pudding, and sprinkle with coconut before serving. YIELD: 8 servings (serving size: about 1 cup).

Per serving: CAL 209 (10% from fat); FAT 2.3g (sat 1.6g); PRO 1.9g; CARB 44.5g; FIB 1.6g; CHOL 1mg; IRON 0.5mg; SOD 182mg; CALC 35mg

APPLE BROWN BETTY

POINTS value: 3

prep: 22 minutes • cook: 1 hour

A betty is a classic American dessert consisting of layers of spiced fruit and buttered breadcrumbs. We used whole wheat French bread to make the crumbs.

1½ cups coarse fresh whole wheat breadcrumbs
1 teaspoon ground cinnamon, divided
⅛ teaspoon salt
3 tablespoons granulated sugar
3 tablespoons unsalted butter, melted and divided
2 pounds McIntosh apples, peeled, cored, and cut into 1-inch chunks
3 tablespoons light brown sugar
4 tablespoons apple cider, divided
1 teaspoon grated fresh lemon rind
2 teaspoons fresh lemon juice
⅛ teaspoon ground allspice
Cooking spray

1. Preheat oven to 375°.
2. Combine breadcrumbs, ½ teaspoon cinnamon, salt, granulated sugar, and 2 tablespoons butter.
3. Combine apple, remaining ½ teaspoon cinnamon, remaining 1 tablespoon butter, brown sugar, 2 tablespoons cider, and next 3 ingredients in a large bowl.
4. Sprinkle half of crumb mixture in bottom of an 8-inch square baking dish coated with cooking spray. Spoon apple filling over crumb mixture, and sprinkle remaining crumb mixture over apple; spoon remaining 2 tablespoons cider over crumbs.

5. Cover and bake at 375° for 45 minutes. Uncover and bake an additional 15 minutes or until lightly browned and bubbly. YIELD: 8 servings (serving size: about ⅔ cup).

Per serving: CAL 144 (30% from fat); FAT 4.8g (sat 2.8g); PRO 1.3g; CARB 26.1g; FIB 2.1g; CHOL 11mg; IRON 0.6mg; SOD 89mg; CALC 20mg

PLUM-BERRY CRUMBLE

POINTS value: 5

prep: 19 minutes • cook: 45 minutes other: 15 minutes

A crumble is a baked fruit mixture that is topped with a sweet crumbly pastry.

1 pound plums, pits removed and cut into eighths (about 5 plums)
1 quart strawberries, quartered (about 3 cups)
1 cup blueberries
¼ cup packed brown sugar
2 tablespoons lemon juice
1 teaspoon vanilla extract
Cooking spray
1 cup regular oats
¾ cup all-purpose flour
1 teaspoon ground cinnamon
¼ teaspoon salt
6 tablespoons chilled butter, cut into small pieces
½ cup turbinado sugar

1. Preheat oven to 375°.
2. Combine plums and next 5 ingredients in an 11 x 7–inch baking dish coated with cooking spray.
3. Combine oats and next 3 ingredients in a medium bowl. Cut in butter with a pastry blender or 2 knives

until mixture resembles coarse meal. Add turbinado sugar, stirring well.
4. Sprinkle oat mixture over fruit mixture. Bake at 375° for 45 minutes or until topping is lightly browned and fruit mixture is bubbly. Let stand 15 minutes before serving. YIELD: 9 servings (serving size: ⅔ cup).

Per serving: CAL 253 (31% from fat); FAT 8.7g (sat 5g); PRO 3.5g; CARB 42.9g; FIB 3.7g; CHOL 20mg; IRON 1.5mg; SOD 123mg; CALC 27mg

à la mode

Nothing beats a warm cobbler or crumble topped with vanilla ice cream. A ¼-cup portion of vanilla fat-free ice cream has a *POINTS* value of 1.

CHOCOLATE CREAM PIE

POINTS value: 5

prep: 9 minutes • cook: 8 minutes
other: 3 hours and 5 minutes

Adding melted dark chocolate chips to a store-bought pudding mix is the secret to this decadent shortcut cream pie.

2   cups fat-free milk
2   (1.3-ounce) packages sugar-free chocolate cook-and-serve pudding mix
¼   cup dark chocolate chips
1   (6-ounce) reduced-fat graham cracker crust
1   (8-ounce) container frozen fat-free whipped topping, thawed

1. Combine milk and pudding mix in a medium saucepan, stirring well with a whisk. Cook over medium heat 8 minutes or until mixture comes to a boil, stirring constantly. Remove from heat, and add chocolate chips, stirring until chocolate melts. Place pan in an ice-water bath for 5 minutes or until cool, stirring often.
2. Pour filling into crust. Cover surface of filling with plastic wrap, and chill at least 3 hours. Spread whipped topping over pie before serving.
YIELD: 8 servings (serving size: 1 slice).

Per serving: CAL 214 (24% from fat); FAT 5.8g (sat 1.8g); PRO 3.8g; CARB 34.5g; FIB 0.4g; CHOL 1mg; IRON 0.3mg; SOD 253mg; CALC 77mg

DARK CHOCOLATE LIME TARTS

POINTS value: 6

(pictured on page 52)

prep: 9 minutes • cook: 16 minutes
other: 2 hours

The contrast between the sweet, rich chocolate filling and the tart lime rind is a thrill for the taste buds.

⅓   cup sugar
¼   cup cocoa
¼   cup cornstarch
2   cups fat-free milk
2   large eggs
4   ounces dark chocolate, melted
1   tablespoon grated fresh lime rind
8   (3-inch) graham cracker tart shells
½   cup frozen fat-free whipped topping, thawed
Lime slices (optional)

1. Combine first 3 ingredients in a medium saucepan; add milk, stirring with a whisk until combined. Cook over medium heat 8 to 9 minutes or until thick, stirring constantly.
2. Place eggs in a small bowl; stir lightly with a whisk to combine. Gradually add one-fourth of hot milk mixture to eggs, stirring constantly. Add to remaining hot milk mixture in pan, stirring constantly. Bring mixture to a simmer over medium-low heat, stirring constantly. Cook 3 minutes. Remove from heat; stir in melted chocolate and lime rind.
3. Spoon mixture evenly into tart shells. Cover the surface of filling of each tart with plastic wrap, and chill 2 hours or until thoroughly chilled. Remove tarts from aluminum pans before serving, if desired. Top each tart with 1 tablespoon whipped topping and, if desired, a lime slice. YIELD: 8 servings (serving size: 1 tart).

Per serving: CAL 292 (38% from fat); FAT 12.4g (sat 4.3g); PRO 5.9g; CARB 42g; FIB 2.7g; CHOL 56mg; IRON 1.6mg; SOD 197mg; CALC 88mg

test kitchen secret

Graham cracker tart shells are fragile and break easily when removed from the aluminum pans. Use kitchen shears to cut through the aluminum pans in 4 or 5 places; then peel down the aluminum. Gently remove the shells.

CHERRY MERINGUE TARTS

POINTS value: 3

prep: 13 minutes
cook: 1 hour and 7 minutes
other: 30 minutes

Many traditional meringue recipes bake at a very low temperature to keep the meringue shells from browning. They also call for an overnight cooling period in the oven to help the meringues develop a crisp texture. This version takes a shortcut and calls for baking them at a higher temperature and eliminating the long cooling period in the oven. The result is a crisp, lightly browned meringue. If you don't want to use liqueur, use 2 additional table-spoons of cherry or another fruit juice.

2   large egg whites
⅓   cup plus 2 tablespoons sugar, divided
1   (12-ounce) package frozen pitted dark sweet cherries, thawed
2   tablespoons crème de cassis (black currant–flavored liqueur) or kirsch (cherry brandy)
1   teaspoon cornstarch
1   teaspoon vanilla extract
¼   teaspoon ground cinnamon
⅛   teaspoon salt
½   ounce white chocolate, shaved

1. Preheat oven to 300°.
2. To prepare meringues, cover a large baking sheet with parchment paper. Draw 4 (3½-inch) circles on paper. Turn paper over, and lay flat on pan.
3. Place egg whites in a medium bowl; beat with a mixer at high speed until foamy. Gradually add ⅓ cup

sugar, 1 tablespoon at a time, beating until stiff peaks form. Divide egg white mixture evenly among the 4 drawn circles. Shape meringues into nests with 1-inch sides using the back of a spoon.
4. Bake at 300° for 1 hour or until meringues are lightly browned and dry. Remove from oven, and let cool completely (about 30 minutes) on pan. Carefully remove meringues from paper.
5. While meringues cool, drain cherries, reserving all liquid. Combine reserved cherry juice, 2 tablespoons sugar, crème de cassis, and next 4 ingredients in a small saucepan, stirring well with a whisk. Stir in cherries. Cook over medium heat 7 minutes or until mixture is thick and bubbly, stirring constantly. Remove from heat, and let cool completely.
6. Place meringues on dessert plates. Spoon cherry mixture evenly into meringue shells; sprinkle with shaved white chocolate. YIELD: 4 servings (serving size: 1 meringue shell, ¼ cup plus 2 tablespoons cherry mixture, and 1½ teaspoons white chocolate).

Per serving: CAL 185 (5% from fat); FAT 1g (sat 0.9g); PRO 2.5g; CARB 39.5g; FIB 1.9g; CHOL 0mg; IRON 0mg; SOD 106mg; CALC 15mg

---

beating egg whites

To get better volume when beating egg whites, place the whole unbroken egg in a bowl of warm water for 5 minutes to bring the egg white to room temperature.

NO-COOK BUTTERSCOTCH-ALMOND LAYER CAKE

POINTS value: 4

prep: 8 minutes • cook: 6 minutes
other: 8 hours and 10 minutes

1   (1-ounce) package sugar-free butterscotch instant pudding mix
1   cup fat-free milk
2   cups frozen reduced-calorie whipped topping, thawed and divided
1   (10-ounce) loaf frozen low-fat pound cake (such as Sara Lee)
⅓   cup fat-free hazelnut-flavored coffee creamer
¼   cup slivered almonds, toasted

1. Prepare pudding mix according to package directions using 1 cup fat-free milk. Cover and chill 10 to 15 minutes or until firm. Fold 1 cup whipped topping into pudding.
2. Remove cake from loaf pan and slice cake lengthwise into 4 slices. Brush coffee creamer evenly over each slice. Return 1 cake slice to bottom of loaf pan; top with ½ cup pudding mixture, spreading to edge of slice. Repeat process with remaining cake slices and pudding mixture, ending with pudding. Top with remaining 1 cup whipped topping.
3. Cover and chill at least 8 hours. Sprinkle with toasted almonds just before serving. Cut into slices. YIELD: 8 servings (serving size: 1 slice).

Per serving: CAL 196 (25% from fat); FAT 5.5g (sat 2.6g); PRO 3.2g; CARB 33.9g; FIB 0.9g; CHOL 1mg; IRON 1.9mg; SOD 226mg; CALC 56mg

CARROT CUPCAKES

POINTS value: 5

prep: 15 minutes • cook: 21 minutes
other: 30 minutes

The addition of crushed pineapple makes these cupcakes extra moist. To get a more tender cake, grate your own carrot instead of using a package of preshredded matchstick carrots.

⅔ cup granulated sugar
¼ cup canola oil
1 large egg
1 teaspoon vanilla extract
1 cup grated carrot (about 4 small)
1 (8-ounce) can crushed
    pineapple in juice, drained
1 cup all-purpose flour
1 teaspoon baking soda
¾ teaspoon ground cinnamon
¼ teaspoon salt
Cream Cheese Frosting (recipe
    at right)

1. Preheat oven to 350°.
2. Place 12 paper muffin cup liners in muffin cups; set aside.
3. Place first 4 ingredients in a large bowl; stir well with a whisk until blended. Stir in carrot and pineapple.
4. Lightly spoon flour into a dry measuring cup; level with a knife. Combine flour and next 3 ingredients in a medium bowl, stirring until blended. Add flour mixture to sugar mixture, stirring just until moist. Spoon batter evenly into prepared muffin cups, filling half full. Bake at 350° for 21 minutes or until a wooden pick inserted in center of cupcake comes out clean. Remove cupcakes from pans; cool on a wire rack.
5. Spread about 1½ tablespoons

Cream Cheese Frosting on top of each cupcake. YIELD: 1 dozen (serving size: 1 cupcake).

Per serving: CAL 218 (38% from fat); FAT 9.3g (sat 3.2g); PRO 3.8g; CARB 30.2g; FIB 0.7g; CHOL 31mg; IRON 0.7mg; SOD 251mg; CALC 24mg

RED VELVET CUPCAKES

POINTS value: 5

(pictured on page 51)

prep: 11 minutes • cook: 16 minutes
other: 30 minutes

All of the key ingredients for a traditional red velvet cake—cocoa, buttermilk, vinegar, and red food coloring—are here in these colorful cupcakes. They will be a hit for Christmas, Valentine's Day, the Fourth of July, or any other special occasion where red and white are the colors of choice.

¾ cup granulated sugar
2½ tablespoons vegetable shortening
1 large egg
1 cup all-purpose flour
1½ tablespoons unsweetened cocoa
½ teaspoon baking soda
½ teaspoon salt
½ cup low-fat buttermilk
1 tablespoon red food coloring
1 teaspoon white vinegar
½ teaspoon vanilla extract
¼ teaspoon almond extract
Cream Cheese Frosting

1. Preheat oven to 350°.
2. Place 12 paper muffin cup liners in muffin cups. Set aside.
3. Combine granulated sugar and shortening in a bowl; beat with a

mixer at medium speed until well blended. Add egg; beat until creamy.
4. Lightly spoon flour into a dry measuring cup; level with a knife. Combine flour, cocoa, baking soda, and salt in a medium bowl. Combine buttermilk and next 4 ingredients in a small bowl. Add flour mixture and buttermilk mixture alternately to sugar mixture, beginning and ending with flour mixture, stirring with a whisk just until smooth. Spoon batter evenly into prepared muffin cups. Bake at 350° for 16 to 18 minutes or until a wooden pick inserted in center of cupcake comes out clean. Cool completely on a wire rack.
5. Spread about 1½ tablespoons Cream Cheese Frosting over tops of cupcakes. YIELD: 1 dozen (serving size: 1 cupcake).

Per serving: CAL 200 (33% from fat); FAT 7.3g (sat 3.6g); PRO 4.1g; CARB 29.9g; FIB 0.5g; CHOL 32mg; IRON 0.7mg; SOD 252mg; CALC 30mg

CREAM CHEESE FROSTING
POINTS value: 1

We loved this luscious frosting slathered over both of these cupcakes.

1 (8-ounce) package ⅓-less-fat
    cream cheese
¾ cup powdered sugar
½ teaspoon vanilla extract

1. Combine all ingredients in a medium bowl; beat with a mixer at medium speed until smooth. YIELD: 1¼ cups.

Per tablespoon: CAL 46 (47% from fat); FAT 2.4g (sat 1.6g); PRO 1.2g; CARB 4.9g; FIB 0g; CHOL 8mg; IRON 0mg; SOD 51mg; CALC 8mg

DELICATE CHAI TEA CAKE

POINTS value: 4

prep: 14 minutes • cook: 23 minutes
other: 1 hour

The exotic flavors of chai tea and the sweetness of ripe pears elevate a simple cake to special-occasion status.

Cooking spray
1⅓ cups water
3 spiced chai tea bags
2 tablespoons water
2 teaspoons cornstarch
2 tablespoons sugar
¼ teaspoon almond extract
1 (9-ounce) package white cake mix (such as Jiffy)
1 large egg white
1 ripe pear, thinly sliced
⅓ cup sliced almonds, toasted

1. Preheat oven to 350°.
2. Coat a 9-inch round cake pan with cooking spray, and line with parchment paper. Set pan aside.
3. Bring 1⅓ cups water to a boil in a saucepan; remove from heat and add tea bags. Cover and let steep 2 minutes; discard tea bags. Remove ½ cup tea from pan, and pour into a shallow bowl; place in freezer 10 minutes or until cool (do not freeze). Reserve remaining tea in pan.
4. Combine 2 tablespoons water and cornstarch in a small bowl; add to remaining tea in pan. Stir in sugar. Bring to a boil over medium-high heat, stirring constantly. Boil 1 minute or until mixture thickens. Remove from heat; stir in almond extract, and set aside.
5. Combine cake mix, egg white, and ½ cup cooled tea. Beat with a mixer at low speed 30 seconds; beat at medium speed 3 minutes. Pour batter into prepared pan. Bake at 350° for 17 minutes or until a wooden pick inserted in center comes out clean. Cool cake in pan 10 minutes on a wire rack. Remove from pan, and carefully peel off parchment paper. Cool completely on a wire rack.
6. Place cake on a plate. Arrange pear slices in a spoke pattern on top. Spoon glaze over pear, allowing some to run over sides. Sprinkle with almonds. Refrigerate, uncovered, until ready to serve. YIELD: 8 servings (serving size: 1 wedge).

Per serving: CAL 186 (26% from fat); FAT 5.4g (sat 1.2g); PRO 3.3g; CARB 32g; FIB 1.7g; CHOL 0mg; IRON 0.8mg; SOD 224mg; CALC 25mg

OVERNIGHT BANANA-CARROT CAKE

POINTS value: 4

prep: 22 minutes • cook: 30 minutes
other: 9 hours

Cantaloupe is the secret ingredient in this surprising cake. Prepare and chill the frosting while the cake cools.

3 cups coarsely chopped cantaloupe, divided
½ cup water
1 (18-ounce) package carrot cake mix (such as Betty Crocker)
3 large eggs
2 tablespoons canola oil
Cooking spray
2 ripe bananas, sliced
Fluffy Cheesecake Frosting
¼ teaspoon ground nutmeg

1. Preheat oven to 350°.
2. Combine 1½ cups cantaloupe and water in a blender, and process until smooth. Combine pureed cantaloupe, cake mix, eggs, and oil in a large bowl. Beat with a mixer at low speed 30 seconds; beat at medium speed 2 minutes. Pour batter into a 13 x 9–inch baking pan coated with cooking spray. Top batter with remaining 1½ cups cantaloupe, lightly pressing cantaloupe into batter.
3. Bake at 350° for 30 minutes or until a wooden pick inserted in center comes out clean. Cool cake completely in pan on a wire rack.
4. Place banana slices on top of cake. Top with Fluffy Cheesecake Frosting, and sprinkle with nutmeg. Cover and chill 8 hours. YIELD: 20 servings (serving size: 1 piece).

Per serving: CAL 194 (34% from fat); FAT 7.3g (sat 2.1g); PRO 4.5g; CARB 27.4g; FIB 1.4g; CHOL 56mg; IRON 0.9mg; SOD 256mg; CALC 71mg

FLUFFY CHEESECAKE FROSTING
POINTS value: 1

½ cup (4 ounces) tub-style light cream cheese, softened
1 (1-ounce) package sugar-free cheesecake instant pudding mix
2 cups fat-free milk
2 cups frozen fat-free whipped topping, thawed

1. Combine first 3 ingredients in a medium bowl. Beat with a mixer at low speed 2 minutes or until thick. Fold in whipped topping. Cover and chill 1 hour. YIELD: 4 cups.

Per 3 tablespoons: CAL 35 (23% from fat); FAT 0.9g (sat 0.6g); PRO 1.3g; CARB 4.8g; FIB 0g; CHOL 3mg; IRON 0mg; SOD 64mg; CALC 35mg

DOUBLE-CHOCOLATE BUNDT CAKE

POINTS value: 6

(pictured on page 54)

prep: 16 minutes • cook: 45 minutes
other: 15 minutes

Dutch process cocoa makes this tender cake exceptionally dark and rich.

Baking spray with flour
1¾ cups all-purpose flour
1   cup granulated sugar
¾   cup Dutch process cocoa
1½ teaspoons baking powder
1½ teaspoons baking soda
1   teaspoon salt
2   large eggs
1   cup low-fat buttermilk
⅔   cup packed brown sugar
⅔   cup strong brewed coffee
¼   cup canola oil
1   tablespoon vanilla extract
1   cup semisweet chocolate
     minichips
1   tablespoon sifted powdered
     sugar

1. Preheat oven to 350°.
2. Heavily coat a 12-cup nonstick Bundt pan with baking spray; set aside.
3. Lightly spoon flour into dry measuring cups; level with a knife. Combine flour and next 5 ingredients in a medium bowl. In a large bowl, beat eggs and next 5 ingredients with a mixer at medium speed 1 minute or until just combined. Add flour mixture to egg mixture; beat at high speed 1 minute. Stir in chocolate minichips.
4. Pour batter into prepared pan. Bake at 350° for 45 minutes or until a wooden pick inserted in center comes out clean. Cool in pan 15 minutes on a wire rack. Remove cake from pan; cool completely on wire rack. Dust with powdered sugar.
YIELD: 16 servings (serving size: 1 slice).

Per serving: CAL 250 (41% from fat); FAT 11.4g (sat 2.5g); PRO 3.9g; CARB 42.2g; FIB 1.8g; CHOL 27mg; IRON 2.6mg; SOD 186mg; CALC 57mg

PEAR-DATE UPSIDE-DOWN CAKE

POINTS value: 5

(pictured on page 57)

prep: 22 minutes • cook: 32 minutes
other: 5 minutes

A spice cake studded with chopped dates forms the base for syrup-coated pears in this old-fashioned skillet dessert.

1½ tablespoons butter
¼   cup pear nectar
⅓   cup packed brown sugar
¼   teaspoon ground cinnamon
2   pears, peeled, cored, and sliced
1   cup all-purpose flour
1   teaspoon baking powder
¼   teaspoon baking soda
½   teaspoon ground cinnamon
¼   teaspoon ground nutmeg
¼   teaspoon salt
¼   cup butter, softened
⅓   cup granulated sugar
⅓   cup packed brown sugar
1   large egg
1   teaspoon vanilla extract
¼   cup pear nectar
¼   cup 1% low-fat milk
½   cup chopped dates
2½ cups vanilla fat-free ice cream
     (optional)

1. Preheat oven to 350°.
2. Melt 1½ tablespoons butter in a 9-inch cast-iron skillet, and add ¼ cup pear nectar, ⅓ cup brown sugar, and ¼ teaspoon cinnamon, stirring until combined. Bring to a boil, and cook over medium heat 1 minute or until syrupy, stirring constantly. Arrange pear slices in a circular pattern over syrupy mixture.
3. Lightly spoon flour into a dry measuring cup, and level with a knife. Combine flour, baking powder, and next 4 ingredients in a medium bowl.
4. Place ¼ cup butter, granulated sugar, and ⅓ cup brown sugar in a medium bowl; beat with a mixer at medium speed until well blended (about 3 minutes). Add egg and vanilla; beat well.
5. Combine ¼ cup pear nectar and milk. Add flour mixture to butter mixture alternately with milk mixture, beginning and ending with flour mixture. Stir in dates.
6. Spoon batter over pears, spreading batter to edges. Bake at 350° for 28 to 30 minutes or until a wooden pick inserted in center comes out clean. Cool in pan 5 minutes. Loosen cake from sides of pan using a narrow metal spatula. Carefully invert onto a plate. Cut into wedges; serve warm. Top each serving with ¼ cup ice cream, if desired. YIELD: 10 servings (serving size: 1 wedge).

Per serving: CAL 246 (26% from fat); FAT 7.2g (sat 4.2g); PRO 2.6g; CARB 44.5g; FIB 1.9g; CHOL 38mg; IRON 1.1mg; SOD 192mg; CALC 77mg

TRIPLE-LAYER MOCHA TOFFEE CAKE

POINTS value: 6

prep: 24 minutes • cook: 20 minutes
other: 1 hour

In this dramatic dessert, three dark chocolate cake layers are brushed with an espresso mixture, frosted with chocolate whipped topping, and sprinkled with chocolate toffee bars.

Cooking spray
1½ cups sifted cake flour
⅓ cup Dutch process cocoa (such as Hershey's Special Dark)
1½ teaspoons baking powder
¼ teaspoon salt
⅔ cup 1% low-fat milk
3 tablespoons light stick butter
3 large eggs
1½ cups plus 2 tablespoons sugar, divided
2 teaspoons vanilla extract
2 teaspoons instant espresso granules
3 tablespoons coffee liqueur
3 tablespoons water
1 (8-ounce) container frozen chocolate whipped topping, thawed
3 (1.4-ounce) chocolate-covered toffee bars, finely chopped

1. Preheat oven to 350°.
2. Line 3 (8-inch) cake pans with parchment paper; coat with cooking spray. Set pans aside.
3. Sift together flour and next 3 ingredients.
4. Combine milk and butter in a 2-cup glass measure. Microwave at HIGH 1 to 1½ minutes or until mixture is very hot.
5. Beat eggs and 1½ cups sugar with a mixer at high speed 5 minutes or until egg mixture is pale yellow and thick. Add flour mixture, milk mixture, and vanilla. Beat 30 seconds or until well combined (batter will be thin). Quickly pour batter evenly into prepared cake pans.
6. Bake at 350° for 18 to 20 minutes or until cake starts to pull away from sides of pan and springs back when pressed in the center. Cool in pans on wire racks 10 minutes. Remove from pans, and cool completely.
7. Combine espresso granules, coffee liqueur, remaining 2 tablespoons sugar, and 3 tablespoons water in a 1-cup glass measure. Microwave at HIGH 1 minute or until sugar dissolves. Brush coffee mixture over cake layers, allowing syrup to soak into cake.
8. Place 1 cake layer on a cake plate. Spread with about 1 cup whipped topping; sprinkle with ¼ cup chopped toffee bars. Repeat procedure twice with remaining ingredients, ending with toffee bars. YIELD: 16 servings (serving size: 1 slice).

Per serving: CAL 246 (32% from fat); FAT 8.7g (sat 4.8g); PRO 3.2g; CARB 40.7g; FIB 0.7g; CHOL 47mg; IRON 1.8mg; SOD 143mg; CALC 57mg

dutch process cocoa

Dutch process cocoa has been treated with an alkali to neutralize the acidity of cocoa. Its flavor is lighter, sweeter, and less bitter than regular cocoa. Because the alkali affects cocoa's interaction with leavening agents, it won't react to baking soda and can only be used in recipes that call for baking powder.

RASPBERRY–CHOCOLATE TRUFFLE CHEESECAKE

POINTS value: 6
(pictured on back cover)

prep: 19 minutes • cook: 2 hours
other: 10 hours

1 (13.7-ounce) package fat-free fudge brownie mix (such as No Pudge!)
½ cup vanilla fat-free yogurt
2 large egg whites, divided
Cooking spray
1 (24-ounce) carton 1% low-fat cottage cheese
1 (8-ounce) package ⅓-less-fat cream cheese, softened
¾ cup sugar
⅓ cup Dutch process cocoa
¼ cup all-purpose flour
¼ teaspoon salt
1 teaspoon instant coffee granules
2 tablespoons hot water
¾ cup seedless raspberry fruit spread
3 ounces bittersweet chocolate, chopped and melted
3 large eggs
1 teaspoon vanilla extract

1. Preheat oven to 350°.
2. Prepare brownie mix according to package directions using yogurt and 1 egg white. Spread batter into an 8-inch square baking pan coated with cooking spray. Bake at 350° for 35 to 40 minutes or until done. Cool completely in pan on a wire rack.
3. Reduce oven temperature to 325°.
4. Combine cottage cheese and cream cheese in a food processor, and process 2 minutes or until smooth. Add sugar, cocoa, flour, and salt. Process 30 seconds or just until blended, scraping down sides of bowl if needed.

5. Combine coffee granules and hot water. Stir in raspberry spread and melted chocolate. Add raspberry mixture, remaining egg white, eggs, and vanilla to cream cheese mixture in processor; process just until combined.

6. Crumble brownie evenly into a 9-inch springform pan coated with cooking spray. Press brownie firmly to form a compact crust.

7. Pour batter over crust. Bake at 325° for 1 hour and 20 minutes or until almost set. Turn off oven; leave cake in oven 1 hour. Remove from oven; run a knife around edge. Cool completely in pan on a wire rack. Cover and chill at least 8 hours. YIELD: 16 servings (serving size: 1 wedge).

Per serving: CAL 284 (22% from fat); FAT 6.9g (sat 3.8g); PRO 11.7g; CARB 45.7g; FIB 0.8g; CHOL 52mg; IRON 2.2mg; SOD 386mg; CALC 94mg

PEANUT BUTTER AND JELLY GEMS

POINTS value: 1

prep: 31 minutes
cook: 10 minutes per batch
other: 30 minutes plus 2 minutes per batch

⅓ cup butter, softened
¾ cup packed dark brown sugar
½ cup granulated sugar
⅓ cup egg substitute
3 tablespoons chunky peanut butter
2 teaspoons vanilla extract
⅓ cup chopped dry-roasted peanuts
1½ cups all-purpose flour
½ teaspoon baking soda
½ teaspoon salt
Cooking spray
9 tablespoons strawberry fruit spread

1. Beat butter with a mixer at high speed until creamy; add brown sugar, beating well. Add granulated sugar and next 3 ingredients; beat until fluffy. Stir in peanuts.

2. Lightly spoon flour into dry measuring cups; level with a knife. Combine flour, baking soda, and salt in a bowl; stir into peanut butter mixture. Cover dough, and chill 30 minutes.

3. Preheat oven to 350°.

4. Shape dough into 1-inch balls; place 2 inches apart on baking sheets coated with cooking spray. Press thumb in center of each ball to make an indentation.

5. Bake at 350° for 10 to 12 minutes or until lightly browned. Press centers again with thumb while cookies are still warm; fill center of each cookie with about ½ teaspoon fruit spread. Cool on pans 2 minutes. Remove from pans, and cool completely on wire racks. YIELD: 56 cookies (serving size: 1 cookie).

Per serving: CAL 59 (32% from fat); FAT 2.1g (sat 0.9g); PRO 0.9g; CARB 9.3g; FIB 0.2g; CHOL 3mg; IRON 0.3mg; SOD 55mg; CALC 5mg

measuring cookie dough

A spring-handled cookie scoop makes measuring dough easy. Manufacturers label scoops in different ways. Some are labeled with a number. The higher the number, the smaller the scoop. Be sure to use a scoop that drops the amount of dough called for in the recipe, or the yield will be incorrect. A #70 scoop holds a level tablespoon of dough.

FUDGY CHOCOLATE-CHERRY BITES

POINTS value: 1

prep: 10 minutes • cook: 16 minutes
other: 2 minutes per batch

These chewy, fudgy little cookies offer big chocolate flavor with a hint of sweet cherries and coffee.

1¼ cups sifted powdered sugar
⅓ cup unsweetened cocoa
½ teaspoon espresso powder
⅛ teaspoon salt
2 large egg whites
1½ teaspoons vanilla extract
½ cup dried sweet cherries, coarsely chopped
½ cup chopped pecans or walnuts
Cooking spray

1. Preheat oven to 300°.

2. Combine first 6 ingredients in a large bowl. Beat with a mixer at low speed until combined. Beat at medium speed 2 minutes. Stir in cherries and nuts.

3. Spoon 1 level tablespoon batter into miniature muffin cups coated with cooking spray. Bake at 300° for 16 minutes or until puffed and crisp on top. Let stand 2 to 5 minutes before removing from pan. Cool on a wire rack. YIELD: 21 cookies (serving size: 1 cookie).

Note: Store in an airtight container up to 2 days.

Per serving: CAL 62 (32% from fat); FAT 2.2g (sat 0.3g); PRO 1g; CARB 10.1g; FIB 1.1g; CHOL 0mg; IRON 0.3mg; SOD 20mg; CALC 8mg

PECAN PIE SQUARES

POINTS value: 5

(pictured on page 50)

prep: 10 minutes • cook: 53 minutes

Take this bar-cookie version of pecan pie to your next holiday gathering. These squares have a rich, buttery crust and a sweet nutty filling that earned them our Test Kitchens' highest rating. But they only have one-third of the calories and 75% less fat than a slice of traditional pecan pie.

1	cup all-purpose flour
¼	cup granulated sugar
⅛	teaspoon salt
¼	cup butter, cut into small pieces
	Cooking spray
¾	cup packed brown sugar
1	cup light corn syrup
1	large egg
4	large egg whites
¾	cup finely chopped pecans
1	teaspoon vanilla extract

1. Preheat oven to 350°.
2. Lightly spoon flour into a dry measuring cup; level with a knife. Combine flour, granulated sugar, and salt in a medium bowl. Cut in butter with a pastry blender or 2 knives until mixture resembles coarse meal. Press flour mixture evenly into bottom of an 8-inch square baking pan coated with cooking spray, using a piece of plastic wrap to press mixture firmly into pan. Remove plastic wrap. Bake at 350° for 20 minutes or until lightly browned.
3. Combine brown sugar and corn syrup in a medium saucepan; bring to a boil over medium heat, stirring gently.
4. Combine egg and egg whites in a medium bowl. Stir one-fourth warm syrup mixture into eggs; add to remaining warm syrup mixture. Stir in pecans and vanilla. Pour mixture over crust.
5. Bake at 350° for 30 minutes or until set (the filling will puff up as it bakes but will deflate as it becomes set). Remove from oven; cool completely in pan on a wire rack. Cut into squares. YIELD: 16 servings (serving size: 1 square).

Per serving: CAL 211 (31% from fat); FAT 7.3g (sat 2.3g); PRO 2.7g; CARB 35.8g; FIB 0.8g; CHOL 21mg; IRON 0.8mg; SOD 74mg; CALC 20mg

BLUEBERRY-WALNUT OATMEAL COOKIES

POINTS value: 2

(pictured on opposite page)

prep: 25 minutes
cook: 10 minutes per batch

Crunchy and sweet, these fruited fiber-filled cookies are perfect for a snack or even for a breakfast on the go.

1½	cups all-purpose flour
1	teaspoon baking soda
½	teaspoon salt
½	cup (4 ounces) ⅓-less-fat cream cheese, softened
6	tablespoons unsalted butter, softened
¾	cup packed light brown sugar
½	cup granulated sugar
1	large egg
2	teaspoons vanilla extract
2½	cups regular oats
1	cup dried blueberries
1	cup chopped walnuts

1. Preheat oven to 350°.
2. Lightly spoon flour into dry measuring cups; level with a knife. Combine flour, baking soda, and salt.
3. Beat cream cheese and butter with a mixer at medium speed until fluffy. Add sugars, beating until blended. Add egg and vanilla, beating just until blended. Gradually add flour mixture to butter mixture, stirring just until combined. Fold in oats, blueberries, and walnuts. Drop by tablespoonfuls 2 inches apart onto baking sheets.
4. Bake at 350° for 10 minutes or until lightly browned. Remove from pans, and cool completely on wire racks. YIELD: 45 cookies (serving size: 1 cookie).

Per serving: CAL 105 (36% from fat); FAT 4.2g (sat 1.5g); PRO 2.2g; CARB 14.7g; FIB 1.2g; CHOL 11mg; IRON 0.6mg; SOD 70mg; CALC 10mg

Blueberry-Walnut Oatmeal Cookies,
opposite page

Pecan Pie Squares, *page 48*

Red Velvet Cupcakes, *page 43*

Dark Chocolate Lime
Tarts, *page 41*

Chai Tea Latte Ice Cream, *page 38*

Double-Chocolate
Bundt Cake, *page 45*

Coffee–Ice Cream Punch,
page 25

Irish Soda Bread with Raisins, *page 30*

Pumpkin Custards
with Brittle Topping, *page 39*

Pear-Date Upside-Down
Cake, *page 45*

Grilled Rosemary Flatbreads,
page 32

Parmesan-Basil Biscuits, *page 29*

Asian-Style Lettuce Wraps, *page 23*

Pomegranate Fizzer, *page 24*

Steak Crostini with
Avocado-Horseradish
Mayonnaise,
page 22

Crab Cakes over Mixed Greens with Lemon Dressing, *page 73*

Amberjack with Mango-Banana
Salsa, *page 66*

Cranberry-Glazed Salmon, *page 69*

fish & shellfish ▸▸

AMBERJACK WITH MANGO-BANANA SALSA

POINTS value: 6
(pictured on page 63)

prep: 17 minutes • cook: 33 minutes
other: 2 hours and 30 minutes

Amberjack is a lean, firm-fleshed white fish. If it's not available, substitute grouper or mahimahi. The flavorful fish and fruit salsa are also great served as fish tacos—just break the fish into pieces and serve in tortillas along with the salsa.

1½ cups pineapple-orange juice
6   tablespoons brown sugar
6   tablespoons dark rum
3   tablespoons low-sodium soy sauce
1½ tablespoons lime juice
1½ tablespoons canola oil
1½ teaspoons crushed red pepper
4   (6-ounce) amberjack fillets (about ½ inch thick)
¼   teaspoon salt
Cooking spray
Mango-Banana Salsa

1. Combine first 7 ingredients in a medium bowl, stirring until sugar dissolves. Pour half of juice mixture into a large heavy-duty zip-top plastic bag; add fish. Seal bag, and marinate in refrigerator 2 hours, turning bag once.
2. Place remaining juice mixture in a small saucepan; bring to a boil. Reduce heat to medium; cook 20 minutes or until mixture is reduced to ¼ cup. Set aside.
3. Prepare grill.
4. Remove fish from marinade; discard marinade. Sprinkle fish with salt.

Place fish on grill rack coated with cooking spray; grill 5 minutes on each side or until fish flakes easily when tested with a fork. Drizzle reduced juice mixture evenly over fish. Serve with Mango-Banana Salsa.
YIELD: 4 servings (serving size: 1 fillet, 1 tablespoon juice mixture, and ½ cup Mango-Banana Salsa).

Per serving: CAL 313 (12% from fat); FAT 4.2g (sat 0.6g); PRO 33.2g; CARB 33.4g; FIB 2.2g; CHOL 124mg; IRON 2.4mg; SOD 378mg; CALC 44mg

MANGO-BANANA SALSA

POINTS value: 0

1   cup chopped mango
¼   cup finely chopped red bell pepper
¼   cup finely chopped red onion
¼   cup chopped fresh cilantro
2   tablespoons fresh lime juice
2   teaspoons minced jalapeño pepper
1½ teaspoons grated peeled fresh ginger
2   teaspoons honey
1   cup diced banana (about 1 medium)

1. Combine first 8 ingredients in a medium bowl. Let stand 30 minutes.
2. Stir in banana just before serving.
YIELD: 2 cups.

Per tablespoon: CAL 10 (0% from fat); FAT 0g (sat 0g); PRO 0.1g; CARB 2.6g; FIB 0.3g; CHOL 0mg; IRON 0mg; SOD 0mg; CALC 1mg

PECAN-CRUSTED CATFISH

POINTS value: 7

prep: 12 minutes • cook: 20 minutes

If you can't find pecan meal, place about ½ cup of pecan halves in a food processor and process until they're finely ground. Adding ground pecans to the breadcrumbs creates a nutty, crispy coating for this oven-fried fish.

1   large egg white
1   teaspoon lemon juice
1   teaspoon cornstarch
¼   teaspoon garlic salt
¼   teaspoon chili powder
⅛   teaspoon ground red pepper
½   cup dry breadcrumbs
⅓   cup pecan meal
4   (6-ounce) catfish fillets
Cooking spray
4   lemon wedges

1. Preheat oven to 425°.
2. Combine first 6 ingredients in a shallow dish; stir well. Combine breadcrumbs and pecan meal in another shallow dish. Pat fish dry. Dip fish in egg white mixture, and dredge in breadcrumb mixture, pressing firmly to coat. Spray fish with cooking spray.
3. Place fish on a baking sheet coated with cooking spray. Bake at 425° for 20 minutes or until fish flakes easily when tested with a fork. Serve with lemon wedges. YIELD: 4 servings (serving size: 1 fillet and 1 lemon wedge).

Per serving: CAL 303 (50% from fat); FAT 16.8g (sat 3.4g); PRO 28.9g; CARB 7.8g; FIB 0.9g; CHOL 80mg; IRON 1.4mg; SOD 229mg; CALC 35mg

COD WITH
TANGY TARTAR SAUCE

POINTS value: 5

prep: 8 minutes • cook: 9 minutes

Cod is a cold-water fish that's a good source of omega-3 fatty acids—helpful fats that can help prevent heart disease. With the fish's crispy golden brown coating and a simple homemade tartar sauce, this is sure to become a family favorite.

¼   cup flour
1   teaspoon kosher salt
½   teaspoon freshly ground black pepper
¼   teaspoon paprika
4   (6-ounce) cod fillets
Cooking spray
Tangy Tartar Sauce

1. Combine first 4 ingredients in a shallow dish. Pat fish dry. Dredge both sides of fish in flour mixture, shaking off excess flour.
2. Heat a large nonstick skillet over medium-high heat. Coat pan with cooking spray. Place fish in pan, reduce heat to medium, and cook 5 minutes. Turn fish, and cook 4 minutes or until fish flakes easily when tested with a fork. Serve with Tangy Tartar Sauce. YIELD: 4 servings (serving size: 1 fillet and 3 tablespoons sauce).

Per serving: CAL 227 (25% from fat); FAT 6.2g (sat 1.2g); PRO 32g; CARB 8.8g; FIB 0.4g; CHOL 81mg; IRON 0.9mg; SOD 450mg; CALC 69mg

TANGY TARTAR SAUCE

POINTS value: 1

⅓   cup fat-free sour cream
¼   cup light mayonnaise
2   tablespoons drained dill pickle relish
1   teaspoon chopped fresh parsley
1   teaspoon drained capers, chopped
½   teaspoon finely grated fresh lemon rind
1   teaspoon fresh lemon juice
¼   teaspoon garlic powder
Dash of ground red pepper

1. Combine all ingredients in a small bowl, stirring well. YIELD: ¾ cup.

Per tablespoon: CAL 27 (57% from fat); FAT 1.7g (sat 0.3g); PRO 0.5g; CARB 2.4g; FIB 0.1g; CHOL 3mg; IRON 0mg; SOD 80mg; CALC 14mg

FLOUNDER MILANESE

POINTS value: 6

prep: 22 minutes • cook: 9 minutes

Top tender pan-fried flounder fillets with a simple Italian-style green salad.

1   large egg
1   large egg white
⅔   cup dry breadcrumbs
¾   teaspoon salt, divided
½   teaspoon freshly ground black pepper, divided
4   (6-ounce) flounder fillets
2   tablespoons olive oil, divided
4   cups mixed baby greens
2   plum tomatoes, diced
½   cup thinly sliced red onion
1   tablespoon fresh lemon juice
1   teaspoon white wine vinegar
½   teaspoon Dijon mustard
3   tablespoons minced fresh parsley

1. Combine egg and egg white in a shallow bowl, stirring with a whisk. Combine breadcrumbs, ½ teaspoon salt, and ¼ teaspoon pepper in another shallow bowl. Pat fillets dry. Dip fillets in egg, letting excess egg drip off. Lightly dredge fillets in breadcrumb mixture.
2. Heat 2 teaspoons oil in a large nonstick skillet over medium heat. Add 2 fillets; cook 2 minutes on each side or until fish flakes easily when tested with a fork. Transfer fillets to a serving platter. Repeat procedure with 1 teaspoon olive oil and remaining fillets.
3. Combine greens, tomato, and onion in a bowl. Combine remaining 1 tablespoon olive oil, remaining ¼ teaspoon salt, remaining ¼ teaspoon pepper, lemon juice, vinegar, and mustard, stirring well with a whisk. Pour dressing over greens; toss to coat. Top fillets with greens mixture, and sprinkle with parsley. YIELD: 4 servings (serving size: 1 fillet and 1 cup salad greens).

Per serving: CAL 290 (32% from fat); FAT 10.4g (sat 1.8g); PRO 36.1g; CARB 12.3g; FIB 2.4g; CHOL 108mg; IRON 2.3mg; SOD 689mg; CALC 95mg

GROUPER TACOS WITH MANGO SALSA

POINTS value: 4

prep: 25 minutes • cook: 15 minutes

Before assembling the tacos, toss 2 or 3 tablespoons of the juices that settle from the salsa with the angel hair slaw to moisten the slaw and distribute the flavors. For ease of preparation, 1 (24-ounce) jar of sliced mango will give you the 1½ cups needed for the salsa.

4   (6-ounce) grouper fillets (about 1¼ to 1½ inches thick)
6   tablespoons fresh lime juice, divided
2   garlic cloves, minced
¾   teaspoon ground cumin, divided
½   teaspoon salt, divided
½   teaspoon freshly ground black pepper, divided
1½   cups diced peeled mango
⅓   cup chopped red onion
¼   cup chopped fresh cilantro
2   large garlic cloves, minced
2½   tablespoons minced seeded jalapeño pepper (about 1 large)
Cooking spray
12   (5½-inch) corn tortillas
1½   cups angel hair slaw

1. Prepare grill.
2. Place fish in a shallow baking dish; sprinkle with 2 tablespoons lime juice and 2 minced garlic cloves. Sprinkle with ½ teaspoon cumin, ¼ teaspoon salt, and ¼ teaspoon black pepper. Set aside.
3. Combine diced mango, next 4 ingredients, remaining ¼ cup lime juice, and remaining ¼ teaspoon each of cumin, salt, and black pepper in a large bowl; toss well, and set aside.

4. Place fish on grill rack coated with cooking spray. Grill 7 to 8 minutes on each side or until fish flakes easily when tested with a fork. Flake fish into bite-sized pieces with fork.
5. Warm tortillas according to package directions.
6. Top each tortilla with about ¼ cup fish, 2 tablespoons mango salsa, and 2 tablespoons slaw. YIELD: 6 servings (serving size: 2 tacos).

Per serving: CAL 228 (9% from fat); FAT 2.4g (sat 0.3g); PRO 24.7g; CARB 29.1g; FIB 3.5g; CHOL 42mg; IRON 1.3mg; SOD 270mg; CALC 66mg

SWEET-AND-SOUR FISH KEBABS

POINTS value: 4

prep: 24 minutes • cook: 12 minutes
other: 30 minutes

A simple marinade featuring lime juice, brown sugar, and crushed red pepper adds a tangy sweetness to the mild-flavored grouper. These colorful kebabs are great for an informal patio dinner.

½   cup fresh lime juice
1½   tablespoons dark brown sugar
½   teaspoon crushed red pepper
1½   pounds grouper fillets, cut into 1-inch pieces
½   teaspoon kosher salt
¼   teaspoon freshly ground black pepper
1   large red bell pepper, cut into 1-inch pieces
1½   cups cubed pineapple (about ½ cored pineapple)
1   small red onion, cut into 1-inch pieces
Cooking spray

1. Combine first 3 ingredients in a small bowl, stirring well with a whisk.
2. Sprinkle fish with salt and black pepper. Thread fish, bell pepper, pineapple, and onion alternately onto 8 (8-inch) metal skewers. Place kebabs in a shallow dish; add marinade. Cover and chill 30 minutes.
3. Prepare grill.
4. Remove kebabs from dish, reserving marinade. Place marinade in a small saucepan, and bring to a boil; remove from heat. Place kebabs on grill rack coated with cooking spray. Grill 10 minutes or until fish flakes easily when tested with a fork, turning kebabs occasionally and basting with reserved marinade. YIELD: 4 servings (serving size: 2 kebabs).

Per serving: CAL 222 (8% from fat); FAT 2g (sat 0.4g); PRO 34g; CARB 17.2g; FIB 1.3g; CHOL 63mg; IRON 2mg; SOD 329mg; CALC 68mg

kebab tips

Size matters: To ensure even cooking when grilling kebabs, make sure the pieces of food are all roughly the same size.

Skewers: If you're using wooden skewers instead of metal ones, soak the wooden skewers in water for at least 30 minutes. Wooden skewers should be discarded after use.

☑. HERB-ROASTED FISH AND POTATOES

POINTS value: 8

prep: 17 minutes • cook: 49 minutes

Fresh herbs and lemon flavor both the roasted potatoes and tender fish in this hearty one-dish meal. We tested with thick fresh halibut fillets, but you can substitute any other firm white fish fillets. Cut back on the baking time if your fillets are thinner than 1 inch.

2½ tablespoons chopped fresh parsley
2   tablespoons olive oil
2   teaspoons chopped fresh oregano
2   teaspoons chopped fresh thyme
½   teaspoon salt
¼   teaspoon black pepper
3   large garlic cloves, crushed
1   pound red potatoes, cut into 1-inch cubes
½   cup coarsely chopped red onion
Cooking spray
1   teaspoon grated fresh lemon rind
1   tablespoon fresh lemon juice
4   (6-ounce) halibut fillets (about 1 to 1½ inches thick)

1. Preheat oven to 400°.
2. Combine first 7 ingredients, stirring well. Place potato and onion in a 13 x 9–inch baking pan coated with cooking spray; toss with 2 tablespoons olive oil mixture. Bake at 400° for 35 to 40 minutes or until tender, stirring after 25 minutes.
3. While potato bakes, stir lemon rind and lemon juice into remaining olive oil mixture. Brush olive oil mixture evenly over fish; cover and let stand while potato finishes baking.
4. Arrange fish over potato in pan. Bake at 400° for 14 to 16 minutes or until fish flakes easily when tested with a fork. YIELD: 4 servings (serving size: 1 fillet and ½ cup potato mixture).

Per serving: CAL 363 (28% from fat); FAT 11.1g (sat 1.6g); PRO 38.5g; CARB 25.8g; FIB 2.5g; CHOL 54mg; IRON 2.5mg; SOD 394mg; CALC 111mg

CRANBERRY-GLAZED SALMON

POINTS value: 9

(pictured on page 64)

prep: 10 minutes • cook: 10 minutes

Cranberries are not just for the holidays. Keep a jar of cranberry chutney on hand to add spicy sweetness to meals year-round. Serve this saucy salmon with a medley of white and wild rice.

⅔   cup cranberry chutney
1   teaspoon grated fresh orange rind
2   tablespoons fresh orange juice
2   teaspoons low-sodium soy sauce
½   teaspoon dry mustard
4   (6-ounce) salmon fillets
Cooking spray
½   teaspoon salt
⅛   teaspoon freshly ground black pepper

1. Preheat broiler.
2. Combine first 5 ingredients in a small bowl, stirring well.
3. Place fish, skin sides down, on a broiler pan coated with cooking spray. Sprinkle fish with salt and pepper. Spread cranberry mixture evenly over fish. Broil 10 minutes or until fish flakes easily when tested with a fork. YIELD: 4 servings (serving size: 1 fillet).

Per serving: CAL 386 (31% from fat); FAT 13.2g (sat 3.1g); PRO 36.5g; CARB 25.2g; FIB 0.1g; CHOL 87mg; IRON 1.6mg; SOD 436mg; CALC 24mg

salmon: wild or farmed?

Farmed Atlantic salmon is the type of salmon most often available in supermarkets, but you may see wild salmon in the peak months of April to October. It's sometimes difficult to distinguish wild from farmed, but some farmed salmon are fed carotene pigments to deepen their color, creating an orange hue. Wild salmon's flesh ranges from light pink (pinks) to a deep red (sockeyes). When sold whole, wild salmon is usually labeled as such.

Wild salmon has a greater range of flavors—from rich, distinctive king salmon to delicately flavored pink. The flavor of farmed salmon will vary depending on the feed mixture each farm uses, but the end result is usually a midrange mild taste. Salmon, both wild and farmed, is a rich source of omega-3 fatty acids. These fats have been shown to help prevent heart disease. There is a slight difference in the amount of total fat between wild and farmed: A 6-ounce fillet of Atlantic wild salmon has 10.8 grams of fat; a 6-ounce fillet of farmed has 13.1 grams.

SPICY ORANGE-GLAZED SALMON

POINTS value: 7

prep: 11 minutes • cook: 8 minutes
other: 15 minutes

Spice up a weeknight meal with this sweet-hot, citrusy salmon dish. Using frozen individually packaged salmon fillets is a great option for convenient dinners and saves you a last-minute stop at the fish market.

¼   cup chopped fresh cilantro
¼   cup thawed orange juice
     concentrate, undiluted
1   teaspoon olive oil
¼   teaspoon ground cumin
¼   teaspoon chili powder
¼   teaspoon salt
¼   teaspoon freshly ground black
     pepper
1   medium jalapeño pepper,
     seeded and minced
4   (6-ounce) salmon fillets
     (1¼ inches thick)
Cooking spray

1. Combine first 8 ingredients in a small bowl; stir well with a whisk.
2. Place fish in a shallow dish; pour orange juice mixture over fish, reserving 1 tablespoon orange juice mixture. Cover and marinate in refrigerator 15 minutes.
3. Prepare grill.
4. Remove fish from marinade; discard marinade. Place fish, skin sides down, on grill rack coated with cooking spray; grill 4 to 5 minutes on each side or until fish flakes easily when tested with a fork. Remove fish from grill, and brush evenly with reserved 1 tablespoon orange

juice mixture. YIELD: 4 servings (serving size: 1 fillet).

Per serving: CAL 287 (44% from fat); FAT 14g (sat 3.2g); PRO 36.4g; CARB 1.6g; FIB 0.2g; CHOL 87mg; IRON 0.7mg; SOD 231mg; CALC 24mg

GRILLED SALMON WITH RED ONION RELISH

POINTS value: 8

prep: 15 minutes • cook: 8 minutes
other: 10 minutes

Strongly flavored Mediterranean-style ingredients, such as balsamic vinegar, olives, capers, and feta cheese, are good matches for succulent salmon.

2   tablespoons balsamic vinegar
2   teaspoons extravirgin olive oil
½   teaspoon kosher salt
½   teaspoon freshly ground black
     pepper
4   (6-ounce) salmon fillets (1 inch
     thick)
1   small red onion, cut into
     ⅓-inch-thick slices
Cooking spray
2   tablespoons crumbled feta
     cheese
2   tablespoons oil-cured olives,
     pitted and chopped
1   teaspoon capers

1. Prepare grill.
2. Combine first 4 ingredients in a small bowl, stirring well with a whisk. Brush 2 tablespoons vinegar mixture on fish; brush remaining vinegar mixture on onion slices. Let stand 10 minutes.
3. Place onion slices and fish, skin

sides down, on grill rack coated with cooking spray. Grill onion 4 minutes on each side or until lightly browned and tender. Grill fish 4 to 6 minutes on each side or until fish flakes easily when tested with a fork.
4. Coarsely chop grilled onion, and place in a large bowl; add cheese, olives, and capers, tossing well. Serve relish with fish. YIELD: 4 servings (serving size: 1 fillet and ¼ cup relish).

Per serving: CAL 333 (48% from fat); FAT 17.9g (sat 4.4g); PRO 37.1g; CARB 4.7g; FIB 0.9g; CHOL 91mg; IRON 0.7mg; SOD 491mg; CALC 49mg

OLIVE-CRUSTED SALMON

POINTS value: 9

prep: 9 minutes • cook: 12 minutes

Plump, juicy kalamata olives in the breadcrumb topping provide a unique Greek accent to the salmon. Substitute any type of olive for a slight variation.

½   cup dry breadcrumbs
¼   cup pitted kalamata olives,
     chopped
2   teaspoons grated fresh lemon
     rind
½   teaspoon dried thyme
2   garlic cloves, minced
1   tablespoon olive oil
4   (6-ounce) salmon fillets
Cooking spray
½   teaspoon salt
¼   teaspoon black pepper
Lemon wedges

1. Preheat oven to 400°.
2. Combine first 5 ingredients in a medium bowl. Add olive oil; stir well.

3. Place fillets, skin sides down, in a baking pan coated with cooking spray; lightly coat fillets with cooking spray. Sprinkle with salt and pepper. Top each fillet with about ¼ cup breadcrumb mixture, pressing breadcrumb mixture onto fillets. Bake at 400° 12 to 15 minutes or until fish flakes easily when tested with a fork. Serve with lemon wedges. YIELD: 4 servings (serving size: 1 fillet).

Per serving: CAL 384 (46% from fat); FAT 19.5g (sat 4g); PRO 38.3g; CARB 11.9g; FIB 0.9g; CHOL 87mg; IRON 1.6mg; SOD 607mg; CALC 57mg

SNAPPER PROVENÇALE

POINTS value: 6

prep: 11 minutes • cook: 20 minutes

4   (6-ounce) snapper or other
     firm white fish fillets
Cooking spray
1   tablespoon plus 1 teaspoon
     olive oil, divided
½   teaspoon kosher salt
½   teaspoon freshly ground black
     pepper
½   cup chopped onion (½ small)
½   cup sliced mushrooms
2   garlic cloves, minced
1   large tomato, chopped
¼   cup pitted kalamata olives,
     chopped
2   tablespoons capers
2   tablespoons chopped fresh
     basil

1. Preheat oven to 425°.
2. Place fish in an 11 x 7–inch baking dish coated with cooking spray; drizzle with 1 tablespoon oil, and sprinkle with salt and pepper. Bake

at 425° for 20 minutes or until fish flakes easily when tested with a fork.
3. While fish bakes, heat remaining 1 teaspoon oil in a large nonstick skillet over medium-high heat. Add onion, mushrooms, and garlic; sauté 5 minutes or until tender. Add tomato, olives, and capers. Cook, uncovered, 3 minutes or until thoroughly heated, stirring frequently. Spoon mixture over cooked fish, and sprinkle with basil. YIELD: 4 servings (serving size: 1 fillet and ½ cup vegetable mixture).

Per serving: CAL 255 (33% from fat); FAT 9.4g (sat 1.5g); PRO 36.1g; CARB 5.5g; FIB 1.3g; CHOL 63mg; IRON 0.7mg; SOD 612mg; CALC 73mg

PAN-FRIED TILAPIA WITH MAQUE CHOUX

POINTS value: 6

prep: 12 minutes • cook: 17 minutes

We spiced up a traditional maque choux (pronounced "mock-shoe"), a dish from southern Louisiana, and served it with pan-fried fish.

3   ears shucked corn
1   tablespoon butter
½   cup chopped onion (½ small)
½   cup grape tomatoes, quartered
½   cup chopped poblano chile
½   cup chopped celery
1   garlic clove, minced
½   to 1 teaspoon ground red pepper
½   teaspoon dried thyme
½   teaspoon salt, divided
½   teaspoon black pepper, divided
½   cup fat-free, less-sodium
     chicken broth
4   (6-ounce) tilapia fillets
1   tablespoon olive oil

1. Cut kernels from ears of corn in a medium bowl to catch juices.
2. Melt butter in a large skillet over medium heat. Add corn, onion, and next 4 ingredients; cook 4 minutes, stirring occasionally. Stir in red pepper, thyme, ¼ teaspoon salt, ¼ teaspoon black pepper, and chicken broth. Bring to a simmer, and cook 3 minutes. Remove corn mixture from pan; set aside, and keep warm.
3. Wipe pan clean with a paper towel. Sprinkle fish with remaining ¼ teaspoon salt and ¼ teaspoon black pepper. Heat oil in pan over medium-high heat. Add fish; cook 3 minutes on each side or until fish flakes easily when tested with a fork.
4. Spoon maque choux onto plates; top with fish. YIELD: 4 servings (serving size: ½ cup maque choux and 1 fillet).

Per serving: CAL 299 (31% from fat); FAT 10.2g (sat 3.4g); PRO 37.5g; CARB 17.5g; FIB 3.1g; CHOL 93mg; IRON 1.8mg; SOD 495mg; CALC 39mg

hot pepper tip

Poblano peppers can range from mild to hot. The heat of your poblano pepper may determine how much additional seasoning you need to add to your dish. This is why we give a range of ground red pepper in the recipe for **Pan-Fried Tilapia with Maque Choux** (left). Start with the lower amount, and increase as desired.

GRILLED TUNA AND CORN SALAD

POINTS value: 6

prep: 7 minutes • cook: 26 minutes

Grilling fresh corn caramelizes its natural sugars, making the corn even more flavorful.

3   small ears shucked corn
½   small red onion, cut into
      ½-inch-thick slices
Cooking spray
4   (6-ounce) tuna steaks
1½ tablespoons olive oil, divided
¾   teaspoon kosher salt, divided
¾   teaspoon freshly ground black
      pepper, divided
2   tablespoons chopped fresh basil
1½ tablespoons cider vinegar

1. Prepare grill.
2. Coat corn and onion with cooking spray; place on grill rack coated with cooking spray. Cover and grill corn 20 minutes, turning 3 times. Grill onion 10 minutes or until tender, turning once.
3. Brush fish with 1 tablespoon oil; sprinkle with ½ teaspoon salt and ½ teaspoon pepper. Place fish on grill rack; grill 3 minutes on each side or until desired degree of doneness.
4. Cut kernels from ears of corn in a medium bowl. Add onion, remaining ½ tablespoon oil, remaining ¼ teaspoon salt, remaining ¼ teaspoon pepper, basil, and vinegar, stirring to combine. Serve fish with corn salad. YIELD: 4 servings (serving size: 1 steak and ½ cup corn salad).

Per serving: CAL 274 (25% from fat); FAT 7.6g (sat 1.4g); PRO 39.4g; CARB 11.7g; FIB 1.8g; CHOL 80mg; IRON 2.5mg; SOD 425mg; CALC 56mg

---

mercury in fish

Certain fish contain high levels of a form of mercury that can cause chronic fatigue and memory loss in adults and harm an unborn child's developing nervous system. Eating these fish occasionally poses no real health risk. However, if you're pregnant, considering pregnancy, or nursing, it's best NOT to eat the following fish:

- Halibut
- King mackerel
- Largemouth bass
- Marlin
- Oysters (from the Gulf of Mexico)
- Sea bass
- Shark
- Swordfish
- Tilefish
- Tuna
- Walleye
- White croaker

PAN-SEARED TUNA WITH FENNEL-PEPPER MÉLANGE

POINTS value: 7

prep: 16 minutes • cook: 11 minutes

Fragrant fennel, sweet red bell pepper, and salty olives comprise a juicy vegetable medley that's spooned over seared fresh tuna. There's a good bit of the vegetable mixture—about ¾ cup per serving—so it functions as a vegetable side dish rather than simply a topping.

2   tablespoons extravirgin olive
      oil, divided
1   fennel bulb, thinly sliced
1   red bell pepper, thinly sliced
1   small red onion, thinly sliced
¼   cup orange juice
12   pitted kalamata olives,
      quartered
1   tablespoon drained capers
¾   teaspoon salt, divided
¾   teaspoon freshly ground black
      pepper, divided
4   (6-ounce) tuna steaks
      (1¼ inches thick)

1. Heat 1 teaspoon oil in a large nonstick skillet over medium-high heat. Add fennel, bell pepper, and onion; sauté 4 to 5 minutes or until golden brown and just tender. Reduce heat to low; add orange juice, and cook 30 seconds or until liquid evaporates, stirring constantly. Remove from heat, and stir in olives, capers, ¼ teaspoon salt, ¼ teaspoon black pepper, and 2 teaspoons oil. Transfer fennel mixture to a bowl; set aside, and keep warm. Wipe pan clean with a paper towel.
2. Sprinkle fish with remaining ½ teaspoon salt and remaining ½ teaspoon black pepper. Heat remaining 1 tablespoon oil in pan over medium-high heat. Add fish to pan, and cook 2 to 3 minutes on each side or until desired degree of doneness. Transfer to plates, and spoon fennel mixture over fish. YIELD: 4 servings (serving size: 1 steak and ¾ cup fennel mixture).

Per serving: CAL 309 (35% from fat); FAT 12g (sat 1.9g); PRO 39g; CARB 10.8g; FIB 2.9g; CHOL 80mg; IRON 2.9mg; SOD 778mg; CALC 92mg

GRILLED TUNA WITH PUTTANESCA SALSA

POINTS value: 4

prep: 14 minutes • cook: 6 minutes
other: 30 minutes

A puttanesca sauce is a spicy mixture of tomatoes, onions, capers, olives, and garlic. We've added the fresh flavors of basil and lemon to our salsa version and served it over thick tuna steaks.

½ cup chopped fresh basil, divided
2 teaspoons grated fresh lemon rind
2 tablespoons lemon juice
3 garlic cloves, minced and divided
4 (6-ounce) tuna steaks (1 inch thick)
2 cups chopped tomato (about 2 large)
¼ cup pitted kalamata olives, coarsely chopped
1 tablespoon drained capers
¼ teaspoon black pepper, divided
Cooking spray
½ teaspoon salt

1. Combine ¼ cup basil, lemon rind, lemon juice, and 2 minced garlic cloves in a shallow dish. Add fish, and turn to coat. Cover and chill 30 minutes.
2. Combine tomato, olives, capers, remaining 1 minced garlic clove, remaining ¼ cup basil, and ⅛ teaspoon pepper in a medium bowl.
3. Prepare grill.
4. Place fish on grill rack coated with cooking spray. Grill 3 to 4 minutes on each side or until desired degree of doneness. Sprinkle fish with salt and remaining ⅛ teaspoon pepper.

Serve with salsa. YIELD: 4 servings (serving size: 1 steak and ½ cup salsa).

Per serving: CAL 223 (17% from fat); FAT 4.2g (sat 0.9g); PRO 38.8g; CARB 6.3g; FIB 1.7g; CHOL 80mg; IRON 2.7mg; SOD 560mg; CALC 77mg

CRAB CAKES OVER MIXED GREENS WITH LEMON DRESSING

POINTS value: 6
(pictured on page 62)

prep: 10 minutes • cook: 18 minutes

These tender, tasty crab cakes—served on a bed of crisp greens and topped with a tangy dressing—received our Test Kitchens' highest rating.

2 tablespoons Dijon mustard, divided
3 tablespoons water
½ teaspoon grated fresh lemon rind
3 tablespoons fresh lemon juice
2 tablespoons olive oil
1 tablespoon minced shallots
½ teaspoon sugar
½ teaspoon salt
½ teaspoon black pepper
¼ cup light mayonnaise
3 tablespoons chopped green onions
1 tablespoon Worcestershire sauce
1 large egg, lightly beaten
1¼ cups panko (Japanese breadcrumbs), divided
1 pound lump crabmeat, drained and shell pieces removed
Cooking spray
4 teaspoons olive oil, divided
1 (10-ounce) package spring mix salad greens

1. Combine 1 tablespoon Dijon mustard and next 8 ingredients in a medium bowl; stir well with a whisk. Cover and chill.
2. Combine remaining 1 tablespoon Dijon mustard, mayonnaise, and next 3 ingredients in a large bowl; stir with a whisk. Gently fold in ¼ cup breadcrumbs and crabmeat. Shape mixture into 12 (½-inch-thick) patties. Dredge patties in remaining 1 cup breadcrumbs. Coat both sides of patties with cooking spray.
3. Heat 2 teaspoons oil in a large nonstick skillet coated with cooking spray over medium heat. Add 6 patties, and cook 4 minutes on each side or until browned. Remove from pan; keep warm. Repeat procedure with remaining 2 teaspoons oil and patties. Serve over greens; drizzle with dressing. YIELD: 6 servings (serving size: 2 crab cakes, 1½ cups mixed greens, and 2 tablespoons dressing).

Per serving: CAL 259 (51% from fat); FAT 14.8g (sat 3.1g); PRO 18.2g; CARB 13.1g; FIB 1.4g; CHOL 102mg; IRON 1.2mg; SOD 673mg; CALC 124mg

lump crabmeat

In recipes that call for fresh crabmeat, lump crabmeat (also called backfin or jumbo) is the most desirable. It's taken from the center of the body and is in large pieces. Flake crabmeat is light and dark meat from the center and the legs, and it comes in smaller pieces.

WHOLE WHEAT SPAGHETTI AND CLAM SAUCE

POINTS value: 6

prep: 6 minutes • cook: 15 minutes

Using white wine and lemon juice instead of clam juice in the sauce gives it a fresh, clean flavor that's often hard to get with canned clams.

8   ounces uncooked whole wheat
     spaghetti
2   teaspoons olive oil
1   cup minced onion
4   teaspoons minced garlic
1   (14.5-ounce) can diced
     tomatoes, drained
¼   teaspoon salt
¼   teaspoon freshly ground black
     pepper
⅔   cup dry white wine (such as
     sauvignon blanc or chardonnay)
1   tablespoon fresh lemon juice
⅓   cup minced fresh parsley
2   (10-ounce) cans baby clams,
     drained

1. Cook pasta according to package directions, omitting salt and fat; drain.
2. While pasta cooks, heat oil in a nonstick skillet over medium heat. Add onion, and sauté 4 minutes or until tender. Add garlic; sauté 1 minute. Add tomatoes, salt, and pepper. Cook 3 minutes, stirring often. Add wine and lemon juice; reduce heat, and simmer 3 minutes. Stir in parsley and clams. Combine pasta and sauce, and toss well to coat. YIELD: 4 servings (serving size: about 1⅔ cups).

Per serving: CAL 316 (15% from fat); FAT 5.4g (sat 1g); PRO 18.1g; CARB 52.7g; FIB 8.7g; CHOL 44mg; IRON 16.1mg; SOD 523mg; CALC 118mg

STEAMED MUSSELS WITH FENNEL AND TOMATOES

POINTS value: 5

prep: 23 minutes • cook: 20 minutes

Serve with slices of crusty bread to soak up every drop of the savory broth.

4   teaspoons olive oil
1   cup finely chopped onion
     (about 1 small)
⅔   cup finely chopped fennel bulb
     (about ½ small bulb)
4   plum tomatoes, seeded and
     diced (about 1½ cups)
3   cloves garlic, minced
¼   teaspoon salt
¼   teaspoon freshly ground black
     pepper
1   cup dry white wine
3   pounds mussels, scrubbed and
     debearded
¼   cup finely chopped fresh
     parsley

1. Heat oil in a large Dutch oven over medium-high heat; add onion and fennel. Cook 5 minutes or until tender, stirring often. Add tomato and next 3 ingredients, and cook 3 minutes or until tomato softens, stirring often. Add wine, and bring to a boil. Add mussels; cover and simmer 10 minutes or until shells open. Remove from heat; discard any unopened shells. Place mussels in wide, shallow bowls; ladle broth over mussels. Sprinkle with parsley. YIELD: 6 servings (serving size: about 15 mussels and ½ cup broth).

Per serving: CAL 256 (30% from fat); FAT 8.4g (sat 1.4g); PRO 28.2g; CARB 16.3g; FIB 2g; CHOL 64mg; IRON 9.7mg; SOD 770mg; CALC 94mg

SEARED SCALLOPS WITH HERB SAUCE

POINTS value: 4

prep: 11 minutes • cook: 7 minutes

Remove the cast-iron skillet from the heat when preparing the sauce so you won't burn the herbs and create a bitter flavor.

1½   pounds large sea scallops
     (12 scallops)
¼   teaspoon kosher salt
¼   teaspoon freshly ground black
     pepper
2   teaspoons olive oil, divided
1   tablespoon chopped shallots
½   cup chardonnay or other dry
     white wine
1   tablespoon grated fresh lemon
     rind
1   tablespoon chopped fresh parsley
1   tablespoon chopped fresh chives
1   tablespoon chopped fresh basil

1. Pat scallops dry with paper towels; sprinkle with salt and pepper. Heat 1 teaspoon oil in a large cast-iron skillet over high heat. Add scallops to pan; cook 3 minutes on each side or until browned. Transfer scallops to a serving platter; keep warm.
2. Remove pan from heat, and add remaining 1 teaspoon oil. Add shallots, and sauté 1 minute or until tender. Stir in wine and remaining ingredients, scraping pan to loosen browned bits. Pour sauce over scallops, and serve immediately. YIELD: 4 servings (serving size: 3 scallops and 1½ tablespoons sauce).

Per serving: CAL 175 (19% from fat); FAT 3.7g (sat 0.5g); PRO 28.8g; CARB 5.3g; FIB 0.3g; CHOL 56mg; IRON 0.8mg; SOD 395mg; CALC 50mg

☑ SCALLOPS PROVENÇALE

POINTS value: 4

prep: 9 minutes • cook: 19 minutes

1½   pounds large sea scallops
      (12 scallops), cut in half
      horizontally
2   teaspoons olive oil
⅓   cup minced shallots or onion
1⅔   cups sliced mushrooms
½   teaspoon salt
¼   teaspoon freshly ground black
      pepper
1   tablespoon minced garlic
2   teaspoons tomato paste
1   (14.5-ounce) can diced
      tomatoes, drained
1½   teaspoons minced fresh or
      ½ teaspoon dried thyme
¼   cup minced fresh basil or parsley
2   teaspoons fresh lemon juice

1. Pat scallops dry with paper towels.
Heat oil in a large nonstick skillet
over medium–high heat. Add scallops
to pan, and cook 3 minutes on each
side or until browned. Remove from
pan, set aside, and keep warm.
2. Reduce heat to medium; add
shallots, mushrooms, salt, and pepper
to pan, and sauté 3 minutes. Stir in
garlic and tomato paste; cook 1
minute, stirring often. Add tomatoes
and thyme. Reduce heat to low, and
simmer 6 minutes, stirring often.
3. Return scallops to pan, and cook
2 to 3 minutes or until thoroughly
heated. Stir in basil and lemon juice.
YIELD: 4 servings (serving size: 6
scallop halves and ½ cup sauce).

Per serving: CAL 212 (18% from fat); FAT 4.2g
(sat 0.5g); PRO 30.3g; CARB 11.5g; FIB 1.9g;
CHOL 56mg; IRON 1.4mg; SOD 656mg;
CALC 65mg

TOMATO-FETA SHRIMP WITH PASTA

POINTS value: 6

prep: 6 minutes • cook: 17 minutes

8   ounces uncooked fusilli (short
      twisted pasta)
2   (14.5-ounce) cans diced
      tomatoes with garlic and
      onion, undrained
Olive oil–flavored cooking spray
½   cup chopped onion
⅓   cup dry white wine
1   tablespoon chopped fresh
      oregano
¾   pound frozen cooked, peeled,
      and deveined medium shrimp,
      thawed
5   tablespoons crumbled feta
      cheese

1. Cook pasta according to package
directions, omitting salt and fat. Drain.
2. While pasta cooks, drain 1 can
diced tomatoes; discard liquid.
Combine drained tomatoes with
remaining 1 can tomatoes; set aside.
3. Heat a large nonstick skillet over
medium–high heat. Coat pan with
cooking spray. Add onion, and sauté
2 minutes or until tender. Add tomatoes, wine, and oregano. Bring to a
simmer; cook 5 minutes, stirring frequently. Stir in shrimp; cook 1 minute
or until mixture is thoroughly heated.
4. Divide pasta among plates; top
evenly with shrimp mixture. Sprinkle
with cheese. YIELD: 5 servings (serving
size: 1 cup pasta, ¾ cup shrimp mixture, and 1 tablespoon cheese).

Per serving: CAL 316 (14% from fat); FAT 5g
(sat 1.8g); PRO 23.4g; CARB 45.3g; FIB 2.7g;
CHOL 112mg; IRON 5.3mg; SOD 854mg;
CALC 119mg

SHRIMP AND WHITE BEANS

POINTS value: 5

prep: 8 minutes • cook: 12 minutes

*Create a rustic Italian-style meal by
serving this hearty dish with ciabatta
and a glass of chilled white wine.*

2   teaspoons olive oil, divided
1¼   pounds large shrimp, peeled
      and deveined
3   garlic cloves, minced
½   cup chopped onion
1   (15-ounce) can cannellini
      beans, rinsed and drained
⅓   cup dry white wine
1   pint grape tomatoes, halved
1   (6-ounce) package fresh baby
      spinach
½   teaspoon freshly ground black
      pepper
¼   teaspoon crushed red pepper
¼   teaspoon salt

1. Heat 1 teaspoon olive oil in a
large nonstick skillet over medium-
high heat. Add shrimp, and cook 3
minutes or until done, stirring occasionally. Remove shrimp from pan;
set aside, and keep warm.
2. Heat remaining 1 teaspoon olive
oil in pan. Add garlic and onion, and
sauté 2 minutes. Add beans and wine;
bring to a simmer, and add tomatoes.
Cook 2 minutes, stirring occasionally.
Stir in spinach, and cook 1 minute
or just until spinach wilts.
3. Add shrimp and juices, peppers,
and salt, stirring to combine. YIELD: 4
servings (serving size: 1¾ cups).

Per serving: CAL 260 (15% from fat); FAT 4.3g
(sat 0.8g); PRO 34.4g; CARB 20.5g; FIB 6g;
CHOL 276mg; IRON 7.1mg; SOD 625mg;
CALC 126mg

☑ CILANTRO-GARLIC SHRIMP

POINTS value: 5

prep: 4 minutes • cook: 7 minutes

This shrimp is sensational as a stand-alone entrée, or you can combine it with crisp greens for a main-dish salad.

1   tablespoon olive oil
1¼ pounds large shrimp, peeled and deveined
6   garlic cloves, minced
½   cup coarsely chopped fresh cilantro
2   teaspoons fresh lemon juice
¼   teaspoon salt
¼   teaspoon freshly ground black pepper

1. Heat oil in a large nonstick skillet over medium-high heat. Add shrimp and garlic; sauté 5 minutes or until shrimp are done.
2. Add cilantro and remaining ingredients; cook 1 minute or until cilantro wilts. YIELD: 3 servings (serving size: about 1 cup).

Per serving: CAL 238 (26% from fat); FAT 6.8g (sat 1.2g); PRO 40g; CARB 2.5g; FIB 0.2g; CHOL 369mg; IRON 6mg; SOD 619mg; CALC 88mg

---

storing fresh cilantro

To keep fresh cilantro fresh longer, wash it in cold water and spin it dry in a salad spinner soon after purchase. Wrap it in paper towels, place in a plastic bag, and store in the refrigerator's vegetable drawer up to 5 days.

☑ BLACKENED SHRIMP WITH CITRUS SALSA

POINTS value: 5

prep: 27 minutes • cook: 10 minutes

We tested with fresh citrus fruit, but you can use refrigerated bottled grapefruit sections to cut down on prep time.

1   cup chopped orange sections (about 2 oranges)
1   cup chopped ruby red grapefruit sections (about 1 grapefruit)
⅓   cup chopped green onions
2   tablespoons minced seeded jalapeño pepper
2   tablespoons chopped fresh cilantro
2   tablespoons salt-free blackening seasoning
¼   teaspoon salt
2   pounds large shrimp, peeled and deveined
4   teaspoons olive oil, divided

1. Combine first 5 ingredients in a medium bowl; cover and chill.
2. Combine seasoning, salt, and shrimp in a large zip-top plastic bag. Seal bag, and shake well to coat.
3. Heat 2 teaspoons oil in a large nonstick skillet over medium-high heat. Add half of shrimp; cook 2 minutes on each side or until done. Remove from pan. Repeat procedure with remaining 2 teaspoons oil and remaining shrimp. Serve warm with salsa. YIELD: 4 servings (serving size: about 12 shrimp and ½ cup salsa).

Per serving: CAL 263 (24% from fat); FAT 6.9g (sat 1.2g); PRO 37.2g CARB 12.6g; FIB 2.9g; CHOL 336mg; IRON 6mg; SOD 538mg; CALC 108mg

---

☑ GRILLED SHRIMP WITH CHERMOULA SAUCE

POINTS value: 7

prep: 8 minutes • cook: 6 minutes

This herbed Moroccan sauce is a classic with fish, but it makes a wonderful sauce for grilled meats of any kind.

½   teaspoon kosher salt
2   garlic cloves, minced
3   tablespoons olive oil
⅓   cup chopped fresh cilantro
2   tablespoons chopped fresh parsley
⅓   cup fresh lemon juice
½   teaspoon ground cumin
½   teaspoon ground coriander
1   teaspoon paprika
⅛   teaspoon ground red pepper
1½ pounds peeled jumbo shrimp with tails (24 shrimp)
Olive oil–flavored cooking spray

1. Prepare grill.
2. Combine salt and garlic, chopping mixture with a large knife to create a paste. Transfer mixture to a small bowl; add oil, stirring with a whisk. Add cilantro and next 6 ingredients; stir with a whisk.
3. Thread 6 shrimp onto each of 4 (12-inch) metal skewers; lightly coat with cooking spray. Place skewers on grill rack coated with cooking spray. Cover and grill 3 minutes on each side or until done. YIELD: 4 servings (serving size: 1 skewer and 2½ tablespoons sauce).

Per serving: CAL 282 (43% from fat); FAT 13.6g (sat 2.1g); PRO 34.9g; CARB 4.4g; FIB 0.5g; CHOL 259mg; IRON 4.4mg; SOD 490mg; CALC 100mg

meatless main dishes ▶▶

EASY HUEVOS RANCHEROS

POINTS value: 7

prep: 8 minutes • cook: 6 minutes

Serve our lightened version of "rancher's eggs" with avocado slices, sour cream, and chopped fresh cilantro, if desired.

1   (10-ounce) can diced tomatoes and green chiles, drained
2   tablespoons chopped fresh cilantro
2   teaspoons fresh lime juice
1   (15-ounce) can black beans, rinsed and drained
1   tablespoon butter
4   large eggs
4   (8-inch) flour tortillas
½   cup (2 ounces) preshredded reduced-fat 4-cheese Mexican blend cheese

1. Combine tomatoes, cilantro, and lime juice in a small bowl; set aside.
2. Place black beans in a small microwave-safe dish; partially mash beans with a fork. Cover and microwave at HIGH 2 minutes.
3. Melt butter in a large nonstick skillet. Add eggs; cook over medium-high heat 1 to 2 minutes on each side or until done (do not break yolks).
4. Warm tortillas according to package directions. Spread beans evenly over tortillas; top each with 1 egg. Top with tomato mixture and cheese. YIELD: 4 servings (serving size: 1 tortilla, ⅓ cup beans, 1 egg, ¼ cup tomato mixture, and 2 tablespoons cheese).

Per serving: CAL 351 (35% from fat); FAT 13.7g (sat 5.2g); PRO 19g; CARB 37.1g; FIB 4.2g; CHOL 224mg; IRON 3.7mg; SOD 709mg; CALC 254mg

ASPARAGUS-MUSHROOM OMELET

POINTS value: 6

prep: 11 minutes • cook: 13 minutes

This hearty veggie-cheese omelet is perfect for brunch or whenever you're craving "breakfast for dinner."

1   teaspoon olive oil, divided
Cooking spray
1   cup sliced mushrooms
½   cup chopped asparagus (about 6 spears)
2   tablespoons chopped green onions
4   large eggs
1   large egg white
2   teaspoons chopped fresh parsley
¼   teaspoon salt
⅛   teaspoon freshly ground black pepper
½   cup (2 ounces) reduced-fat shredded Swiss cheese

1. Heat ½ teaspoon oil in a medium nonstick skillet coated with cooking spray over medium-high heat. Add mushrooms, asparagus, and green onions; sauté 5 minutes or until crisp-tender. Remove from pan, set aside, and keep warm.
2. Combine eggs, egg white, and next 3 ingredients in a bowl, stirring well with a whisk. Heat remaining ½ teaspoon oil in pan. Add egg mixture to pan; cook until edges begin to set (about 2 minutes). Gently lift edges of omelet with a spatula, and tilt pan so uncooked portion flows underneath. Continue cooking until center is just set (about 4 minutes).
3. Spoon vegetable mixture evenly over half of omelet, and sprinkle cheese over vegetable mixture. Loosen omelet with spatula, and fold in half. Cut omelet in half crosswise, and serve immediately. YIELD: 2 servings (serving size: ½ of omelet).

Per serving: CAL 241 (52% from fat); FAT 13.9g (sat 4.4g); PRO 24.1g; CARB 4.9g; FIB 1.3g; CHOL 432mg; IRON 3mg; SOD 533mg; CALC 330mg

SOUTHWESTERN FRITTATA

POINTS value: 2

prep: 7 minutes • cook: 16 minutes

The ingredients are the same as those in huevos rancheros, but we've combined them in a new way to create a hearty frittata.

Cooking spray
4   (5-inch) corn tortillas, chopped
1   (15-ounce) can black beans, rinsed and drained
1   (4.5-ounce) can chopped green chiles, drained
½   teaspoon minced garlic
4   large egg whites, lightly beaten
1   large egg, lightly beaten
¼   teaspoon salt
⅛   teaspoon black pepper
½   cup (2 ounces) 50% reduced-fat shredded Cheddar cheese with jalapeño peppers (such as Cabot)
2   tablespoons chopped cilantro
6   tablespoons salsa
6   tablespoons fat-free sour cream

1. Preheat oven to 400°.
2. Heat a 10-inch ovenproof skillet over medium-high heat. Coat pan

with cooking spray; add tortilla pieces, and sauté 2 minutes or until lightly browned. Stir in black beans, chiles, and garlic. Cook 1 minute or until thoroughly heated.

3. Combine egg whites, egg, salt, and black pepper, stirring with a whisk; pour over tortilla mixture. Sprinkle with cheese. Bake at 400° for 13 minutes or just until set. Sprinkle with cilantro. Cut into 6 wedges. Serve with salsa and sour cream. YIELD: 6 servings (serving size: 1 wedge, 1 tablespoon salsa, and 1 tablespoon sour cream).

Per serving: CAL 124 (23% from fat); FAT 3.2g (sat 1.3g); PRO 10g; CARB 18.3g; FIB 4.2g; CHOL 43mg; IRON 0.8mg; SOD 525mg; CALC 154mg

ovenproof skillets

To go from stovetop to oven, you need an ovenproof skillet. You can use a cast-iron or a heavy stainless steel skillet. Don't put a nonstick skillet in the oven because the nonstick coating should not be overheated, and many nonstick pans have plastic handles that will melt in the oven.

ROASTED RED BELL PEPPER AND GOAT CHEESE FRITTATA

POINTS value: 4

prep: 15 minutes • cook: 7 minutes

We used a 12-inch ovenproof skillet for testing. If you want a thicker frittata, use a smaller skillet.

2   large eggs
4   large egg whites
2   tablespoons chopped fresh chives
½   teaspoon salt, divided
½   teaspoon freshly ground black pepper, divided
4   teaspoons olive oil
1   cup chopped bottled roasted red bell peppers
4   green onions, chopped
2   garlic cloves, minced
½   cup (2 ounces) crumbled goat cheese

1. Preheat broiler.
2. Combine eggs, egg whites, chives, ¼ teaspoon salt, and ¼ teaspoon pepper in a bowl, stirring with a whisk.
3. Heat oil in an ovenproof skillet over medium heat. Add red bell peppers, onions, garlic, and remaining salt and pepper; sauté 2 minutes. Pour egg mixture over vegetables. As mixture starts to cook, gently lift edges of frittata with a spatula, and tilt pan so uncooked portion flows underneath. Cook 2 minutes; remove from heat.
4. Sprinkle cheese over frittata. Broil 2 minutes or until set and lightly browned. Cut into 4 wedges. YIELD: 4 servings (serving size: 1 wedge).

Per serving: CAL 160 (65% from fat); FAT 11.5g (sat 4.4g); PRO 10.3g; CARB 3.9g; FIB 0.5g; CHOL 117mg; IRON 1mg; SOD 563mg; CALC 74mg

WHITE VEGETARIAN PIZZA

POINTS value: 5

prep: 12 minutes • cook: 25 minutes

1   cup broccoli florets
2   teaspoons olive oil
1   cup chopped red bell pepper
¼   cup chopped red onion
2   garlic cloves, minced
1   (8-ounce) package presliced portobello mushrooms
¼   teaspoon kosher salt
¼   teaspoon crushed red pepper
½   (24-ounce) package prebaked pizza crust (such as Mama Mary's)
Olive oil–flavored cooking spray
1½   cups (6 ounces) shredded part-skim mozzarella cheese, divided
2   tablespoons chopped fresh basil

1. Preheat oven to 450°.
2. Cook broccoli in boiling water 3 minutes or until tender. Drain and plunge in ice water; drain and chop.
3. Heat oil in a large nonstick skillet over medium-high heat. Add bell pepper and next 3 ingredients; sauté 5 minutes or until tender. Add broccoli, salt, and crushed red pepper; cook 2 minutes or until thoroughly heated. Remove from heat; drain.
4. Lightly coat crust with cooking spray; place on a baking sheet. Sprinkle ¾ cup cheese over crust; top with vegetable mixture and remaining ¾ cup cheese. Reduce oven temperature to 425°; bake 8 minutes or until crust is golden and cheese melts. Sprinkle with basil. Cut into 8 slices. YIELD: 8 servings (serving size: 1 slice).

Per serving: CAL 219 (37% from fat); FAT 9.1g (sat 3.1g); PRO 10.1g; CARB 25g; FIB 1.9g; CHOL 12mg; IRON 1.9mg; SOD 302mg; CALC 187mg

DEEP-DISH TACO PIZZA

POINTS value: 5

prep: 5 minutes • cook: 20 minutes
other: 5 minutes

This family-pleasing dish is a cross between a pizza and a casserole, but the flavors may remind you of a beefy taco.

1   (12-ounce) package frozen meatless burger crumbles, thawed
½   cup frozen chopped onion
1   (14.5-ounce) can diced tomatoes and green chiles, drained
1   teaspoon salt-free Mexican seasoning
1   (13.8-ounce) can refrigerated pizza crust dough
Cooking spray
1   cup (4 ounces) shredded part-skim mozzarella cheese
½   cup refrigerated fresh salsa
½   cup fat-free sour cream

1. Preheat oven to 425°.
2. Cook burger crumbles and onion in a large nonstick skillet over medium-high heat 6 minutes or until crumbles are thoroughly heated.

Add tomatoes and seasoning; cook 1 minute, stirring frequently.
3. Unroll pizza crust dough. Press into bottom and halfway up sides of a 13 x 9–inch baking dish coated with cooking spray. Spoon burger mixture over pizza crust dough.
4. Bake at 425° for 10 minutes. Top with cheese, and bake 3 to 4 minutes or until cheese melts and edges of crust are browned. Let stand 5 minutes before slicing. Top with salsa and sour cream. YIELD: 8 servings (serving size: 1 slice).

Per serving: CAL 251 (20% from fat); FAT 5.6g (sat 2.1g); PRO 16.2g; CARB 32.6g; FIB 2.3g; CHOL 11mg; IRON 3.3mg; SOD 745mg; CALC 130mg

FOLD-OVER QUESADILLAS

POINTS value: 7

prep: 10 minutes • cook: 8 minutes

There's no reason to think of quesadillas as mere appetizers when they make such a quick and easy meal. When preparing the quesadillas, keep the tortillas covered to prevent them from drying out and cracking when you fold them.

1   (4.5-ounce) can chopped green chiles
4   (8-inch) flour tortillas
1½ cups (6 ounces) shredded part-skim mozzarella cheese
⅓   cup finely chopped red onion
½   teaspoon ground cumin
Cooking spray
½   cup fat-free sour cream
¼   cup refrigerated fresh salsa
¼   cup chopped fresh cilantro

1. Spoon 2 tablespoons green chiles over half of each tortilla, spreading evenly. Sprinkle cheese, onion, and cumin over chiles. Fold each tortilla in half.
2. Heat a large nonstick skillet over medium heat. Coat pan with cooking spray. Add 2 quesadillas, and cook 2 minutes. Turn and cook 2 minutes or until cheese melts. Remove from pan, and keep warm. Repeat with remaining quesadillas. Cut each quesadilla into 3 wedges. Serve with sour cream, salsa, and cilantro. YIELD: 4 servings (serving size: 3 wedges, 2 tablespoons sour cream, 1 tablespoon salsa, and 1 tablespoon cilantro).

Per serving: CAL 302 (30% from fat); FAT 9.9g (sat 4.7g); PRO 16g; CARB 34.5g; FIB 1.4g; CHOL 30mg; IRON 1.2mg; SOD 643mg; CALC 461mg

BLACK BEAN AND CORN TOSTADAS

POINTS value: 5

prep: 10 minutes • cook: 10 minutes

To save time, buy prechopped onion and bell pepper in the produce section, as well as a bag of shredded lettuce.

5   (5½-inch) corn tortillas
Cooking spray
2   teaspoons canola oil
⅓   cup diced onion
⅓   cup diced green bell pepper
1   (15.5-ounce) can black beans, rinsed and drained
1   cup frozen whole-kernel corn, thawed
¾   cup refrigerated fresh salsa
1½   teaspoons chili powder
½   teaspoon dried oregano
½   teaspoon ground cumin
¼   teaspoon salt
⅛   teaspoon coarsely ground black pepper
1¼   cups shredded iceberg lettuce
10   tablespoons refrigerated fresh salsa
5   tablespoons fat-free sour cream
¾   cup (3 ounces) reduced-fat shredded Cheddar cheese
5   teaspoons minced fresh cilantro

1. Preheat oven to 350°.
2. Coat tortillas with cooking spray; place on a baking sheet. Bake at 350° for 10 minutes or until crisp, turning after 7 minutes.
3. While tortillas bake, heat oil in a large nonstick skillet over medium-high heat. Add onion and bell pepper; sauté 4 minutes or until onion is lightly browned. Stir in beans and next 7 ingredients. Cook 2 minutes.
4. Place tortillas on plates. Top each tortilla with about ½ cup bean mixture, ¼ cup lettuce, 2 tablespoons salsa, 1 tablespoon sour cream, about 2 tablespoons cheese, and 1 teaspoon cilantro. YIELD: 5 servings (serving size: 1 tostada).

Per serving: CAL 238 (26% from fat); FAT 7.1g (sat 2.8g); PRO 10.7g; CARB 32g; FIB 5.7g; CHOL 16mg; IRON 1.6mg; SOD 427mg; CALC 188mg

LENTIL PATTIES WITH YOGURT SAUCE

POINTS value: 7

prep: 14 minutes • cook: 32 minutes

Since you need only ¼ cup of cooked rice for the patties, we suggest using a microwavable pouch of precooked rice. Measure out ¼ cup and add it to the lentil mixture. Save the rest of the rice for another use. You can also use brown rice instead of white, if you prefer.

¾   cup dried lentils
4   cups water
⅓   cup dry breadcrumbs
2   teaspoons ground cumin
½   teaspoon crushed red pepper
¼   teaspoon kosher salt
¼   teaspoon freshly ground black pepper
2   garlic cloves, chopped
¼   cup cooked white rice
3   tablespoons olive oil, divided
2   large egg whites
Cooking spray
Yogurt Sauce

1. Place lentils and 4 cups water in a large saucepan; bring to a boil. Cover, reduce heat, and simmer 20 minutes or until lentils are tender. Drain well.
2. Combine breadcrumbs and next 5 ingredients in a food processor; process until blended. Add lentils, rice, 1 tablespoon oil, and egg whites; process until coarsely chopped.
3. Divide mixture into 8 (¼-cup) portions, and shape each into a ¼-inch-thick patty.
4. Heat remaining oil in a large nonstick skillet over medium-high heat. Coat pan with cooking spray. Add patties; cook 3 minutes on each side or until browned. Serve with Yogurt Sauce. YIELD: 4 servings (serving size: 2 patties and ¼ cup sauce).

Per serving: CAL 330 (39% from fat); FAT 14.2g (sat 2.5g); PRO 17.3g; CARB 35.4g; FIB 9.4g; CHOL 107mg; IRON 5.1mg; SOD 411mg; CALC 143mg

YOGURT SAUCE
POINTS value: 0

1   (6-ounce) carton plain fat-free yogurt
½   cup chopped cucumber
2   tablespoons chopped fresh parsley
2   tablespoons chopped fresh cilantro
1   teaspoon grated fresh lemon rind
¼   teaspoon salt
¼   teaspoon freshly ground black pepper

1. Combine all ingredients, stirring until well blended. YIELD: 1 cup.

Per tablespoon: CAL 7 (0% from fat); FAT 0g (sat 0g); PRO 0.8g; CARB 1.1g; FIB 0.1g; CHOL 0mg; IRON 0mg; SOD 47mg; CALC 20mg

CHEESE-FILLED EGGPLANT ROLLS

***POINTS* value: 6**

prep: 16 minutes • cook: 42 minutes

Thin slices of tender baked eggplant filled with cheese and baked in marinara sauce make a satisfying meal. For an additional POINTS value of 2, serve over ½-cup portions of spaghetti.

1   medium eggplant (about 1 pound), trimmed
Cooking spray
2   tablespoons olive oil
½   teaspoon kosher salt
½   teaspoon freshly ground black pepper
1   cup bottled marinara sauce, divided
½   cup part-skim ricotta cheese
½   cup (4 ounces) goat cheese
1   tablespoon chopped fresh parsley
½   cup (2 ounces) shredded part-skim mozzarella cheese

1. Preheat oven to 450°.
2. Cut eggplant lengthwise into 8 (¼-inch-thick) slices.
3. Coat a large baking sheet with cooking spray. Place eggplant slices on pan; brush slices with olive oil, and sprinkle with salt and pepper. Bake at 450° for 12 minutes or until tender; cover and keep warm.
4. Reduce oven temperature to 375°.
5. Spread ⅔ cup sauce in an 8-inch square baking dish coated with cooking spray. Combine ricotta cheese, goat cheese, and parsley in a small bowl. Spread 2 tablespoons ricotta mixture onto each eggplant slice. Roll up slices, and place, seam sides down, in dish. Spoon remaining ⅓ cup sauce

evenly over rolls, and sprinkle with mozzarella cheese. Cover and bake at 375° for 25 minutes; uncover and bake an additional 5 minutes or until cheese is browned and bubbly. YIELD: 4 servings (serving size: 2 rolls).

Per serving: CAL 270 (62% from fat); FAT 18.7g (sat 8.1g); PRO 13.9g; CARB 14.8g; FIB 3.9g; CHOL 34mg; IRON 0.9mg; SOD 706mg; CALC 194mg

TWICE-BAKED POTATOES

***POINTS* value: 8**

prep: 12 minutes
cook: 1 hour and 4 minutes

These loaded baked potatoes make a great weeknight meal.

4   medium baking potatoes (about 8 ounces each)
1   teaspoon olive oil
3   green onions, thinly sliced
2   garlic cloves, minced
1   (10-ounce) package frozen chopped spinach, thawed, drained, and squeezed dry
½   cup grated fresh Parmesan cheese, divided
1   cup part-skim ricotta cheese
½   cup light sour cream
¾   teaspoon salt
¼   teaspoon freshly ground black pepper
Cooking spray
Salsa (optional)

1. Preheat oven to 450°.
2. Rinse potatoes; pierce several times with a fork. Bake at 450° for 45 minutes or until tender.
3. Heat oil in a large nonstick skillet over medium-high heat; add onions

and garlic. Cook 1 minute or until soft. Add spinach; cook 2 minutes or until thoroughly heated. Remove from pan, and place in a large bowl.
4. When potatoes are cool enough to handle, cut in half lengthwise, and scoop out pulp, leaving a ¼-inch-thick shell. Add pulp to spinach mixture; stir in ¼ cup Parmesan cheese and next 4 ingredients. Place potato shells in an 11 x 7–inch baking dish coated with cooking spray. Spoon filling evenly into potato shells. Bake 15 minutes or until thoroughly heated and lightly browned. Top with remaining ¼ cup Parmesan cheese and, if desired, salsa. YIELD: 4 servings (serving size: 2 stuffed potato halves).

Per serving: CAL 382 (29% from fat); FAT 12.5g (sat 6.9g); PRO 20.8g; CARB 52.3g; FIB 6.2g; CHOL 45mg; IRON 3.4mg; SOD 869mg; CALC 437mg

hot potato tips

Microwave: If you want to microwave the potatoes instead of baking them in the oven in step 2, use this tip from the United States Potato Board: Place potatoes in a microwave-safe dish (no need to pierce). Cover dish with microwave-safe plastic wrap; poke a small hole in the plastic wrap to vent. Microwave at HIGH for 8 minutes or until potatoes are done. Use oven mitts to carefully remove dish from microwave and use oven mitts or tongs to remove plastic wrap.

Make ahead: To make Twice-Baked Potatoes ahead, freeze the potato halves after filling them. To serve, bake frozen stuffed potatoes at 350° for 55 minutes.

MEXICAN LASAGNA

POINTS value: 6

prep: 18 minutes • cook: 40 minutes
other: 10 minutes

To prevent the foil from sticking to the lasagna, use nonstick foil or coat one side of regular foil with cooking spray.

1   (10-ounce) package frozen chopped spinach, thawed, drained, and squeezed dry
1   cup part-skim ricotta cheese
1   (16-ounce) can pinto beans, rinsed and drained
1   (15-ounce) can black beans, rinsed and drained
6   (5-inch) corn tortillas
Cooking spray
2   cups refrigerated fresh salsa
1   (8-ounce) block 50% reduced-fat Cheddar cheese with jalapeño peppers, shredded

1. Preheat oven to 425°.
2. Combine spinach and ricotta cheese in a small bowl. In a separate bowl, combine beans.
3. Cut 3 corn tortillas into pieces, and arrange in a solid layer to cover bottom of an 8-inch square baking dish coated with cooking spray. Top with half each of beans, salsa, spinach mixture, and cheese. Repeat layers with remaining ingredients.
4. Cover and bake at 425° for 25 minutes; uncover and bake an additional 15 minutes. Let stand 10 minutes before serving. YIELD: 6 servings (serving size: ⅙ of casserole).

Per serving: CAL 303 (32% from fat); FAT 10.7g (sat 6.2g); PRO 22.8g; CARB 29.2g; FIB 7.6g; CHOL 37mg; IRON 2.5mg; SOD 765mg; CALC 449mg

PENNE ALLA VODKA

POINTS value: 5

prep: 4 minutes • cook: 21 minutes

Pasta with a creamy vodka-tomato sauce is a popular American-Italian dish. We've lightened it by using fat-free half-and-half and less olive oil, and we've increased the fiber by using multigrain pasta. The vodka adds a hint of dryness and perhaps a little sophistication, but you could substitute a dry white wine.

10   ounces multigrain penne (such as Barilla Plus)
½   cup fat-free half-and-half
1   teaspoon all-purpose flour
1   tablespoon olive oil
1   (14.5-ounce) can diced tomatoes, undrained
¼   cup vodka
¼   teaspoon crushed red pepper
2   garlic cloves, minced
⅔   cup grated Parmesan cheese

1. Cook pasta according to package directions, omitting salt and fat. Drain.
2. While pasta cooks, combine ¼ cup half-and-half and flour, stirring with a whisk until smooth. Add remaining ¼ cup half-and-half.
3. Heat oil in a large nonstick skillet over medium-high heat. Add tomatoes and next 3 ingredients, and cook 5 minutes. Add half-and-half mixture; cook 3 minutes or until thick, stirring occasionally.
4. Place pasta in a large bowl; add tomato mixture and cheese. Toss well. YIELD: 7 servings (serving size: 1 cup).

Per serving: CAL 245 (23% from fat); FAT 6.2g (sat 2.6g); PRO 12.4g; CARB 32.6g; FIB 3.9g; CHOL 11mg; IRON 1.5mg; SOD 304mg; CALC 174mg

TORTELLINI PRIMAVERA

POINTS value: 6

prep: 15 minutes • cook: 20 minutes

Give a taste of spring to a package of cheese tortellini by adding fresh asparagus, yellow squash, and zucchini. Intensify the flavors with pesto, garlic, and sun-dried tomatoes.

1   (9-ounce) package fresh three-cheese tortellini
1   cup (1-inch) sliced asparagus (about 14 spears)
1   cup cubed yellow squash (about 1 large)
1   cup cubed zucchini (about 1 small)
½   cup sliced drained oil-packed sun-dried tomato halves
2   tablespoons commercial pesto
2   teaspoons minced garlic
2   tablespoons minced fresh basil
2   tablespoons grated fresh Parmesan cheese

1. Cook tortellini in boiling water 8 minutes. Add asparagus, yellow squash, and zucchini to pasta; cook 2 minutes. Drain pasta and vegetables, reserving ¼ cup cooking liquid.
2. While pasta cooks, heat a large nonstick skillet over medium-high heat. Add tomatoes, pesto, and garlic; reduce heat to medium-low, and cook 1 to 2 minutes or until thoroughly heated, stirring constantly. Add reserved cooking liquid, pasta, vegetables, and basil; toss. Sprinkle with cheese. YIELD: 4 servings (serving size: 1½ cups).

Per serving: CAL 312 (31% from fat); FAT 10.9g (sat 3.4g); PRO 13.6g; CARB 41.6g; FIB 4.6g; CHOL 25mg; IRON 1.8mg; SOD 416mg; CALC 138mg

SOBA NOODLES
WITH VEGETABLES

POINTS value: 8

prep: 7 minutes • cook: 20 minutes

Soba are Japanese noodles made from a combination of buckwheat and wheat flour. Look for them in the Asian-foods section of the supermarket or at an Asian grocery store. They have a dark brownish gray color and a slightly nutty flavor. If you can't find shiitake mushrooms, use an 8-ounce package of sliced button mushrooms.

8	ounces uncooked soba (buckwheat noodles)
1	tablespoon canola oil
1	tablespoon minced peeled fresh ginger
1	tablespoon minced garlic
1	cup sliced onion
1	cup sliced red bell pepper
2	(3½-ounce) packages shiitake mushrooms, trimmed and sliced
¼	teaspoon salt
1	cup trimmed and halved snow peas
½	cup mirin (sweet rice wine)
¼	cup low-sodium soy sauce
2	teaspoons dark sesame oil

1. Cook noodles according to package directions; drain, reserving 1 tablespoon pasta water. Keep noodles warm.
2. Heat canola oil in a large nonstick skillet over medium-high heat. Add ginger and garlic; sauté 30 seconds. Add onion and bell pepper; cook 3 minutes or until golden brown, stirring often. Add mushrooms, salt, and reserved 1 tablespoon pasta water; cook 2 minutes or until mushrooms are tender, stirring frequently. Stir in snow peas, and cook 1 minute.
3. Combine mirin, soy sauce, and sesame oil in a small bowl, stirring with a whisk. Add mirin mixture and noodles to pan; toss to combine. Serve immediately. YIELD: 4 servings (serving size: 1½ cups).

Per serving: CAL 400 (18% from fat); FAT 8g (sat 0.7g); PRO 11.1g; CARB 63.8g; FIB 4.8g; CHOL 0mg; IRON 3.6mg; SOD 755mg; CALC 44mg

PAN-SEARED ASIAN TOFU
WITH CABBAGE

POINTS value: 4

prep: 15 minutes • cook: 17 minutes
other: 10 minutes

A sweet-salty sesame and ginger sauce pumps up the flavor of tofu and sautéed cabbage. Keep prep time to a minimum by using a preshredded coleslaw mix for the cabbage.

1	(14-ounce) package reduced-fat tofu, drained
2	tablespoons light brown sugar
1	tablespoon sesame seeds, toasted
½	teaspoon ground ginger
¼	teaspoon salt
⅛	teaspoon garlic powder
3	tablespoons low-sodium soy sauce
½	teaspoon hot sauce
4	teaspoons canola oil, divided
¼	teaspoon crushed red pepper
¼	cup diagonally cut green onions
1	(16-ounce) cabbage-and-carrot coleslaw
¼	cup chopped fresh cilantro

1. Cut tofu crosswise into 8 (½-inch-thick) slices. Place tofu slices on several layers of heavy-duty paper towels. Cover tofu with additional paper towels. Place a cutting board on top of tofu. Let stand 10 minutes.
2. While tofu stands, combine brown sugar and next 6 ingredients in a small bowl.
3. Heat 3 teaspoons oil in a large nonstick skillet over medium-high heat. Add tofu; cook 3 to 4 minutes on each side or until browned. Remove from pan, and place tofu in a shallow dish; top with half of brown sugar sauce. Cover and keep warm.
4. Reduce heat to medium. Add remaining 1 teaspoon oil, red pepper, and green onions to pan; sauté 1 minute. Add coleslaw to pan, and sauté 6 minutes or just until soft.
5. Divide slaw mixture among plates. Top with tofu, and drizzle evenly with remaining sauce. Sprinkle with cilantro. YIELD: 4 servings (serving size: ¾ cup slaw mixture, 2 slices tofu, and about 2 teaspoons sauce).

Per serving: CAL 219 (42% from fat); FAT 10.3g (sat 0.4g); PRO 13.6g; CARB 19.8g; FIB 5.2g; CHOL 0mg; IRON 5.9mg; SOD 579mg; CALC 112mg

preparing tofu

Pressing the tofu between paper towels removes excess moisture, allowing more flavor to be absorbed while cooking. It also encourages the tofu to brown faster.

Tofu is also more receptive to flavor if you heat it first. If you marinate tofu straight from the package, not much flavor will penetrate the surface.

meats ▶▶

BARE BURRITO

POINTS value: 8

prep: 5 minutes • cook: 10 minutes

When you omit the tortilla from a burrito and make a meal of the filling, you reduce the POINTS value by 2. Precooked rice, preshredded cheese, and preshredded lettuce are all great time-savers.

1	pound ground sirloin
½	cup chopped onion
½	cup chopped green bell pepper
1	(8¾-ounce) can no-salt-added whole-kernel corn, drained
1	(4.4-ounce) package precooked brown rice
1	cup salsa
½	teaspoon coarsely ground black pepper
4	cups shredded iceberg lettuce
¼	cup (1 ounce) reduced-fat shredded Cheddar cheese
¼	cup reduced-fat sour cream

1. Cook first 3 ingredients in a large nonstick skillet over medium-high heat until browned, stirring to crumble beef. (Drain if necessary, and return to pan.) Stir in corn and next 3 ingredients. Cook 2 minutes until thoroughly heated, stirring frequently.
2. Divide lettuce evenly among plates. Top with beef mixture, cheese, and sour cream. YIELD: 4 servings (serving size: 1 cup lettuce, 1 cup beef mixture, 1 tablespoon cheese, and 1 tablespoon sour cream).

Per serving: CAL 362 (39% from fat); FAT 15.6g (sat 6.8g); PRO 29.2g; CARB 26g; FIB 3.5g; CHOL 86mg; IRON 3.3mg; SOD 541mg; CALC 123mg

POBLANO PICADILLO CASSEROLE

POINTS value: 7

prep: 22 minutes • cook: 57 minutes
other: 15 minutes

Picadillo, a popular dish in many Spanish-speaking countries, consists of ground meat, tomatoes, garlic, onion, and, often, olives and raisins. This casserole version gets an extra punch of rich flavor from roasted poblano chiles.

4	large poblano chiles, seeded and halved
	Cooking spray
1	(3½-ounce) bag boil-in-bag brown rice (such as Success)
1	pound ground sirloin
½	cup chopped onion
1	garlic clove, minced
1	(14.5-ounce) can no-salt-added diced tomatoes, undrained
1	(8-ounce) can no-salt-added tomato sauce
½	cup water
2	tablespoons raisins
2	tablespoons chopped pimiento-stuffed olives
2	tablespoons slivered almonds, toasted
½	teaspoon salt
½	teaspoon ground cumin
½	teaspoon ground cinnamon
¼	teaspoon black pepper
½	cup (2 ounces) shredded part-skim mozzarella cheese

1. Preheat broiler.
2. Place poblano chile halves, skin sides up, on a foil-lined baking sheet coated with cooking spray; flatten with hand. Broil 16 minutes or until blackened. Place chiles in a zip-top plastic bag; seal. Let stand 10 minutes. Peel and discard skins; cut chile halves into strips to measure ¾ cup. Reserve any remaining chile for another use.
3. While chile stands, cook brown rice according to package directions, omitting salt and fat; drain well.
4. Preheat oven to 350°.
5. Cook beef, onion, and garlic in a Dutch oven over medium-high heat until browned, stirring to crumble beef. (Drain if necessary, and return beef mixture to pan.) Add rice, diced tomatoes, and next 9 ingredients. Bring to a boil; cook, uncovered, 3 minutes.
6. Spoon 3 cups beef mixture into an 11 x 7–inch baking dish coated with cooking spray. Top with chile strips and remaining beef mixture. Bake, uncovered, at 350° for 20 minutes or until bubbly.
7. Remove from oven; sprinkle with cheese. Cover loosely with foil; let stand 5 minutes or until cheese melts. YIELD: 6 servings (serving size: about 1 cup).

Per serving: CAL 338 (31% from fat); FAT 11.6g (sat 4.2g); PRO 22.1g; CARB 36.8g; FIB 4g; CHOL 55mg; IRON 3.2mg; SOD 372mg; CALC 115mg

MEXICAN SKILLET SUPPER

POINTS value: 6

prep: 13 minutes • cook: 27 minutes

You can't beat a one-skillet supper when it comes to easy cleanup. Plus, these ingredients are items you probably already have on hand.

2 (3½-ounce) bags boil-in-bag brown rice (such as Success)
½ pound ground sirloin
1 (16-ounce) can light red kidney beans, rinsed and drained
1 (14.5-ounce) can diced tomatoes and green chiles, undrained
1 (1.25-ounce) package 40%-less-sodium taco seasoning
¾ cup frozen whole-kernel corn
¾ cup water
6 tablespoons reduced-fat sour cream
6 tablespoons finely chopped fresh cilantro

1. Cook brown rice according to package directions, omitting salt and fat; drain well.
2. While rice cooks, heat a large nonstick skillet over medium-high heat. Add beef; cook 5 minutes or until browned, stirring to crumble. (Drain if necessary, and return beef to pan.) Stir in beans and next 4 ingredients, and bring to a boil. Cover, reduce heat, and simmer 12 minutes or until slightly thick, stirring occasionally.
3. Serve beef mixture over rice, and top with sour cream and cilantro.

YIELD: 6 servings (serving size: ½ cup rice, ⅔ cup beef mixture, 1 tablespoon sour cream, and 1 tablespoon cilantro).

Per serving: CAL 292 (18% from fat); FAT 5.7g (sat 2.3g); PRO 14.5g; CARB 42.4g; FIB 4.8g; CHOL 30mg; IRON 2.6mg; SOD 710mg; CALC 54mg

BEEF KEEMA

POINTS value: 7

prep: 6 minutes • cook: 18 minutes

Keema is an Indian-style ground meat dish made with either lamb or beef. The spiced beef mixture is thick and chili-like and is traditionally served with an Indian flatbread called naan. We've used store-bought pita bread as an easy-to-find alternative.

1½ teaspoons olive oil
1 cup chopped onion (about ¾ small)
3 garlic cloves, minced
½ teaspoon minced peeled fresh ginger
1 pound ground sirloin
1¼ teaspoons ground cumin
1¼ teaspoons ground coriander
½ teaspoon salt
¼ teaspoon ground turmeric
¼ teaspoon black pepper
⅛ teaspoon ground cinnamon
¾ cup chopped plum tomato (2 medium)
½ cup frozen green peas
3 tablespoons plain low-fat yogurt
1 (6-inch) whole wheat pita, cut into fourths
4 lime wedges

ground beef

To make sure you're buying lean ground beef, read the label to determine the percentage of fat rather than relying on the name of the specific cut. The percentage of lean to fat is usually listed on the label near the name of the cut. For example, "85/15" means that the ground beef is 85% lean and 15% fat.

Ground sirloin (or extralean) = ground beef with 10% fat or less

Ground round = ground beef with 15% fat

Ground chuck = ground beef with 20% fat

Regular ground beef = 30% fat (the maximum amount)

1. Heat oil in a large nonstick skillet over medium-high heat. Add onion, garlic, and ginger; sauté 4 minutes. Add beef; cook 8 minutes or until browned, stirring to crumble beef. (Drain, if necessary, and return beef mixture to pan.)
2. Stir in cumin and next 5 ingredients, and cook 1 minute over medium-high heat, stirring often. Stir in tomato, peas, and yogurt. Cook 4 minutes or until thoroughly heated. Serve with pita wedges and lime wedges. YIELD: 4 servings (serving size: ¾ cup beef mixture, 1 pita wedge, and 1 lime wedge).

Per serving: CAL 316 (40% from fat); FAT 14.1g (sat 5g); PRO 27.1g; CARB 20.4g; FIB 3.9g; CHOL 74mg; IRON 3.9mg; SOD 493mg; CALC 61mg

☑ BEEF AND BOK CHOY

POINTS value: 4

prep: 17 minutes • cook: 10 minutes
other: 10 minutes

Bok choy is a relative of Chinese cabbage and resembles a bunch of wide-stalked celery with its crunchy white stalks and tender dark green leaves. Its mild flavor partners well with this Asian-style beef. Serve the meat mixture over rice or Chinese-style noodles.

1½   pounds flank steak
⅓   cup rice wine vinegar
⅓   cup low-sodium soy sauce
2   tablespoons chopped green onions
1   tablespoon grated peeled fresh ginger
½   teaspoon crushed red pepper
2   garlic cloves, minced
2½   cups thinly sliced bok choy
2   tablespoons sesame seeds, toasted

1. Cut steak diagonally across grain into thin slices; set aside. Combine vinegar and next 5 ingredients in a large zip-top plastic bag; add steak, and seal bag. Let stand 10 minutes.
2. Heat a large nonstick skillet over medium-high heat; add steak and marinade. Cook 4 minutes or until browned. Add bok choy; sauté 3 minutes or until tender. Sprinkle with sesame seeds. YIELD: 6 servings (serving size: ⅔ cup).

Per serving: CAL 195 (36% from fat); FAT 7.7g (sat 2.4g); PRO 26.3g; CARB 3.3g; FIB 0.5g; CHOL 37mg; IRON 6.7mg; SOD 557mg; CALC 64mg

MEAT JUN

POINTS value: 8

prep: 8 minutes • cook: 30 minutes
other: 1 hour

This Korean dish is popular in Hawaii. It's marinated beef that's coated with an egg-flour mixture, fried, and served with a dipping sauce. We pan-fried the meat in a small amount of oil instead of deep-frying and still got a crispy coating.

1   pound top sirloin steak
4   green onions, sliced
¼   cup low-sodium soy sauce
2   tablespoons dark sesame oil
2   garlic cloves, minced
¼   cup low-sodium soy sauce
2   teaspoons sesame seeds, toasted
1   teaspoon rice vinegar
1   teaspoon sesame oil
1   green onion, sliced
1   garlic clove, minced
2   (3½-ounce) bags boil-in-bag brown rice (such as Success)
2   large eggs
2   large egg whites
¾   cup all-purpose flour
2   tablespoons canola oil, divided

1. Cut steak diagonally across grain into ¼-inch-thick slices. Combine steak and next 4 ingredients in a large zip-top plastic bag; seal bag, and chill at least 1 hour. Remove steak from bag; discard marinade.
2. Combine ¼ cup soy sauce and next 5 ingredients; set aside.
3. Cook rice according to package directions, omitting salt and fat; drain.
4. Lightly beat eggs and egg whites in a medium bowl. Dredge steak strips in flour; dip in beaten egg (do not return steak to flour).

5. Heat 1 tablespoon oil in a large nonstick skillet. Add steak, in batches, and cook 2 minutes on each side or until golden, adding 1 teaspoon additional oil to pan for each batch. Serve steak with sauce and rice. YIELD: 6 servings (serving size: 2 ounces steak, 1½ tablespoons sauce, and ½ cup rice).

Per serving: CAL 377 (34% from fat); FAT 14.1g (sat 2.5g); PRO 25.1g; CARB 38.8g; FIB 2.4g; CHOL 117mg; IRON 5.5mg; SOD 625mg; CALC 45mg

FIVE-SPICE BEEF

POINTS value: 7

prep: 28 minutes • cook: 16 minutes
other: 20 minutes

Five-spice powder is a staple in Chinese cooking and an ideal accent for beef.

1   pound sirloin steak (1 inch thick), cut diagonally across grain into wafer-thin strips
1   tablespoon Chinese five-spice powder
¼   cup low-sodium soy sauce, divided
1   cup fat-free, less-sodium beef broth
¾   cup green bell pepper, seeded and chopped (about ½ small)
½   cup red bell pepper, seeded and chopped (about ½ small)
½   cup onion, chopped
¼   cup diced celery
1   (8-ounce) can sliced water chestnuts, drained
1   (8.8-ounce) package precooked brown rice
2   tablespoons coarsely chopped cashews

1. Place steak in a large zip-top plastic bag. Combine five-spice powder and 3 tablespoons soy sauce in a small bowl; pour over steak. Seal bag; chill at least 20 minutes.

2. Heat a large nonstick skillet or wok over medium-high heat. Add steak and marinade to pan; stir-fry 4 minutes or until browned on all sides. Remove steak from pan; set aside, and keep warm.

3. Add broth and next 5 ingredients to pan; cook over medium heat 7 minutes or until vegetables are tender. Return steak to pan; stir in remaining 1 tablespoon soy sauce, and cook until thoroughly heated.

4. While vegetable mixture simmers, heat rice in microwave oven according to package directions.

5. Spoon steak mixture over rice, and sprinkle with cashews. YIELD: 4 servings (serving size: 1 cup steak mixture, about ½ cup rice, and 1½ teaspoons cashews).

Per serving: CAL 335 (23% from fat); FAT 8.7g (sat 2.4g); PRO 29.5g; CARB 34.5g; FIB 4.1g; CHOL 69mg; IRON 5.7mg; SOD 752mg; CALC 50mg

☑ GRILLED STEAK WITH BALSAMIC PEPPERS

POINTS value: 4

prep: 8 minutes • cook: 20 minutes

Add Mediterranean flair as well as color to your grilled steaks with a bell pepper and onion medley. As with roasting, grilling peppers brings out their natural sweetness.

1	small red bell pepper, halved and seeded
1	small yellow bell pepper, halved and seeded
1	small green bell pepper, halved and seeded
1	medium onion, cut into ¼-inch rings
Cooking spray	
1	tablespoon chopped fresh rosemary
3	tablespoons balsamic vinegar
1	teaspoon olive oil
1	garlic clove, minced
4	(4-ounce) beef tenderloin steaks, trimmed (1 inch thick)
½	teaspoon salt
¾	teaspoon freshly ground black pepper

1. Prepare grill.

2. Place bell peppers and onion on grill rack coated with cooking spray, and grill 10 to 12 minutes or until tender. Slice bell peppers into ¼-inch-thick strips, and cut onion rings in half. Place in a medium bowl, and toss with rosemary and next 3 ingredients; set aside.

3. Sprinkle steaks evenly with salt and black pepper. Grill 5 minutes on each side or until desired degree of doneness. Serve vegetable mixture with steaks. YIELD: 4 servings (serving size: 1 steak and ¾ cup vegetable mixture).

Per serving: CAL 185 (39% from fat); FAT 8.1g (sat 2.7g); PRO 18.9g; CARB 8.8g; FIB 1.5g; CHOL 54mg; IRON 2.8mg; SOD 337mg; CALC 22mg

how hot?

The best way to measure the temperature of an open fire is the time-honored hand test. Simply hold your hand about 3 inches above the grate, and then time how long you can keep your hand there before you're forced to withdraw it:

■ **1 to 2 seconds**—the fire is hot and perfect for searing a steak or grilling shrimp.

■ **3 seconds**—indicates medium-high heat, which is great for most fish.

■ **4 to 5 seconds**—signifies a medium range, which is ideal for most chicken and vegetables.

■ **7 to 8 seconds**—indicates the temperature is low and perfect for grilling delicate vegetables and fruit.

HUNTER'S-STYLE BEEF PIE

POINTS value: 7

(pictured on page 135)

prep: 25 minutes
cook: 1 hour and 25 minutes

Reminiscent of a homestyle chicken pot pie, this hearty pie is filled with a savory mixture of wine-braised beef and tender vegetables. You can substitute an additional ½ cup beef broth for the wine if you prefer.

1   tablespoon olive oil
1   pound boneless sirloin steak, trimmed and cut into ½-inch cubes
1¾ cups chopped onion (about 1 medium)
2   garlic cloves, minced
1½ cups fat-free, less-sodium beef broth
½   cup merlot or other dry red wine
2   tablespoons no-salt-added tomato paste
1   tablespoon low-sodium Worcestershire sauce
1½ cups sliced carrot (about 5 medium)
1   cup sliced mushrooms
2   thyme sprigs
2   tablespoons all-purpose flour
3   tablespoons water
½   teaspoon salt
¼   teaspoon black pepper
Cooking spray
½   (15-ounce) package refrigerated pie dough (such as Pillsbury)

1. Heat oil in a Dutch oven over medium-high heat. Add steak, onion, and garlic; cook 5 minutes or until steak is browned. Add beef broth and next 3 ingredients to pan; stir well to combine. Bring to a boil; reduce heat, and simmer, uncovered, 25 minutes, stirring occasionally.
2. Stir in carrot, mushrooms, and thyme; cover and simmer 30 minutes.
3. Combine flour and water in a small bowl, stirring with a whisk; add to steak mixture in pan. Cook over medium heat 2 minutes or until thick. Remove and discard thyme; stir in salt and pepper.
4. Preheat oven to 425°.
5. Spoon steak filling into a 9-inch deep-dish pie plate coated with cooking spray. Unroll pie dough; cut small slits in center to vent, and place over filling. Fold edges under; flute.
6. Bake at 425° for 17 to 18 minutes or until lightly browned. YIELD: 6 servings (serving size: 1 wedge).

Per serving: CAL 327 (40% from fat); FAT 14.5g (sat 5.3g); PRO 19.8g; CARB 29.2g; FIB 2g; CHOL 53mg; IRON 2.7mg; SOD 545mg; CALC 35mg

cooking with wine basics

Quality While the wine you cook with does not have to be expensive, it needs to be of good quality because it will contribute its flavors to the final dish.

Timing The type of recipe will determine when in the cooking process the wine should be added. For the most impact, add the wine at the end of the cooking process, such as when deglazing a pan to make a flavorful sauce. This will allow some of the water and alcohol to evaporate and will concentrate the wine's acidity, sugar, and flavors. But if you're cooking a stew, it's best to add the wine at the beginning to allow the wine time to blend with the other ingredients and flavors.

Less is more You don't need a lot of wine in the dish to get big flavor. If you decide to add wine to a recipe that does not call for wine, substitute the wine for a portion of one of the other liquid ingredients, such as water or broth.

Burn-off factor The longer the cooking time, the more alcohol that evaporates, leaving the wine's flavor behind. (Note that not all of the alcohol evaporates; after simmering for 2½ hours, 5 percent of the alcohol will still remain.)

Temperature High temperatures can cause some of the flavor elements to disappear from the wine, so it's a good idea to limit cooking time and temperatures.

Substitutions If you prefer not to use wine in a recipe, you can substitute an equal amount of fat-free, less-sodium chicken broth for white wine or less-sodium beef broth for red wine in savory recipes.

Cooking wine Cooking wines aren't recommended because they have salt and food coloring added, and they usually have an inferior flavor.

BURGUNDY POT ROAST

POINTS value: 5

prep: 23 minutes
cook: 5 hours and 6 minutes

Burgundy adds a rich depth of flavor to this traditional pot roast. You can substitute a dry red wine, such as merlot or cabernet sauvignon, for the Burgundy. If you prefer not to use wine, use 1 cup of less-sodium beef broth.

2   teaspoons olive oil
1   (4-pound) sirloin tip roast, trimmed
2   teaspoons salt
1   teaspoon freshly ground black pepper
4   cups sliced onion
4   garlic cloves, minced
1   (14-ounce) can less-sodium beef broth
1   cup Burgundy or other dry red wine
4   thyme sprigs
7   carrots, sliced into 1-inch pieces
5   celery stalks, coarsely chopped
1   pound red potatoes, coarsely chopped
3   plum tomatoes, chopped
3   tablespoons all-purpose flour

1. Preheat oven to 325°.
2. Heat oil in a large Dutch oven over medium-high heat. Sprinkle roast evenly with salt and pepper. Add roast to pan; cook 8 minutes or until browned on all sides. Remove roast from pan.
3. Add onion and garlic to pan, and sauté 6 minutes or until tender. Return roast to pan. Add broth, wine, and thyme to pan; bring to a simmer. Cover and bake at 325° for 1 hour.
4. Add carrot and next 3 ingredients to pan. Cover and bake an additional 3½ hours or until vegetables and roast are tender. Remove roast and vegetables to a serving dish, reserving juices in pan; discard thyme sprigs.
5. Combine flour and ½ cup pan juices in a small bowl, stirring with a whisk. Return mixture to pan. Bring to a simmer over medium heat; cook 15 minutes or until thick. Slice or shred roast; serve with vegetables and gravy. YIELD: 16 servings (serving size: 3 ounces roast, ½ cup vegetable mixture, and ¼ cup gravy).

Per serving: CAL 239 (36% from fat); FAT 9.5g (sat 3.3g); PRO 25.1g; CARB 12.6g; FIB 2.1g; CHOL 66mg; IRON 2.3mg; SOD 430mg; CALC 55mg

VEAL WITH MUSHROOM SAUCE

POINTS value: 7

prep: 5 minutes • cook: 15 minutes

A splash of dry sherry and a sprinkle of nutmeg enhance the rich, creamy sauce.

6   ounces uncooked egg noodles
1   pound veal cutlets (about ¼ inch thick)
½   teaspoon salt
¼   teaspoon black pepper
2   teaspoons olive oil, divided
1   (8-ounce) package presliced mushrooms
1   (5-ounce) can evaporated fat-free milk
¾   cup fat-free, less-sodium chicken broth
2   tablespoons all-purpose flour
¼   teaspoon ground nutmeg
2   tablespoons dry sherry

1. Cook noodles according to package directions, omitting salt and fat. Drain.
2. While noodles cook, place veal between 2 sheets of plastic wrap; pound to an even thickness using a meat mallet or small heavy skillet. Sprinkle salt and pepper over both sides of veal.
3. Heat 1 teaspoon oil in a large nonstick skillet over medium-high heat. Add half of veal, and cook 1 minute on each side or until lightly browned. Remove from pan, and keep warm. Repeat procedure with remaining 1 teaspoon oil and veal.
4. Add mushrooms to pan. Cook over medium-high heat 3 minutes or until tender. Combine milk and next 3 ingredients, stirring well with a whisk. Add milk mixture to pan. Reduce heat to medium, and cook 4 minutes or until thick, stirring constantly. Stir in sherry. Add reserved veal and juices to pan; cook 1 minute or until thoroughly heated. Serve over noodles. YIELD: 4 servings (serving size: 3 ounces veal, ½ cup sauce, and 1 cup noodles).

Per serving: CAL 364 (16% from fat); FAT 6.5g (sat 1.5g); PRO 34.8g; CARB 40.2g; FIB 2.1g; CHOL 124mg; IRON 3.1mg; SOD 426mg; CALC 124mg

VEAL WITH MUSTARD CREAM SAUCE

POINTS value: 4

prep: 1 minute • cook: 12 minutes

Serve these tender veal cutlets topped with a tangy cream sauce alongside asparagus and mashed potatoes.

1   pound veal cutlets
½   teaspoon salt
½   teaspoon black pepper
2   teaspoons olive oil, divided
½   cup fat-free, less-sodium chicken broth
⅔   cup fat-free half-and-half
4   teaspoons Dijon mustard
2   teaspoons lemon juice
¼   cup chopped fresh parsley

1. Place veal between 2 sheets of plastic wrap; pound to ¼-inch thickness using a meat mallet or small heavy skillet. Sprinkle both sides of veal with salt and pepper.
2. Heat 1 teaspoon oil in a large nonstick skillet over medium-high heat. Add half of veal, and cook 1 minute on each side or until lightly browned. Remove veal from pan; keep warm. Repeat procedure with remaining 1 teaspoon oil and veal.
3. Add chicken broth to pan, scraping pan to loosen browned bits. Stir in half-and-half, mustard, and lemon juice. Reduce heat, and simmer 6 to 7 minutes or until sauce is slightly thick. Spoon sauce over veal, and sprinkle with chopped parsley. YIELD: 4 servings (serving size: about 3 ounces veal and 5 tablespoons sauce).

Per serving: CAL 172 (23% from fat); FAT 4.4g (sat 0.9g); PRO 24.7g; CARB 4.8g; FIB 0.2g; CHOL 88mg; IRON 1.2mg; SOD 542mg; CALC 39mg

MOROCCAN LAMB CHOPS WITH COUSCOUS PILAF

POINTS value: 8

prep: 18 minutes • cook: 11 minutes
other: 5 minutes

Lamb is well suited for the North African flavors in this dish. For added flavor, stir golden raisins into the couscous pilaf.

2   teaspoons sweet paprika
1½   teaspoons ground cumin
1   teaspoon garlic salt
1   teaspoon ground coriander
½   teaspoon ground cinnamon
8   (4-ounce) lamb loin chops, trimmed
1   tablespoon olive oil
¾   cup fat-free, less-sodium chicken broth
¼   cup fresh orange juice
½   cup grated carrot
⅔   cup uncooked couscous
¼   cup minced green onions
Cooking spray

1. Prepare grill.
2. Combine paprika and next 4 ingredients in a small bowl; stir well to combine. Reserve 1½ teaspoons spice mixture, and set aside.
3. Brush lamb chops with olive oil; rub 4½ teaspoons spice mixture on both sides of lamb chops. Set lamb chops aside.
4. Combine chicken broth, orange juice, carrot, and reserved 1½ teaspoons spice mixture in a medium saucepan, and bring to a boil. Stir in couscous and green onions. Remove from heat; cover and let stand 5 minutes or until liquid is absorbed. Fluff mixture with a fork; keep warm.

5. Place lamb chops on grill rack coated with cooking spray. Grill 4 to 5 minutes on each side or until desired degree of doneness. Serve lamb chops with couscous. YIELD: 4 servings (serving size: 2 chops and ¾ cup couscous).

Per serving: CAL 385 (33% from fat); FAT 14.2g (sat 4.9g); PRO 35.9g; CARB 26.4g; FIB 2.4g; CHOL 95mg; IRON 3.3mg; SOD 458mg; CALC 51mg

GRILLED CURRY-GINGER LAMB CHOPS

POINTS value: 8

prep: 12 minutes • cook: 14 minutes
other: 3 hours

Curry and ginger are two spices that always work with lamb. Here, the lamb is marinated in a pastelike mixture made with those spices and apricot preserves. We recommend grilling over medium heat for this recipe so that the sweet apricot mixture doesn't burn.

⅓   cup apricot preserves
3   tablespoons curry powder
3   tablespoons grated peeled fresh ginger
1   tablespoon olive oil
½   teaspoon kosher salt
½   teaspoon black pepper
8   (4-ounce) lamb loin chops, trimmed
Cooking spray
Cilantro sprigs (optional)

1. Combine first 6 ingredients in a medium bowl, and spread over lamb. Place lamb in a shallow dish;

cover and marinate in refrigerator at least 3 hours.

2. Prepare grill.

3. Coat lamb with cooking spray. Place lamb on grill rack. Grill 7 to 8 minutes on each side or until desired degree of doneness. Garnish with cilantro, if desired. YIELD: 4 servings (serving size: 2 chops).

Per serving: CAL 340 (38% from fat); FAT 14.5g (sat 4.9g); PRO 32.1g; CARB 20.8g; FIB 1.3g; CHOL 95mg; IRON 4.4mg; SOD 344mg; CALC 57mg

on the "lamb"

Today, lamb is leaner than ever. And because lamb cuts are leaner, it's very important that you watch the cooking time and temperature carefully, or your meat will be overcooked and tough. For the best flavor and tenderness, cook lamb only until it's pink: medium-rare (145°) or medium (160°). Most of the fat on lamb is on the outside, not inside the meat, so if you cook the lamb to 180° or 185° (well done), the meat will be tough and dry.

Lamb loin chops are a very tender cut and are good for grilling, broiling, and pan-roasting. One 4-ounce chop yields about 1½ to 2 ounces of cooked meat, so one serving is 2 (4-ounce) chops.

☑ SONORAN SPICED PORK CHOPS

POINTS value: 4

prep: 5 minutes • cook: 12 minutes

When you need a head start on supper, rub the Mexican-style spice mixture on the chops the day before. These pork chops are also great for the grill. The cooking time will be about the same.

2 tablespoons ground cumin
1 tablespoon ground coriander
1 tablespoon paprika
1 tablespoon dried thyme
¾ teaspoon salt
½ teaspoon black pepper
¼ teaspoon ground red pepper
4 (4-ounce) boneless center-cut loin pork chops (about ¾ inch thick)
Cooking spray
4 lemon wedges

1. Prepare broiler.

2. Combine first 7 ingredients in a small bowl; rub spice mixture onto both sides of pork chops.

3. Place chops on rack of a broiler pan coated with cooking spray; broil 6 to 8 minutes on each side or until desired degree of doneness. Serve with lemon wedges. YIELD: 4 servings (serving size: 1 chop).

Per serving: CAL 187 (35% from fat); FAT 7.3g (sat 2.3g); PRO 24.8g; CARB 4.1g; FIB 2.5g; CHOL 65mg; IRON 2.5mg; SOD 493mg; CALC 68mg

PORK CHOPS WITH APRICOT SAUCE

POINTS value: 5

prep: 8 minutes • cook: 16 minutes

With only a can of apricots and a couple of spices, you can transform ordinary pork chops into a sweet and saucy entrée.

½ teaspoon salt
½ teaspoon ground ginger
¼ teaspoon black pepper
4 (4-ounce) boneless center-cut loin pork chops (½ inch thick)
2 teaspoons olive oil
1 (15-ounce) can apricot halves in extralight syrup

1. Combine first 3 ingredients, and sprinkle over both sides of pork chops.

2. Heat oil in large nonstick skillet over medium-high heat. Add pork, and cook 3 minutes on each side or until done. Remove pork from pan; set aside, and keep warm.

3. Drain apricots, reserving syrup. Add 6 tablespoons syrup to pan; cook over medium-high heat 4 to 5 minutes or until mixture is reduced by half, scraping pan to loosen browned bits. Reduce heat to medium. Add remaining ½ cup syrup and apricots; cook 5 minutes or until thoroughly heated. Serve sauce over pork. YIELD: 4 servings (serving size: 1 chop, 2 apricot halves, and about 2 tablespoons sauce).

Per serving: CAL 231 (35% from fat); FAT 9g (sat 2.8g); PRO 24g; CARB 13.5g; FIB 1.7g; CHOL 67mg; IRON 1.2mg; SOD 341mg; CALC 30mg

PARMESAN-CRUSTED PORK CHOPS

POINTS value: 6

prep: 11 minutes • cook: 7 minutes

Enjoy the homestyle goodness of fried pork chops—but with only a fraction of the fat. Parmesan cheese and Italian seasoning pump up the flavor of the breadcrumb coating. Try them with Roasted Green Beans with Bacon and Shallots (page 146). You can prepare the pork chops on the stovetop while the beans roast in the oven.

½   cup Italian-seasoned breadcrumbs
¼   cup grated fresh Parmesan cheese
2   teaspoons Italian seasoning
¼   teaspoon kosher salt
¼   teaspoon freshly ground black pepper
4   (4-ounce) boneless center-cut loin pork chops
2   large egg whites, lightly beaten
2   teaspoons olive oil
1   teaspoon butter
Cooking spray
1   tablespoon fresh lemon juice
2   teaspoons minced fresh parsley (optional)

1. Combine first 5 ingredients in a medium bowl. Place pork chops between 2 sheets of plastic wrap; pound to ¼-inch thickness using a meat mallet or small heavy skillet. Dip chops in egg white; dredge in breadcrumb mixture.
2. Heat oil and butter in a large nonstick skillet coated with cooking spray over medium-high heat until butter melts. Add chops, and cook 3

minutes on each side or until browned. Drizzle with lemon juice. Sprinkle with parsley, if desired. YIELD: 4 servings (serving size: 1 chop).

Per serving: CAL 239 (42% from fat); FAT 11.1g (sat 3.8g); PRO 28g; CARB 5.5g; FIB 0.4g; CHOL 70mg; IRON 1.1mg; SOD 383mg; CALC 98mg

PORK STIR-FRY WITH ORANGE SAUCE

POINTS value: 7
(pictured on page 132)

prep: 16 minutes • cook: 15 minutes

Tossing the pork in soy sauce and letting it stand a few minutes gives this stir-fry its authentic flavor. Look for rice noodles in Asian markets or in the Asian-cooking section of the supermarket.

4   ounces uncooked thin rice noodles
1   pound boneless loin pork chops, trimmed and cut into thin strips
3   tablespoons low-sodium soy sauce, divided
1½ teaspoons cornstarch
¼   cup fat-free, less-sodium chicken broth
3   tablespoons dry sherry
2   tablespoons thawed frozen orange juice concentrate
2   teaspoons grated peeled fresh ginger
⅛   teaspoon crushed red pepper
4   teaspoons canola oil, divided
⅔   cup diagonally cut peeled carrot (about 2 medium)
1   cup sliced red bell pepper
4   green onions, sliced diagonally

1. Cook noodles according to package directions, omitting salt and fat. Drain and keep warm.
2. While noodles cook, combine pork and 1 tablespoon soy sauce in a small bowl. Set aside.
3. Combine remaining 2 tablespoons soy sauce and cornstarch in a small bowl, stirring with a whisk until smooth. Stir in broth and next 4 ingredients. Set aside.
4. Heat 2 teaspoons oil in a large nonstick skillet over medium-high heat. Add pork; cook 2 minutes or until pork just loses its pink color. Remove from pan; set aside.
5. Heat remaining 2 teaspoons oil in pan; add carrot and bell pepper. Sauté 2 minutes or until crisp-tender. Add green onions; cook 2 minutes or until onions wilt. Add soy sauce mixture to pan. Return pork and accumulated juices to pan; sauté 2 minutes or until sauce is thick. Serve over noodles. YIELD: 4 servings (serving size: ¾ cup pork mixture and ½ cup noodles).

Per serving: CAL 341 (24% from fat); FAT 9.1g (sat 2.6g); PRO 27.3g; CARB 33.3g; FIB 2.3g; CHOL 67mg; IRON 2.3mg; SOD 509mg; CALC 48mg

PORK MEDALLIONS WITH DRIED CHERRIES

POINTS value: 5

prep: 5 minutes • cook: 19 minutes

Create a colorful plate by serving the pork and cherry sauce with wild rice and steamed sugar snap peas.

1   (1-pound) pork tenderloin, trimmed
2   teaspoons olive oil
Cooking spray
½   teaspoon salt
¼   teaspoon black pepper
¼   teaspoon dried rubbed sage
½   cup finely chopped onion
¾   cup dry white wine, divided
½   cup fat-free, less-sodium chicken broth
1   tablespoon apple jelly
1   teaspoon cornstarch
¼   teaspoon salt
⅛   teaspoon crushed red pepper
½   cup dried sweet cherries

1. Cut tenderloin crosswise into ¼-inch-thick slices. Heat oil in a large skillet coated with cooking spray over medium–high heat. Combine salt, black pepper, and sage, and sprinkle over both sides of pork medallions. Coat medallions with cooking spray. Add half of pork to pan; cook 3 minutes on each side or until browned. Remove pork from pan; keep warm. Repeat procedure with remaining pork.
2. Recoat pan with cooking spray. Add onion and ¼ cup wine; sauté 2 minutes. Combine remaining ½ cup wine, broth, and next 4 ingredients in a small bowl, stirring until smooth. Add wine mixture and dried cherries to pan. Cook 4 minutes or until thick, stirring constantly. Spoon cherry mixture evenly over pork. YIELD: 4 servings (serving size: 3 ounces pork and 2½ tablespoons sauce).

Per serving: CAL 255 (22% from fat); FAT 6.2g (sat 1.7g); PRO 25g; CARB 22.3g; FIB 2.4g; CHOL 74mg; IRON 2mg; SOD 571mg; CALC 35mg

PORK CUTLETS WITH MANGO CHUTNEY

POINTS value: 6

prep: 15 minutes • cook: 16 minutes

Keep a jar of chutney on hand as an easy way to add a kick to meats and poultry.

1   (1-pound) pork tenderloin, trimmed
¼   teaspoon salt
¼   teaspoon freshly ground black pepper
2   teaspoons olive oil, divided
2   tablespoons chopped shallots
⅓   cup mango chutney
⅓   cup apple cider
1   tablespoon water
¼   teaspoon minced fresh thyme

1. Cut tenderloin crosswise into ½-inch-thick slices; place between 2 sheets of plastic wrap, and pound to ¼-inch thickness using a meat mallet or small heavy skillet. Sprinkle pork with salt and pepper. Heat 1 teaspoon oil in a large nonstick skillet over medium–high heat. Add half of pork, and cook 2 minutes on each side or until golden brown. Remove from pan, and repeat procedure with remaining 1 teaspoon oil and pork.
2. Add shallots to pan, and sauté 1 minute. Remove pan from heat; add chutney, cider, and 1 tablespoon water, scraping pan to loosen browned bits. Return pan to heat, and cook 2 minutes or until sauce is slightly thick. Add pork and accumulated juices to pan. Cook 1 minute or until thoroughly heated. Spoon sauce over pork, and sprinkle with thyme. YIELD: 4 servings (serving size: 3 ounces pork and 2 tablespoons sauce).

Per serving: CAL 252 (22% from fat); FAT 6.2g (sat 1.7g); PRO 24g; CARB 22.5g; FIB 0.1g; CHOL 74mg; IRON 1.5mg; SOD 429mg; CALC 8mg

how to trim a pork tenderloin

You'll need to trim any fat and remove the silver skin from the tenderloin before cooking. The silver skin is the thin, shiny membrane that runs along the surface of the meat. Leaving it on can cause the tenderloin to toughen and lose its shape during cooking.

1. Stretching the membrane with one hand so it's tight, use your other hand to slip the tip of the knife underneath the silvery skin.

2. Slowly slice back and forth, angling the sharp edge of the blade up, rather than down, through the meat. Continue until all the silver skin is removed, and then discard.

BRAISED PORK TENDERLOIN
WITH DRIED FRUIT

POINTS value: 5

prep: 7 minutes • cook: 64 minutes

Capture the flavors of the holidays with this fork-tender pork that's simmered in apple cider with dried fruit and sage.

1	(1-pound) pork tenderloin, trimmed
½	teaspoon salt, divided
¼	teaspoon freshly ground black pepper
¼	teaspoon poultry seasoning
2	teaspoons olive oil, divided
½	cup chopped onion
2	garlic cloves, minced
¾	cup dried apple slices
⅓	cup orange-flavored sweetened dried cranberries
1	cup apple cider
½	cup fat-free, less-sodium chicken broth
½	teaspoon chopped fresh sage

1. Sprinkle pork with ¼ teaspoon salt, pepper, and poultry seasoning. Heat 1 teaspoon oil in a Dutch oven over medium-high heat. Add pork; cook 3 to 4 minutes until browned on all sides. Remove pork from pan.
2. Reduce heat to medium; add remaining 1 teaspoon oil. Add onion and garlic; sauté 2 minutes or just until tender. Add apple and next 3 ingredients; bring to a boil. Return pork and juices to pan. Cover, reduce heat, and simmer 50 minutes or until pork is done, turning after 25 minutes.
3. Remove pork from pan; cover and keep warm. Stir remaining ¼ teaspoon salt and sage into sauce. Bring to a boil; cook 5 minutes or until

slightly reduced. Slice pork, and serve with sauce. YIELD: 4 servings (serving size: 3 ounces pork and ½ cup sauce).

Per serving: CAL 274 (21% from fat); FAT 6.3g; (sat 1.7g); PRO 25.1g; CARB 30g; FIB 2.6g; CHOL 74mg; IRON 1.9mg; SOD 434mg; CALC 24mg

CHILE-RUBBED
PORK TENDERLOIN WITH
QUICK MOLE SAUCE

POINTS value: 4

(pictured on page 139)

prep: 18 minutes • cook: 22 minutes
other: 10 minutes

Mole is a rich, reddish brown sauce usually made with onion, garlic, chiles, and cocoa or bitter chocolate. Our quick version contains tomatoes and simmers only 15 minutes.

1	tablespoon plus 2 teaspoons canola oil, divided
⅓	cup minced onion
2	garlic cloves, minced
1	(14.5-ounce) can Mexican-style stewed tomatoes, undrained
¼	cup water
2	teaspoons espresso powder
2	teaspoons unsweetened cocoa
½	chipotle chile, canned in adobo sauce
4	teaspoons salt-free Mexican seasoning (such as The Spice Hunter), divided
1	teaspoon sugar
¼	teaspoon salt
2	(¾-pound) pork tenderloins, trimmed
Cooking spray	
1	teaspoon kosher salt
¼	teaspoon ground red pepper

1. Heat 2 teaspoons canola oil in a 2½-quart saucepan over medium heat. Add onion and garlic; sauté 3 minutes or until mixture begins to brown. Transfer onion mixture to a blender; add tomatoes, ¼ cup water, espresso powder, cocoa, chile, 1 teaspoon Mexican seasoning, sugar, and ¼ teaspoon salt. Process until smooth, scraping down sides if necessary.
2. Return tomato mixture to pan. Bring to a boil; reduce heat, and simmer, uncovered, 15 minutes or until thick, stirring often.
3. Preheat broiler.
4. While tomato mixture simmers, place pork on a broiler pan coated with cooking spray; brush with remaining 1 tablespoon oil. Combine 1 tablespoon Mexican seasoning, kosher salt, and red pepper; rub over pork. Broil 16 minutes or until a thermometer registers 160° (slightly pink), turning once. Remove from pan; cover with foil, and let stand 10 minutes before slicing. Serve pork with sauce. YIELD: 6 servings (serving size: 3 ounces pork and ¼ cup sauce).

Per serving: CAL 202 (36% from fat); FAT 8g; (sat 1.7g); PRO 24.7g; CARB 7.7g; FIB 1.5g; CHOL 74mg; IRON 1.8mg; SOD 705mg; CALC 23mg

poultry ▶▶

EASY CHICKEN QUESADILLAS

POINTS value: 5

prep: 13 minutes • cook: 9 minutes

1⅓ cups chopped cooked chicken
    breast
1   tablespoon 40%-less-sodium
    taco seasoning
4   (8½-inch) flour tortillas
½   cup fat-free refried beans
¼   cup thinly sliced green onions
1   cup (4 ounces) shredded 50%
    reduced-fat Cheddar cheese
    with jalapeño peppers
¾   cup refrigerated fresh salsa

1. Place chicken in a bowl; sprinkle
with taco seasoning, and toss well.
2. Stack 2 tortillas in a large nonstick
skillet, and place over medium heat;
cook about 30 seconds or until
warm and soft, turning stack once.
Remove tortillas from pan, and
quickly spread half of each tortilla
with 2 tablespoons refried beans. Top
each with 1 tablespoon green onions,
⅓ cup chicken mixture, and ¼ cup
cheese.
3. Fold tortillas in half, and place,
folded edges together, in pan. Cook
2 minutes on each side or until
lightly browned and cheese melts.
Remove from pan, and keep warm.
Repeat procedure with remaining
tortillas, beans, green onions, chicken
mixture, and cheese. Cut each quesadilla into 3 wedges, and serve
immediately with salsa. **YIELD:** 6
servings (serving size: 2 wedges
and 2 tablespoons salsa).

Per serving: CAL 245 (26% from fat); FAT 7.1g
(sat 3.2g); PRO 18.5g; CARB 22.9g; FIB 1.3g;
CHOL 39mg; IRON 1.4mg; SOD 589mg;
CALC 216mg

PIZZA WITH CHICKEN AND ARTICHOKES

POINTS value: 5

prep: 10 minutes • cook: 15 minutes

*To reduce the sodium by 222 milligrams
per serving, use frozen artichoke hearts
instead of canned, and cook them
according to the package directions
before putting them on the pizza.*

1   (10-ounce) Italian cheese-
    flavored thin whole wheat
    pizza crust (such as Boboli)
1¼ cups roasted garlic pasta sauce
    (such as Barilla)
1   (14-ounce) can quartered
    artichoke hearts, drained and
    coarsely chopped
1   (6-ounce) package cooked
    chicken breast strips, coarsely
    chopped
1   cup thinly sliced red bell
    pepper (1 medium)
¾   cup (3 ounces) shredded
    part-skim mozzarella cheese

1. Preheat oven to 450°.
2. Place pizza crust on a 12-inch
pizza pan. Spread pasta sauce over
crust to within 1 inch of edge; top
with artichoke hearts, chicken, and
bell pepper. Sprinkle with cheese.
Bake at 450° for 15 minutes or until
cheese melts. **YIELD:** 6 servings (serving size: 1 wedge).

Per serving: CAL 273 (26% from fat); FAT 7.9g
(sat 2.6g); PRO 18.5g; CARB 35.9g; FIB 6.3g;
CHOL 27mg; IRON 1.6mg; SOD 947mg;
CALC 177mg

CHICKEN, BROCCOLI, AND GNOCCHI WITH PARSLEY PESTO

POINTS value: 8
(pictured on page 136)

prep: 14 minutes • cook: 20 minutes

*Walnuts and parsley replace pine nuts
and fresh basil in this pesto sauce.*

2   garlic cloves, peeled
1   cup fresh flat-leaf parsley
    leaves
¼   cup (1 ounce) grated fresh
    Parmesan cheese
2   tablespoons chopped walnuts,
    toasted
¼   teaspoon salt
¼   teaspoon freshly ground black
    pepper
3   tablespoons extravirgin
    olive oil
1   tablespoon water
2   quarts water
2   cups small broccoli florets
1   (1-pound) package vacuum-
    packed gnocchi (such as Vigo)
2   cups chopped cooked chicken
    breast
2   tablespoons chopped walnuts,
    toasted (optional)
2   tablespoons Parmesan cheese
    (optional)

1. Drop garlic through food chute
with food processor on; process until
minced. Add parsley and next 4
ingredients; process until finely
minced. Gradually add olive oil and
1 tablespoon water, processing just
until blended.
2. Bring 2 quarts water to a boil in
a 4-quart saucepan. Add broccoli,
and cook 2 minutes. Remove 2 cups

gnocchi from package; reserve remaining gnocchi for another use. Add gnocchi to pan, and cook 3 minutes or just until broccoli is tender; drain and place in a large bowl. Add chicken and parsley mixture; toss gently to coat. Sprinkle with 2 tablespoons walnuts and 2 tablespoons Parmesan cheese, if desired. YIELD: 5 servings (serving size: 1 cup).

Per serving: CAL 366 (36% from fat); FAT 14.5g (sat 3.1g); PRO 25.5g; CARB 33.7g; FIB 2.9g; CHOL 56mg; IRON 2.7mg; SOD 557mg; CALC 95mg

CHICKEN SAUSAGE AND COUSCOUS

POINTS value: 8

prep: 3 minutes • cook: 15 minutes
other: 5 minutes

When kitchen time is limited, a one-skillet dinner is always a good idea. This one features savory chicken sausage links served over a bed of spicy couscous.

Cooking spray
1   (12-ounce) package chicken sausage with wild mushrooms and sun-dried tomatoes (such as Gerhard's)
¾   cup finely chopped onion
¼   cup pine nuts
2   cups water
¾   cup uncooked couscous
½   cup raisins
¾   teaspoon curry powder
¼   teaspoon salt
¼   teaspoon crushed red pepper

1. Heat a large nonstick skillet over medium heat. Coat pan with cooking spray. Add sausage to pan; cook 5 to 7 minutes or until browned on all sides. Remove from pan; set aside, and keep warm.
2. Coat pan with cooking spray. Add onion and pine nuts; cook 3 minutes or until pine nuts begin to brown, stirring occasionally. Increase heat to high; add 2 cups water to onion mixture. Bring to a boil, scraping bottom of pan to loosen browned bits. Add couscous and next 4 ingredients, stirring well. Arrange sausage over couscous. Remove from heat. Cover and let stand 5 minutes or until liquid is absorbed. YIELD: 4 servings (serving size: 1 sausage link and 1 cup couscous).

Per serving: CAL 372 (34% from fat); FAT 14.1g (sat 2.8g); PRO 16.4g; CARB 48.4g; FIB 5.5g; CHOL 62mg; IRON 2.2mg; SOD 574mg; CALC 27mg

chicken sausage

Chicken sausage links have about 8 grams of fat and 100 calories per 3-ounce serving. Regular pork sausage links have about 17 grams of fat and 194 calories for the same serving size. Chicken sausage is made with boneless, skinless chicken and flavored with salt, herbs, and spices. There are a number of flavor variations: sun-dried tomatoes and garlic, habanero pepper, and apple.

SLOW-COOKER CHICKEN-SAUSAGE PAELLA

POINTS value: 7

prep: 8 minutes
cook: 4 hours and 40 minutes

1¾   cups uncooked converted rice (such as Uncle Ben's)
2   cups frozen chopped onion
1   (14.5-ounce) can Italian-flavored stewed tomatoes, undrained and chopped
1   (9-ounce) package frozen chopped cooked chicken
½   (14-ounce) package low-fat smoked sausage (such as Healthy Choice), sliced
2   tablespoons bottled minced garlic
1   teaspoon dried thyme
1   teaspoon black pepper
Cooking spray
1   (14-ounce) can fat-free, less-sodium chicken broth
1¾   cups water
½   teaspoon saffron threads
1   cup frozen petite green peas

1. Place first 8 ingredients in a 4-quart electric slow cooker coated with cooking spray. Combine broth, 1¾ cups water, and saffron; add to cooker. Stir well. Cover and cook on LOW 4 hours and 30 minutes.
2. Remove lid; quickly stir in peas. Cover and cook on HIGH 10 minutes. YIELD: 6 servings (serving size: about 1¾ cups).

Per serving: CAL 362 (5% from fat); FAT 2.1g (sat 0.3g); PRO 21.2g; CARB 63.9g; FIB 3.9g; CHOL 30mg; IRON 3.4mg; SOD 852mg; CALC 57mg

THAI CHICKEN CURRY OVER COUSCOUS

POINTS value: 6

prep: 13 minutes • cook: 9 minutes
other: 5 minutes

Sweet fresh pineapple and tart lime juice contrast with fiery red curry paste to create an explosion of flavor. This is a creative way to use leftover chicken.

1	cup water
⅔	cup uncooked couscous
¼	cup light mayonnaise
2	tablespoons plain nonfat yogurt
2	tablespoons honey
1	tablespoon fresh lime juice
1½	cups chopped cooked chicken breast
⅓	cup diced fresh pineapple
¼	cup minced red onion
2	tablespoons chopped fresh cilantro
	Cooking spray
2	tablespoons slivered almonds
2	tablespoons minced fresh ginger
1	teaspoon Thai red curry paste
2½	cups fresh baby spinach

1. Bring 1 cup water to a boil in a medium saucepan. Stir in couscous; cover and remove from heat. Let stand 5 minutes, and fluff with a fork.
2. Combine mayonnaise and next 3 ingredients in a bowl, stirring well. Stir in chicken and next 3 ingredients; set aside.
3. Heat a large nonstick skillet over medium heat. Coat pan with cooking spray. Add almonds, and sauté 3 to 4 minutes or until golden. Add ginger and curry paste; cook 30 seconds or until fragrant. Stir into chicken mixture. Return pan to heat; increase heat to medium-high. Add spinach to pan, and cook 2 minutes or until spinach wilts; stir into chicken mixture. Serve over couscous. YIELD: 4 servings (serving size: about ⅔ cup chicken mixture and about ½ cup couscous).

Per serving: CAL 300 (26% from fat); FAT 8.8g (sat 1.7g); PRO 20.9g; CARB 34.4g; FIB 2.5g; CHOL 50mg; IRON 1.6mg; SOD 215mg; CALC 49mg

SPICY CHICKEN-SPINACH PASTA BAKE

POINTS value: 6

prep: 17 minutes • cook: 56 minutes

We tested this recipe with both fresh and frozen spinach and had much better results with the fresh.

8	ounces uncooked penne
2	teaspoons butter
½	cup chopped onion
4	garlic cloves, minced
¼	cup all-purpose flour
2½	cups 1% low-fat milk
1	(6-ounce) package fresh baby spinach, coarsely chopped
1¼	cups grated fresh Parmesan cheese, divided
½	teaspoon salt
½	teaspoon freshly ground black pepper
2	cups chopped cooked chicken breast
1½	cups salsa
	Cooking spray

1. Preheat oven to 350°.
2. Cook pasta according to package directions, omitting salt and fat. Drain.
3. While pasta cooks, melt butter in a Dutch oven over medium heat. Add onion and garlic; sauté 4 minutes or until tender. Lightly spoon flour into a dry measuring cup; level with a knife. Add flour to pan; cook 1 minute, stirring constantly. Add milk, stirring constantly with a whisk. Cook 11 minutes or until thick. Add spinach, stirring until spinach wilts. Remove from heat; add ¼ cup cheese, salt, and pepper.
4. Stir in chicken, salsa, and ¾ cup cheese. Carefully fold in pasta. Spoon mixture into a 13 x 9-inch baking dish coated with cooking spray. Sprinkle evenly with remaining ¼ cup cheese. Bake at 350° for 39 minutes or until bubbly. YIELD: 8 servings (serving size: 1 cup).

Per serving: CAL 297 (22% from fat); FAT 7.2g (sat 3.8g); PRO 24.4g; CARB 33.3g; FIB 1.9g; CHOL 44mg; IRON 2.3mg; SOD 655mg; CALC 308mg

poached chicken breasts

Keep skinless, boneless chicken breasts on hand, and you can have cooked chicken ready for your recipe in about 20 minutes.

For a yield of about 3 cups chopped, cooked chicken, place 3 (6-ounce) skinless, boneless chicken breasts in a large skillet, and add about 1½ cups water. Bring to a boil. Cover, reduce heat, and simmer 14 minutes or until chicken is no longer pink. Drain. Slice, chop, or shred chicken as directed in the recipe. Chill chicken if required.

You can also cook your chicken in advance to have on hand. Plain cooked chicken with keep in the refrigerator 3 to 4 days or in the freezer 4 months.

CHICKEN TIKKA

POINTS value: 5

prep: 22 minutes • cook: 12 minutes
other: 8 hours and 30 minutes

Sometimes referred to as tandoori chicken, this Indian chicken is marinated in a mixture of yogurt and spices and traditionally cooked in either a clay oven (tandoor) or grilled. We grilled the flavorful chicken on skewers and found it paired well with jasmine or basmati rice. (A ½-cup portion of rice has a POINTS value of 2.)

¼ cup plain low-fat yogurt
2 teaspoons ground coriander
1 teaspoon ground turmeric
1 teaspoon chili powder
1 teaspoon ground ginger
½ teaspoon ground cumin
½ teaspoon salt
⅛ teaspoon ground red pepper
3 garlic cloves, minced
1½ pounds skinless, boneless chicken breast, cut into 1-inch pieces
Cooking spray
8 lime wedges
¼ cup mango chutney

1. Combine first 9 ingredients in a medium bowl. Add chicken; toss to coat well. Cover and marinate in refrigerator 8 hours.
2. Soak 12 (6-inch) wooden skewers in water 30 minutes.
3. Prepare grill.
4. Thread chicken pieces evenly onto skewers. Place skewers on grill rack coated with cooking spray; grill 12 to 13 minutes or until done, turning once. Serve with lime wedges and mango chutney. YIELD: 4 servings

(serving size: 3 skewers, 2 lime wedges, and 1 tablespoon chutney).

Per serving: CAL 246 (16% from fat); FAT 4.3g (sat 1.2g); PRO 35.3g; CARB 14.4g; FIB 0.4g; CHOL 95mg; IRON 1.8mg; SOD 659mg; CALC 45mg

CHICKEN WITH CREAMY HERB GRAVY

POINTS value: 7

prep: 12 minutes • cook: 35 minutes

Crispy whole-grain waffles catch the creamy gravy of this homestyle dish. You can also serve the chicken and gravy over rice or mashed potatoes.

3 teaspoons canola oil, divided
¾ cup chopped celery
¾ cup chopped carrot
½ cup chopped onion
2 garlic cloves, minced
3 tablespoons all-purpose flour
½ teaspoon freshly ground black pepper
½ teaspoon poultry seasoning
¼ teaspoon salt
1 pound skinless, boneless chicken breast, cut into 1-inch pieces
1 (14-ounce) can fat-free, less-sodium chicken broth
1 cup frozen petite green peas
¼ cup 2% reduced-fat milk
1 tablespoon all-purpose flour
¼ cup chopped fresh parsley
4 (1.3-ounce) low-fat multigrain waffles, toasted

1. Heat 1 teaspoon oil in a Dutch oven over medium-high heat. Add celery, carrot, and onion, and sauté

8 minutes or until tender. Add garlic; sauté 2 minutes. Remove from pan, and set aside.
2. Combine 3 tablespoons flour, pepper, poultry seasoning, and salt in a zip-top plastic bag. Add chicken; seal bag, and toss to coat. Heat remaining 2 teaspoons oil in pan; add chicken, and cook 7 minutes, browning on all sides. Add broth to pan, scraping pan to loosen browned bits. Stir in reserved vegetables and peas, and cook 3 minutes or until mixture is thoroughly heated.
3. Combine milk and 1 tablespoon flour, stirring with a whisk. Add to chicken mixture. Bring to a boil over medium-high heat; reduce heat, and simmer 8 minutes or until slightly thick, stirring constantly. Stir in parsley. Serve over waffles. YIELD: 4 servings (serving size: 1¼ cups chicken mixture and 1 waffle).

Per serving: CAL 372 (24% from fat); FAT 9.8g (sat 1.8g); PRO 35.4g; CARB 36.1g; FIB 5.8g; CHOL 91mg; IRON 3.8mg; SOD 780mg; CALC 184mg

chicken broth

Chicken broth, available in cans or cartons, is a staple ingredient in a well-stocked pantry. Use it as the foundation for soups, sauces, or gravies, and you'll have a dish ready in a fraction of the time it would take to make your own broth. Be sure to read the nutrition label, as the sodium and fat contents vary among brands.

CHICKEN SATAY

POINTS value: 6

prep: 13 minutes • cook: 6 minutes
other: 30 minutes

Satay is an Indonesian-style kebab featuring small cubes of meat or poultry; the kebabs are usually served with a spicy peanut sauce. Although satay is often served as an appetizer, this version is hearty enough for a main dish. Complement the chicken with a ½-cup portion of aromatic jasmine rice for a meal with a POINTS value of 8.

12   chicken breast tenders (about 1½ pounds)
3   tablespoons fresh lime juice
1   tablespoon low-sodium soy sauce
2   teaspoons fish sauce
2   garlic cloves, minced
½   teaspoon crushed red pepper
1   tablespoon canola oil
3   tablespoons low-sodium soy sauce
3   tablespoons fresh lime juice
2   tablespoons creamy peanut butter
1   tablespoon honey
1   teaspoon grated peeled fresh ginger
1   garlic clove, minced
Cooking spray

1. Soak 12 (6-inch) wooden skewers in water 30 minutes.
2. While skewers soak, combine first 7 ingredients in a large zip-top plastic bag; seal and gently shake bag to coat chicken. Marinate in refrigerator 15 minutes.
3. Combine soy sauce and next 5 ingredients, stirring with a whisk.

4. Prepare grill.
5. Remove chicken from bag; discard marinade. Thread each chicken tender onto a skewer. Place chicken on grill rack coated with cooking spray. Cover and grill 3 minutes on each side or until done. Serve chicken with peanut sauce. YIELD: 4 servings (serving size: 3 skewers and 1 tablespoon sauce).

Per serving: CAL 270 (29% from fat); FAT 8.7g (sat 1.7g); PRO 37.1g; CARB 9.5g; FIB 0.8g; CHOL 94mg; IRON 1.6mg; SOD 695mg; CALC 25mg

CHICKEN SCHNITZEL

POINTS value: 8

prep: 15 minutes • cook: 14 minutes

Schnitzel, the German word for cutlet, features thin pieces of meat dipped in egg, breaded, and fried. Our lightened version of wiener schnitzel is made with chicken instead of veal and is lightly pan-fried in a small amount of olive oil.

4   (6-ounce) skinless, boneless chicken breast halves
½   teaspoon salt
¼   teaspoon freshly ground black pepper
⅓   cup all-purpose flour
1   tablespoon Dijon mustard
1   large egg
1   cup panko (Japanese breadcrumbs)
2   tablespoons chopped fresh parsley
1   garlic clove, minced
2   tablespoons olive oil, divided
Lemon wedges

1. Cut each chicken breast half in half horizontally through thickest portion of each breast half. Place chicken between 2 sheets of heavy-duty plastic wrap; pound to ⅛-inch thickness using a meat mallet or small heavy skillet. Sprinkle chicken with salt and pepper.
2. Place flour in a shallow baking dish. Combine mustard and egg in another shallow baking dish. Combine panko, parsley, and garlic in a third shallow baking dish. Dredge pounded chicken in flour; dip in mustard mixture, and dredge in panko mixture, pressing firmly to coat.
3. Heat 1 tablespoon oil in a large nonstick skillet over medium-high heat. Add 4 chicken pieces. Cook 3 minutes on each side or until done. Remove chicken, and keep warm. Repeat with remaining 1 tablespoon oil and chicken. Serve with lemon wedges. YIELD: 4 servings (serving size: 2 chicken pieces).

Per serving: CAL 362 (27% from fat); FAT 10.7g (sat 1.9g); PRO 44.1g; CARB 19g; FIB 0.9g; CHOL 152mg; IRON 2.1mg; SOD 516mg; CALC 32mg

pounding chicken breasts

To easily pound chicken breasts, place them between 2 sheets of heavy-duty plastic wrap; pound to desired thickness—usually ¼ to ½ inch thick—using a meat mallet or small heavy skillet.

CHICKEN WITH ORANGE-CHIPOTLE SAUCE

POINTS value: 5

prep: 15 minutes • cook: 21 minutes

To save a little prep time, pound all 4 chicken breasts at one time rather than pounding each breast separately.

4   large navel oranges
4   (6-ounce) skinless, boneless
     chicken breast halves
¼   teaspoon salt
1¼ teaspoons ground cumin,
     divided
Cooking spray
2   tablespoons honey
¾   teaspoon chopped chipotle
     chile, canned in adobo sauce
2   tablespoons chopped fresh
     cilantro
⅛   teaspoon salt

1. Peel and section oranges over a bowl; squeeze membranes to extract juice. Set sections aside; reserve juice. Discard membranes.
2. Place chicken breast halves between 2 sheets of plastic wrap, and pound to ½-inch thickness using a meat mallet or a small heavy skillet. Sprinkle chicken with ¼ teaspoon salt and 1 teaspoon cumin. Heat a large nonstick skillet over medium heat. Coat pan with cooking spray. Add chicken, and cook 7 minutes on each side or until browned and done. Remove from pan, and keep warm.
3. Add orange sections, reserved juice, honey, chile, and remaining ¼ teaspoon cumin to pan; increase heat to medium-high, and cook, uncovered, 7 minutes or until

mixture is reduced to 1 cup. Stir in cilantro and ⅛ teaspoon salt. Serve with chicken. YIELD: 4 servings (serving size: 1 chicken breast half and ¼ cup sauce).

Per serving: CAL 291 (8% from fat); FAT 2.5g (sat 0.6g); PRO 40.7g; CARB 26.7g; FIB 3.4g; CHOL 99mg; IRON 1.7mg; SOD 345mg; CALC 85mg

☑ GRILLED TANDOORI CHICKEN WITH CUCUMBER-TOMATO RAITA

POINTS value: 6

prep: 18 minutes • cook: 12 minutes
other: 1 hour and 25 minutes

Popular in India and central Asia for centuries, tandoori chicken is traditionally a fairly hot dish, but this version is relatively mild and served with raita, a cooling salad. Make the raita ahead so it has time to chill. Use the extra raita as a topping for a pita sandwich.

1⅓ cups Cucumber-Tomato Raita
1   tablespoon fresh lemon juice
1   tablespoon canola oil
1   teaspoon ground coriander
1   teaspoon ground turmeric
2   teaspoons grated peeled fresh
     ginger
½   teaspoon salt
½   teaspoon ground cumin
½   teaspoon freshly ground black
     pepper
2   garlic cloves, minced
4   (6-ounce) skinless, boneless
     chicken breast halves
Cooking spray

1. Prepare Cucumber-Tomato Raita.

2. Combine lemon juice and next 8 ingredients in a small bowl, stirring well to form a paste. Cut 3 diagonal ¼-inch-deep slits across each chicken breast half. Rub spice paste in slits and on all sides of chicken. Cover and let stand 15 minutes.
3. Prepare grill.
4. Place chicken on grill rack coated with cooking spray; grill 6 minutes on each side or until done. Serve with Cucumber-Tomato Raita. YIELD: 4 servings (serving size: 1 chicken breast half and ⅓ cup raita).

Per serving: CAL 273 (28% from fat); FAT 8.6g (sat 1.9g); PRO 38.2g; CARB 8.9g; FIB 1.3g; CHOL 99mg; IRON 2.1mg; SOD 539mg; CALC 130mg

CUCUMBER-TOMATO RAITA
POINTS value: 0

1½ cups plain low-fat yogurt
1   cup chopped seeded tomato
     (about 1 medium)
½   cup grated seeded cucumber,
     squeezed dry (1 small)
2   tablespoons minced fresh mint
¾   teaspoon ground cumin
¼   teaspoon salt

1. Spoon yogurt into a wire mesh strainer lined with several layers of heavy-duty paper towels. Cover with additional paper towels; let stand 10 minutes. Scrape drained yogurt into a bowl using a rubber spatula. Stir in tomato and remaining ingredients. Cover and refrigerate 1 hour. Stir before serving. YIELD: 1⅔ cups (serving size: 1 tablespoon).

Per serving: CAL 10 (18% from fat); FAT 0.2g (sat 0.1g); PRO 0.7g; CARB 1.4g; FIB 0.2g; CHOL 1mg; IRON 0.1mg; SOD 31mg; CALC 20mg

☑ GREEK ISLE CHICKEN

POINTS value: 7

(pictured on page 137)

prep: 10 minutes • cook: 25 minutes

The secret to the rich flavor of this dish is to brown the chicken on both sides until it's golden before finishing it in the oven, creating a well-caramelized crust. Test the pan with a droplet of water to make sure it's hot enough before adding the chicken—the water should sizzle when it hits the pan.

1   lemon, halved
1   pint grape tomatoes
1   (6-ounce) jar Sicilian pitted green olives, drained
1   teaspoon chopped fresh oregano
1   garlic clove, minced
1   tablespoon plus 2 teaspoons olive oil, divided
4   (6-ounce) skinless, boneless chicken breast halves
4   teaspoons salt-free Greek seasoning (such as Cavender's)
Fresh oregano sprigs

1. Preheat oven to 400°.
2. Squeeze 1 lemon half, and reserve juice. Thinly slice other lemon half crosswise, and quarter each slice. Combine quartered lemon slices, tomatoes, and next 3 ingredients in a medium bowl; add 2 teaspoons olive oil, and toss to combine.
3. Sprinkle both sides of chicken evenly with Greek seasoning. Heat remaining 1 tablespoon oil in a large ovenproof skillet over medium-high heat. Add chicken, and cook 2 to 3 minutes on each side or until golden brown. Remove chicken from pan; keep warm.

4. Add reserved lemon juice to pan, scraping pan to loosen browned bits. Add tomato mixture to pan, stirring gently.
5. Place chicken on top of tomato mixture, and place pan in oven. Bake at 400° for 20 to 22 minutes or until chicken is done. Garnish with oregano sprigs, if desired. YIELD: 4 servings (serving size: 1 chicken breast half and ¾ cup tomato mixture).

Per serving: CAL 323 (41% from fat); FAT 14.7g (sat 1.4g); PRO 40.2g; CARB 8.5g; FIB 1.5g; CHOL 99mg; IRON 1.6mg; SOD 835mg; CALC 35mg

CHICKEN WITH MUSHROOMS AND GREEN ONIONS

POINTS value: 5

prep: 4 minutes • cook: 12 minutes

Tomato paste and sage contribute to the rich flavor of the mushroom sauce that cooks along with the chicken. For tips on tomato paste, see the information at right.

2   cups fat-free, less-sodium chicken broth
¼   cup no-salt-added tomato paste
1   teaspoon dried rubbed sage
¼   teaspoon salt
¼   teaspoon coarsely ground black pepper
4   (6-ounce) skinless, boneless chicken breast halves
4   teaspoons Italian-seasoned breadcrumbs
2   teaspoons olive oil
Cooking spray
1   (8-ounce) package presliced mushrooms
4   green onions, thinly sliced

1. Combine first 5 ingredients in a medium bowl, and stir with a whisk. Set aside.
2. Sprinkle chicken evenly with breadcrumbs. Heat oil in a large nonstick skillet coated with cooking spray over medium-high heat. Add chicken, and cook 2 to 3 minutes on each side or until lightly browned. Add mushrooms and reserved broth mixture; cover, reduce heat, and simmer 7 to 8 minutes or until chicken is done. Sprinkle with green onions. YIELD: 4 servings (serving size: 1 chicken breast half and about ⅓ cup mushroom sauce).

Per serving: CAL 260 (17% from fat); FAT 4.9g (sat 1g); PRO 44.1g; CARB 9.2g; FIB 2.2g; CHOL 99mg; IRON 2.6mg; SOD 610mg; CALC 52mg

tomato paste

Tomato paste is a richly flavored tomato concentrate made from ripened tomatoes that have been cooked for several hours, strained, and then reduced. The result is a thick red paste that's perfect for adding hearty flavor to pizza or pasta sauces. When a recipe calls for a small amount of paste, it's convenient to use paste from a tube. However, if you prefer canned paste but don't know what to do with leftover paste, here's a suggestion: Spoon any remaining paste by the tablespoon onto a baking sheet, and freeze. Store the frozen paste in a heavy-duty plastic freezer bag. It'll already be measured and ready for your next recipe.

CHICKEN WITH BÉARNAISE SAUCE

POINTS value: 5

prep: 2 minutes • cook: 16 minutes

The onion and herb–flavored topping is similar to a traditional herb butter. It melts over the hot chicken breast, creating a savory sauce.

½ cup dry white wine
2 tablespoons finely chopped onion
¾ teaspoon dried tarragon
4 (6-ounce) skinless, boneless chicken breast halves
Cooking spray
¼ teaspoon freshly ground black pepper
¼ teaspoon salt, divided
3 tablespoons yogurt-based spread (such as Brummel & Brown)

1. Combine first 3 ingredients in a large nonstick skillet; bring to a boil over medium-high heat. Boil 3 minutes or until liquid is absorbed. Remove from pan, and cool.
2. Coat chicken with cooking spray. Sprinkle both sides of chicken with pepper and ⅛ teaspoon salt. Heat pan over medium-high heat; add chicken, and cook 6 minutes on each side or until done.
3. Combine onion mixture, yogurt-based spread, and remaining ⅛ teaspoon salt; spoon over chicken. Let stand 1 minute before serving. YIELD: 4 servings (serving size: 1 chicken breast half and 1 tablespoon sauce).

Per serving: CAL 226 (23% from fat); FAT 5.9g (sat 1.3g); PRO 39.5g; CARB 1.2g; FIB 0.1g; CHOL 99mg; IRON 1.5mg; SOD 328mg; CALC 26mg

dutch oven facts

A Dutch oven is neither Dutch nor an oven; rather, it's a deep pot with a tight-fitting lid that can go from cooktop to oven. It usually holds 3 to 6 quarts. Some versions come with a long handle, like a skillet. Dutch ovens are frequently used for braising and for making soups, stews, chiles, pot roasts, and pasta.

☑ CHICKEN ESCABECHE

POINTS value: 6

prep: 15 minutes • cook: 41 minutes

*Escabeche is a traditional Spanish poached fish dish. It's usually marinated for at least 24 hours (which almost pickles the vegetables) and served cold. Our chicken version does not marinate and is served warm. We suggest serving it with a ½-cup portion of saffron rice for an added **POINTS** value of 2.*

4 teaspoons olive oil, divided
4 (8-ounce) bone-in chicken breast halves, skinned
½ teaspoon freshly ground black pepper, divided
¼ teaspoon salt
2 cups thinly sliced onion
1½ cups thinly sliced red bell pepper
1 cup sliced carrot
6 garlic cloves, sliced
1½ cups fat-free, less-sodium chicken broth
¼ cup cider vinegar
1 teaspoon dried thyme
3 whole cloves
1 (3-inch) cinnamon stick
¼ cup drained sliced pickled jalapeño pepper

1. Heat 2 teaspoons oil in a large Dutch oven over medium heat. Sprinkle chicken evenly with ¼ teaspoon black pepper and salt. Add chicken to pan; cook 5 minutes on each side or until browned. Remove from pan; set aside.
2. Heat remaining 2 teaspoons oil in pan over medium heat. Add onion, bell pepper, carrot, garlic, and remaining ¼ teaspoon black pepper. Cook over medium heat 5 minutes or until vegetables are crisp-tender, stirring frequently.
3. Add broth and next 4 ingredients to pan; bring to a boil. Return chicken to pan. Cover, reduce heat to low, and simmer 20 minutes or until chicken is done and vegetables are tender.
4. Remove and discard cinnamon stick and cloves. Stir in jalapeño pepper. YIELD: 4 servings (serving size: 1 chicken breast half and about ¾ cup vegetable mixture).

Per serving: CAL 318 (21% from fat); FAT 7.3g (sat 1.3g); PRO 45g; CARB 16.9g; FIB 3.4g; CHOL 105mg; IRON 2.3mg; SOD 670mg; CALC 64mg

EASY CHICKEN CACCIATORE

POINTS value: 8

prep: 12 minutes • cook: 55 minutes

To make this classic dish quicker, we've used skinless bone-in breast halves instead of calling for cutting up a whole chicken. Cacciatore is often served over cooked pasta; a ½-cup portion of regular pasta has a **POINTS** *value of 2, while whole wheat pasta has a* **POINTS** *value of 1.*

2   tablespoons olive oil
4   (8-ounce) bone-in chicken
    breast halves, skinned
1   (8-ounce) package presliced
    mushrooms
3   cups sliced green bell pepper
2   tablespoons chopped shallots
1   teaspoon dried oregano
¼   teaspoon crushed red pepper
2   garlic cloves, minced
1   (26-ounce) jar tomato-basil
    pasta sauce (such as Classico)
2   tablespoons chopped fresh basil

1. Heat oil in a large nonstick skillet over medium-high heat. Add chicken; cook 3 to 4 minutes on each side or until browned. Remove from pan, and set aside.
2. Add mushrooms and next 5 ingredients to pan; cook 8 minutes or until mushrooms are tender. Add pasta sauce; bring to a boil. Return chicken to pan; cover, reduce heat, and simmer 35 minutes or until chicken is done. Stir in basil. YIELD: 4 servings (serving size: 1 chicken breast half and 1 cup sauce).

Per serving: CAL 377 (26% from fat); FAT 11g (sat 1.7g); PRO 48.2g; CARB 22.3g; FIB 5.9g; CHOL 105mg; IRON 3.3mg; SOD 702mg; CALC 163mg

HONEY MUSTARD–GLAZED CHICKEN

POINTS value: 8

prep: 9 minutes • cook: 36 minutes
other: 30 minutes

¼   cup low-sodium soy sauce
2   tablespoons rice vinegar
2   tablespoons honey
1   tablespoon Dijon mustard
1   tablespoon dark sesame oil
2   teaspoons grated peeled fresh
    ginger
2   garlic cloves, minced
2   bone-in chicken breast halves
    (about 1½ pounds)
2   chicken leg quarters (about
    1½ pounds)
Cooking spray

1. Combine first 7 ingredients in a small bowl, stirring with a whisk. Pour into a large zip-top plastic bag. Add chicken; seal bag, and marinate in refrigerator at least 30 minutes, turning occasionally.
2. Preheat oven to 425°.
3. Remove chicken from bag; reserving marinade. Pour marinade into a 1-cup glass measure, and microwave at HIGH 1 minute or until boiling. Arrange chicken in a foil-lined broiler pan coated with cooking spray. Bake at 425° for 35 minutes or until done, basting twice with marinade. Remove skin before serving. YIELD: 4 servings (serving size: 1 chicken breast half or 1 leg quarter).

Per serving: CAL 358 (34% from fat); FAT 13.7g (sat 3.3g); PRO 45.9g; CARB 10.8g; FIB 0.2g; CHOL 140mg; IRON 2.2mg; SOD 710mg; CALC 27mg

LEMON-SAGE ROASTED CHICKEN WITH SAGE PAN SAUCE

POINTS value: 5

prep: 17 minutes
cook: 1 hour and 5 minutes
other: 10 minutes

Lemon and fresh sage are perfect partners for roasted chicken. Roasting a chicken with seasonings tucked between the skin and the meat infuses the chicken with flavor.

2   small lemons
2   garlic cloves, minced
1   (3-pound) whole chicken
6   sage sprigs, divided
Cooking spray
¾   teaspoon salt, divided
½   teaspoon black pepper, divided
1¼ cups fat-free, less-sodium
    chicken broth
2   tablespoons all-purpose flour
1   teaspoon minced sage

1. Preheat oven to 400°.
2. Grate rind from lemons to equal 1 tablespoon. Cut 1 lemon in half; reserve other lemon for another use. Combine lemon rind and garlic in a small bowl, stirring well.
3. Remove and discard giblets and neck from chicken. Trim excess fat. Starting at neck cavity, loosen skin from breast by inserting fingers, gently pushing between skin and meat. Rub garlic mixture under loosened skin. Place 1 sage sprig under skin on each side of breast. Gently press skin to secure. Lift wing tips up and over back; tuck under chicken. Place lemon halves and remaining 4 sage sprigs in cavity. Tie legs together

with kitchen string. Place chicken on rack of a broiler pan coated with cooking spray. Sprinkle with ½ teaspoon salt and ¼ teaspoon pepper. Insert a thermometer into meaty part of thigh, making sure not to touch bone.

4. Bake at 400° for 1 hour or until thermometer registers at least 165° or until desired degree of doneness. Transfer to a platter; cover with foil.

5. Place a zip-top plastic bag inside a 2-cup glass measure. Pour pan drippings into bag, reserving browned bits in bottom of pan. Let drippings stand 10 minutes (fat will rise to top). Seal bag, and carefully snip off 1 bottom corner. Drain pan drippings from bag into measuring cup, stopping before fat layer reaches opening. Reserve 1 tablespoon fat; discard remaining fat.

6. Add enough broth to drippings to equal 1¼ cups; add reserved 1 tablespoon fat and flour, stirring with a whisk until smooth. Pour broth mixture into broiler pan. Cook over medium heat 5 minutes or until thick, scraping pan to loosen browned bits. Remove from heat; stir in remaining ¼ teaspoon salt, remaining ¼ teaspoon pepper, and minced sage.

7. Remove and discard lemon and sage from cavity of chicken. Carefully remove and discard skin from chicken and sage sprigs from breast, reserving garlic mixture. Spread garlic mixture over chicken. Cut chicken into quarters. Serve chicken with sauce. YIELD: 4 servings (serving size: 1 chicken quarter and ¼ cup sauce).

Per serving: CAL 249 (29% from fat); FAT 8g (sat 2.1g); PRO 36.9g; CARB 5.6g; FIB 0.8g; CHOL 116mg; IRON 2.1mg; SOD 752mg; CALC 28mg

COQ AU VIN

POINTS value: 8

prep: 27 minutes • cook: 50 minutes

This is a classic French dish of chicken, mushrooms, onions, and herbs braised in red wine. The rich, savory sauce created during cooking is the most flavorful part of the dish. We suggest serving it with French bread so you can soak up the sauce.

3   thick-cut bacon slices, cut into 1-inch pieces
½   (16-ounce) package frozen white pearl onions, thawed and drained
1   (3-pound) whole chicken
¼   teaspoon salt
½   teaspoon freshly ground black pepper, divided
1   cup chopped onion (about 1 large)
1   (8-ounce) package mushrooms, quartered
3   garlic cloves, minced
2   cups fat-free, less-sodium chicken broth
1½   cups dry red wine (such as pinot noir)
1   tablespoon tomato paste
1   teaspoon dried rosemary
2   tablespoons cornstarch
¼   cup water
1   tablespoon chopped fresh parsley

1. Heat a Dutch oven over medium heat. Add bacon; cook 4 minutes or until crisp. Remove bacon from pan, reserving 1 tablespoon drippings in pan; set bacon aside.

2. Place pearl onions in a microwave-safe dish. Cover dish with lid, and microwave at HIGH 3 minutes or until tender.

3. Remove and discard giblets and neck from chicken. Trim excess fat. Remove skin, and cut chicken into quarters. Sprinkle chicken with ¼ teaspoon salt and ¼ teaspoon pepper.

4. Add chicken and pearl onions to reserved drippings in pan, and cook 4 minutes on each side or until chicken is browned. Remove chicken from pan; keep warm.

5. Add chopped onion to pan, and sauté 3 minutes or until translucent. Add mushrooms; sauté 3 minutes or until tender. Stir in garlic. Add broth, next 3 ingredients, and remaining ¼ teaspoon pepper. Return chicken to pan, and bring to a boil. Cover, reduce heat, and simmer 25 minutes or until chicken is done. Remove chicken from pan, and keep warm.

6. Combine cornstarch and water, stirring with a whisk until smooth. Add to broth mixture, stirring with a whisk. Bring to a boil; reduce heat, and simmer 2 minutes or until slightly thick, stirring constantly. Stir in reserved bacon and parsley. YIELD: 4 servings (serving size: 1 chicken quarter and 1½ cups broth mixture).

Per serving: CAL 379 (24% from fat); FAT 10.2g (sat 3.1g); PRO 42.5g; CARB 29.1g; FIB 1.6g; CHOL 121mg; IRON 3.3mg; SOD 742mg; CALC 73mg

CHICKEN THIGHS WITH TOMATOES AND OLIVES

POINTS value: 7

(pictured on page 140)

prep: 7 minutes • cook: 28 minutes

Serve this one-skillet Mediterranean chicken dish with herbed green beans and a glass of red wine.

8 (3-ounce) skinless, boneless chicken thighs
⅛ teaspoon salt
¼ teaspoon freshly ground black pepper
1½ teaspoons olive oil
3 garlic cloves, minced
¾ cup chopped onion
1 (14.5-ounce) can diced tomatoes with basil, garlic, and oregano, undrained
⅓ cup merlot or other dry red wine
⅓ cup pitted kalamata olives, chopped
¼ cup chopped fresh basil
¼ teaspoon freshly ground black pepper

1. Sprinkle chicken evenly with ⅛ teaspoon salt and ¼ teaspoon pepper. Heat oil in large nonstick skillet over medium-high heat. Add chicken; cook 3 to 4 minutes on each side or until browned. Remove chicken from pan; keep warm.
2. Add garlic and onion to pan, and sauté 2 minutes. Stir in tomatoes and wine; bring to a simmer. Return chicken to pan, and bring to a boil. Cover, reduce heat, and simmer 12 minutes or until chicken is done. Remove chicken from pan, and keep warm. Continue to simmer tomato mixture, uncovered, 5 minutes. Stir in olives, basil, and ¼ teaspoon pepper. YIELD: 4 servings (serving size: 2 chicken thighs and ½ cup sauce).

Per serving: CAL 306 (34% from fat); FAT 11.4g (sat 2.3g); PRO 35g; CARB 14.7g; FIB 1.6g; CHOL 141mg; IRON 2.1mg; SOD 734mg; CALC 38mg

CURRIED CHICKEN THIGHS

POINTS value: 8

prep: 20 minutes • cook: 12 minutes
other: 8 hours

Aromatic and distinctively flavorful, curry powder and fresh ginger add a warm, spicy note to the sweet yogurt mixture that's used to marinate the chicken. Basmati rice is an ideal accompaniment for the grilled chicken and onion.

½ cup plain low-fat yogurt
2 tablespoons honey
2 teaspoons curry powder
1 garlic clove, minced
1 teaspoon grated peeled fresh ginger
8 (3-ounce) skinless, boneless chicken thighs
¾ teaspoon salt
1 red onion, cut into ¼-inch-thick slices
Cooking spray
4 teaspoons fresh lemon juice
2 teaspoons canola oil
2 tablespoons minced fresh cilantro

1. Combine first 5 ingredients in a medium bowl, stirring with a whisk. Pour into a large zip-top plastic bag; add chicken. Seal bag, and marinate in refrigerator 8 hours, turning bag occasionally.
2. Prepare grill.
3. Remove chicken from bag, discarding marinade. Sprinkle chicken with salt, and coat chicken and onion with cooking spray. Place on grill rack coated with cooking spray; cook 6 minutes on each side or until chicken is done. Remove chicken and onion from grill; cut onion slices in half, and separate into strips.
4. Combine lemon juice, oil, and cilantro in a medium bowl. Add onion strips; toss well. Spoon onion mixture onto a serving platter. Top with chicken. YIELD: 4 servings (serving size: 2 chicken thighs and ⅓ cup onion mixture).

Per serving: CAL 319 (44% from fat); FAT 15.5g (sat 3.9g); PRO 31.8g; CARB 12g; FIB 0.7g; CHOL 113mg; IRON 1.9mg; SOD 559mg; CALC 54mg

fresh ginger

Look for fresh ginger in the produce section of your supermarket. Choose the freshest, youngest-looking ginger you can find. Old ginger is fibrous, tough, and flavorless. Store fresh ginger tightly wrapped in plastic wrap in your refrigerator's crisper up to 3 weeks. Use a vegetable peeler or a paring knife to remove the tough skin and reveal the yellowish flesh. To grate ginger, cut a piece big enough to hold comfortably, and use a fine grater.

SAGE-APPLE TURKEY BREAKFAST SAUSAGE

POINTS value: 2

prep: 17 minutes • cook: 23 minutes

One of these turkey sausage patties contains 66 percent less fat than a 1-ounce cooked pork sausage patty. After cooking the patties, you can freeze them in an airtight container and use as needed. Remove a frozen patty from the freezer, wrap it in a paper towel, and microwave at HIGH 30 seconds.

1	teaspoon butter
⅓	cup minced onion
1	tablespoon chopped fresh sage
1½	teaspoons chopped fresh rosemary
1½	teaspoons chopped fresh thyme
1	Granny Smith apple, peeled and diced
1	garlic clove, minced
1¼	pounds ground turkey
1	teaspoon salt
¼	teaspoon black pepper

1. Melt butter in a large nonstick skillet over medium-high heat. Add onion and next 5 ingredients; sauté 6 minutes or until onion is tender. Remove from heat.
2. Combine onion mixture, turkey, salt, and pepper in a medium bowl. Divide mixture into 12 equal portions; shape each portion into a ½-inch-thick patty.
3. Wipe out pan with paper towel. Heat pan over medium heat. Add half of patties; cook 4 minutes on each side or until lightly browned and done. Remove from pan, and keep warm. Repeat procedure with remaining patties. **YIELD:** 12 servings (serving size: 1 patty).

Per serving: CAL 73 (41% from fat); FAT 3.3g (sat 1g); PRO 9.3g; CARB 2g; FIB 0.2g; CHOL 28mg; IRON 0.8mg; SOD 232mg; CALC 4mg

SAUSAGE AND VEGETABLE QUICHE

POINTS value: 8

prep: 13 minutes • cook: 47 minutes
other: 10 minutes

Quiche is not just for breakfast or brunch—this hearty sausage-vegetable pie is a great choice for a weeknight dinner. We've lightened the quiche by using turkey sausage, part-skim mozzarella cheese, and 2% reduced-fat milk instead of cream. We also replaced a whole egg with egg whites.

½	(15-ounce) package refrigerated pie dough
½	pound turkey breakfast sausage
½	cup (1-inch) cut asparagus (5 small spears)
½	cup chopped onion
½	cup diced red bell pepper
½	cup frozen whole-kernel corn
1	garlic clove, minced
¾	cup shredded part-skim mozzarella cheese
1	cup 2% reduced-fat milk
1	large egg
2	large egg whites
⅛	teaspoon salt
⅛	teaspoon black pepper

1. Preheat oven to 400°.
2. Fit dough into a 9-inch pie plate; flute edges. Set aside.

3. Cook sausage in a small skillet over medium heat 6 minutes or until browned, stirring to crumble. Remove sausage from pan; keep warm. Add asparagus and next 4 ingredients to pan, and sauté over medium-high heat 6 to 7 minutes or until vegetables are tender. Spoon vegetable mixture into crust. Sprinkle with sausage and cheese.
4. Combine milk and next 4 ingredients, stirring well with a whisk. Pour egg mixture over sausage and cheese. Place on bottom rack in oven; bake at 400° for 35 minutes or until a knife inserted in center comes out clean. Let stand 10 minutes before cutting into wedges. **YIELD:** 6 servings (serving size: 1 wedge).

Per serving: CAL 324 (47% from fat); FAT 17g (sat 7.9g); PRO 16.1g; CARB 26.4g; FIB 1.2g; CHOL 82mg; IRON 1.1mg; SOD 539mg; CALC 177mg

RUSTIC SKILLET KIELBASA AND VEGETABLES OVER POLENTA

POINTS value: 4

prep: 18 minutes • cook: 13 minutes

Cheesy baked polenta rounds form a hearty base for the colorful mixture of squash, red bell pepper, and sausage slices. Look for tubes of polenta in the produce section.

1 (16-ounce) tube of polenta, cut into 8 pieces
Cooking spray
1 tablespoon grated fresh Parmesan cheese
1 (14-ounce) package turkey kielbasa, cut into thin slices
2 yellow squash, sliced lengthwise
1 red bell pepper, cut into thin strips
¼ cup water
1 tablespoon sugar
1 tablespoon low-sodium Worcestershire sauce
2 tablespoons chopped fresh parsley (optional)

1. Preheat oven to 450°.
2. Place polenta slices on a baking sheet coated with cooking spray. Sprinkle evenly with Parmesan cheese. Bake at 450° for 10 minutes or until lightly browned.
3. While polenta bakes, heat a large nonstick skillet over medium-high heat. Coat pan with cooking spray. Add sausage, and cook 5 minutes or until browned, stirring occasionally. Remove sausage from pan; set aside.
4. Add vegetables to pan, and sauté 3 to 4 minutes or until crisp-tender. Add sausage, ¼ cup water, and sugar;

cook 4 minutes or until liquid is almost absorbed. Add Worcestershire sauce, and cook, stirring constantly, 30 seconds or until sausage and vegetables are glazed. Serve sausage mixture over polenta rounds. Sprinkle with parsley, if desired. YIELD: 4 servings (serving size: 2 polenta rounds and 1¼ cups sausage mixture).

Per serving: CAL 225 (24% from fat); FAT 5.9g (sat 2.9g); PRO 18.1g; CARB 26.3g; FIB 3.7g; CHOL 26mg; IRON 2.3mg; SOD 724mg; CALC 175mg

SAUSAGES WITH BEER-BRAISED ONIONS AND PEPPERS

POINTS value: 4

prep: 12 minutes • cook: 29 minutes

A dark beer gives this dish a more pronounced flavor, but it works with any type of beer. For a sandwich variation, serve the sausage and vegetables on whole wheat hot dog buns.

1 (14-ounce) package turkey kielbasa, cut into 4 pieces
2 teaspoons olive oil
1 red bell pepper, cut into strips
1 yellow bell pepper, cut into strips
2 garlic cloves, minced
1 large onion, vertically sliced
½ cup dark beer (such as Guinness)

1. Heat a large nonstick skillet over medium-high heat. Add kielbasa, and cook 2 minutes on each side or until browned. Remove from pan, and keep warm.

2. Add oil to pan. Add bell peppers, garlic, and onion; sauté 7 minutes or until lightly browned. Place sausage on top of vegetable mixture, and add beer. Bring to a boil; cover, reduce heat, and simmer 15 minutes or until vegetables are tender. Increase heat to medium-high, and cook, uncovered, 3 minutes or until liquid evaporates. YIELD: 4 servings (serving size: 1 sausage piece and ⅔ cup vegetable mixture).

Per serving: CAL 161 (44% from fat); FAT 7.9g (sat 3g); PRO 15.3g; CARB 10.7g; FIB 1.7g; CHOL 25mg; IRON 1.4mg; SOD 501mg; CALC 158mg

slicing onion

When slicing onions, start at the end opposite the root. Onions contain sulfuric compounds that are released when they are peeled or sliced. Those compounds irritate the eyes and produce tears. Since more of these compounds are found in the root, it's best to cut that last. Slice the top off the onion, leaving the root end intact. Remove the papery skin; slice the onion in half vertically. Continue cutting the onion vertically into thin slices.

salads ▶▶

CRANBERRY SALAD

POINTS value: 3

prep: 5 minutes • cook: 2 minutes
other: 4 hours

This fruited salad is great paired with turkey or pork.

2   (0.3-ounce) packages sugar-free black cherry–flavored gelatin
1   cup boiling water
1   cup canned whole-berry cranberry sauce
1   cup ice water
1   (20-ounce) can crushed pineapple in juice, drained
½   cup chopped pecans

1. Combine gelatin and boiling water in an 11 x 7–inch baking dish; stir until gelatin is dissolved. Add cranberry sauce and ice water, stirring well. Add pineapple and pecans; stir. Cover and chill 4 hours or until set. YIELD: 8 servings (serving size: ¾ cup).

Per serving: CAL 129 (38% from fat); FAT 5.4g (sat 0.5g); PRO 1.4g; CARB 21.1g; FIB 2g; CHOL 0mg; IRON 0.5mg; SOD 26mg; CALC 13mg

CARROT SALAD WITH GRAPES

POINTS value: 2

prep: 8 minutes • other: 5 minutes

To get a moist, tender salad, we recommend shredding the carrots yourself.

¼   cup light mayonnaise
2   tablespoons orange juice
1   teaspoon sugar
6   medium carrots, shredded
⅔   cup seedless red grape halves

1. Combine first 3 ingredients in a large bowl, stirring with a whisk until blended. Add carrot and grapes, tossing well to coat. Let stand 5 minutes. YIELD: 4 servings (serving size: ¾ cup).

Per serving: CAL 113 (42% from fat); FAT 5.3g (sat 1.1g); PRO 1.1g; CARB 16.4g; FIB 2.8g; CHOL 5mg; IRON 0.4mg; SOD 184mg; CALC 34mg

GINGER-APPLE SALAD

POINTS value: 2
(pictured on page 134)

prep: 15 minutes • cook: 2 minutes
other: 10 minutes

Crystallized ginger adds a peppery-sweet note to this apple salad, which garnered rave reviews in our Test Kitchens.

2½   cups chopped Granny Smith apple (1 large)
2   cups chopped Gala apple (1 large)
½   cup chopped pecans, toasted
¼   cup dried sweet cherries
3   tablespoons chopped crystallized ginger
2   tablespoons thawed orange juice concentrate
1   tablespoon lemon juice
1   tablespoon honey

1. Combine all ingredients in a large bowl; toss well. Let stand 10 minutes before serving. YIELD: 10 servings (serving size: ½ cup).

Per serving: CAL 93 (42% from fat); FAT 4.3g (sat 0.4g); PRO 1g; CARB 13.9g; FIB 1.7g; CHOL 0mg; IRON 0.4mg; SOD 2mg; CALC 13mg

BROCCOLI SLAW SALAD

POINTS value: 3
(pictured on page 133)

prep: 9 minutes • cook: 7 minutes

What's not to like in a slaw that is the perfect combination of sweet and salty, crisp and creamy? Instead of cabbage, we've used broccoli slaw, which is shredded broccoli stalks.

4   center-cut bacon slices
⅓   cup light mayonnaise
2   tablespoons plain fat-free yogurt
2   teaspoons cider vinegar
1   teaspoon sugar
¼   teaspoon salt
½   teaspoon freshly ground black pepper
1   (12-ounce) package broccoli slaw
½   cup finely chopped red onion
½   cup raisins
2   tablespoons chopped pecans, toasted

1. Cook bacon in a large nonstick skillet over medium heat until crisp. Remove bacon from pan; crumble and set aside.
2. Combine mayonnaise and next 5 ingredients in a bowl. Add broccoli slaw, onion, and raisins; toss to coat. Cover and chill until ready to serve. Sprinkle with bacon and pecans before serving. YIELD: 6 servings (serving size: ¾ cup).

Per serving: CAL 148 (49% from fat); FAT 8.1g (sat 1.6g); PRO 3.9g; CARB 16.8g; FIB 2.9g; CHOL 9mg; IRON 1.6mg; SOD 323mg; CALC 45mg

FENNEL, FETA, AND KALAMATA COLESLAW

POINTS value: 1

prep: 15 minutes

This slaw is made with thinly sliced fennel bulb instead of the traditional cabbage, and, surprisingly, it has no oil or mayonnaise. The amazing flavor comes from feta cheese, olives, and white balsamic vinegar.

1   (1-pound) fennel bulb with stalks
½   cup reduced-fat feta cheese with basil and sun-dried tomatoes
¼   cup thinly sliced red onion
6   pitted kalamata olives, halved
2   tablespoons chopped fresh parsley
1   tablespoon white balsamic vinegar
¼   teaspoon freshly ground black pepper
⅛   teaspoon salt

1. Trim tough outer leaves from fennel; chop feathery fronds to measure 1 tablespoon. Remove and discard stalks. Cut bulb lengthwise into thin slices; cut slices into thin strips.
2. Place fennel bulb strips and 1 tablespoon chopped fronds in a medium bowl; add feta cheese and remaining ingredients. Toss well.
YIELD: 4 servings (serving size: 1 cup).

Per serving: CAL 65 (31% from fat); FAT 2.2g (sat 0.4g); PRO 2.3g; CARB 10.3g; FIB 3.8g; CHOL 1mg; IRON 1mg; SOD 272mg; CALC 72mg

fennel

Fresh fennel has a bulbous base, stalks like celery, and feathery leaves (or fronds) that resemble fresh dill. Like celery, the entire plant is edible. The crisp and slightly sweet bulb is especially delicious when served raw in salads. You can use the fronds as a garnish or chop them and use as you would herbs such as dill or parsley.

Look for small, heavy, white bulbs that are firm and free of cracks, brown spots, or moist areas. The stalks should be crisp, with feathery, bright green fronds. Store fennel bulbs in a perforated plastic bag in the refrigerator up to 5 days.

BLUE CHEESE SLAW

POINTS value: 1

prep: 7 minutes

Blue cheese fans will delight in this revision of basic coleslaw.

3   cups packaged cabbage-and-carrot coleslaw
2   tablespoons crumbled blue cheese
½   cup finely chopped celery
¼   cup diced green bell pepper
⅓   cup reduced-fat blue cheese dressing (such as Naturally Fresh)
¼   teaspoon freshly ground black pepper

1. Combine first 4 ingredients in a large bowl. Add dressing and black pepper, tossing to coat. YIELD: 7 servings (serving size ½ cup).

Per serving: CAL 47 (59% from fat); FAT 3.1g (sat 0.8g); PRO 1.4g; CARB 3.9g; FIB 1g; CHOL 4mg; IRON 0.2mg; SOD 161mg; CALC 31mg

TENDER BIBB, ORANGE, AND BACON SALAD

POINTS value: 3

prep: 20 minutes • cook: 9 minutes

3   tablespoons olive oil
1   tablespoon grated fresh orange rind
2   tablespoons fresh orange juice
1   tablespoon rice vinegar
2   teaspoons chopped fresh flat-leaf parsley
¼   teaspoon salt
¼   teaspoon freshly ground black pepper
8   cups torn Bibb lettuce (2 heads)
1   cup navel orange sections
⅓   cup thinly sliced red onion
¼   cup slivered almonds, toasted
2   cooked bacon slices, crumbled

1. Combine olive oil and next 6 ingredients, stirring well with a whisk.
2. Combine lettuce, orange sections, and onion in a large bowl. Add dressing; toss gently. Top with almonds and bacon. Serve immediately. YIELD: 6 servings (serving size: 1 cup).

Per serving: CAL 136 (69% from fat); FAT 10.4g (sat 1.5g); PRO 3.1g; CARB 10.1g; FIB 2.7g; CHOL 2mg; IRON 1mg; SOD 149mg; CALC 57mg

MESCLUN WITH RED GRAPEFRUIT AND FETA

POINTS value: 1

prep: 11 minutes

Instead of sectioning fresh grapefruit, you can substitute bottled citrus sections.

6   cups mesclun salad greens
1   cup red grapefruit sections
     (about 2 large)
3   tablespoons fresh grapefruit
     juice
2   teaspoons extravirgin olive oil
1   teaspoon honey
¼   teaspoon salt
⅛   teaspoon coarsely ground black
     pepper
¼   cup (1 ounce) crumbled feta
     cheese

1. Combine mesclun and grapefruit sections in a large bowl. Combine grapefruit juice and next 4 ingredients in a small bowl, stirring with a whisk. Pour over salad; toss gently to coat. Divide evenly among plates. Sprinkle each serving with cheese. YIELD: 4 servings (serving size: 1½ cups salad and 1 tablespoon cheese).

Per serving: CAL 81 (46% from fat); FAT 4.1g (sat 1.4g); PRO 2.8g; CARB 9.9g; FIB 2.5g; CHOL 6mg; IRON 1.2mg; SOD 246mg; CALC 89mg

GREEN SALAD WITH CREAMY SALSA DRESSING

POINTS value: 2

prep: 7 minutes

½   cup light ranch dressing
⅓   cup salsa
1   (10-ounce) package torn
     romaine lettuce
20   thin slices cucumber
20   grape tomatoes

1. Combine dressing and salsa; stir well with a whisk. Place lettuce on plates. Top with cucumber and tomatoes. Drizzle with dressing mixture. YIELD: 5 servings (serving size: 1⅔ cups salad and 2 tablespoons dressing).

Per serving: CAL 97 (56% from fat); FAT 6g (sat 0.5g); PRO 1.9g; CARB 9.2g; FIB 2.7g; CHOL 8mg; IRON 0.9mg; SOD 353mg; CALC 38mg

FIELD SALAD WITH TOMATO, FETA, AND OLIVES

POINTS value: 1

prep: 8 minutes

To dice the olives, quarter them lengthwise; then cut crosswise into pieces.

3   tablespoons fat-free Italian
     dressing
¼   teaspoon kosher salt
⅛   teaspoon coarsely ground black
     pepper
2   large pimiento-stuffed olives,
     diced
6   cups mesclun salad greens
8   cherry tomatoes, halved
¼   cup (1 ounce) crumbled feta
     cheese

1. Combine first 4 ingredients in a large bowl. Add mesclun, tomatoes, and cheese; toss gently until greens are thoroughly coated. YIELD: 4 servings (serving size: 1¾ cups).

Per serving: CAL 48 (39% from fat); FAT 2.1g (sat 1.2g); PRO 2.8g; CARB 5.5g; FIB 2.3g; CHOL 7mg; IRON 1.3mg; SOD 422mg; CALC 90mg

TANGY RADICCHIO, ENDIVE, AND SPINACH SALAD

POINTS value: 3

prep: 15 minutes • other: 10 minutes

Combine ruby radicchio, emerald spinach, and creamy white endive for a vibrant salad reminiscent of the Italian flag. The hearts of palm and Gorgonzola definitely make this a company-worthy dish.

¼   cup minced shallots (about 1)
2   tablespoons sherry vinegar
2   tablespoons fresh orange
     juice
⅛   teaspoon kosher salt
⅛   teaspoon freshly ground black
     pepper
3   tablespoons extravirgin
     olive oil
1   tablespoon honey
1   teaspoon Dijon mustard
4   cups loosely packed baby
     spinach
1   small head radicchio, thinly
     sliced
1   Belgian endive, thinly sliced
     crosswise
1   (14-ounce) can hearts of palm,
     drained and sliced
¼   cup (1 ounce) crumbled
     Gorgonzola cheese

1. Combine first 5 ingredients in a large bowl; let stand 10 minutes.
2. Add oil, honey, and Dijon mustard to shallot mixture, stirring with a whisk until well blended. Add spinach and next 3 ingredients, tossing gently to coat. Sprinkle with cheese. YIELD: 6 servings (serving size: 1 cup).

Per serving: CAL 123 (64% from fat); FAT 8.7g (sat 2.1g); PRO 3.2g; CARB 10.5g; FIB 2.8g; CHOL 4mg; IRON 2.1mg; SOD 319mg; CALC 73mg

ZUCCHINI, PARMESAN, AND MÂCHE SALAD

POINTS value: 3
(pictured on page 141)

prep: 7 minutes • other: 15 minutes

This recipe proves that minimalism in the kitchen pays off. Lemon and salty Parmesan cheese pair perfectly with raw zucchini. If mâche is unavailable, substitute baby spinach or arugula.

2   medium zucchini, thinly sliced
¼   cup shaved Parmigiano-Reggiano cheese
2   tablespoons olive oil
½   teaspoon grated fresh lemon rind
1   tablespoon fresh lemon juice (about 1 small lemon)
½   teaspoon kosher salt
¼   teaspoon freshly ground black pepper
1   (3½-ounce) container mâche

1. Combine first 7 ingredients in a large bowl, and toss. Let stand at room temperature 15 minutes.
2. Add mâche, and toss well to coat.

Serve immediately. YIELD: 4 servings (serving size: 1⅓ cups).

Per serving: CAL 117 (71% from fat); FAT 9.2g (sat 2g); PRO 4.8g; CARB 6.4g; FIB 2.3g; CHOL 5mg; IRON 1.1mg; SOD 409mg; CALC 133mg

RUSTIC MEDITERRANEAN TOMATO SALAD

POINTS value: 1

prep: 17 minutes • other: 2 hours

This marinated salad is easy to transport. Just take it in the plastic bag, and transfer it to a serving bowl when you arrive.

1   (14-ounce) can quartered artichoke hearts, drained
2   cups grape tomatoes, halved
¼   cup finely chopped red onion
¼   cup sliced pepperoncini peppers (about 6)
3   ounces part-skim mozzarella cheese, cut into ¼-inch cubes
2   tablespoons chopped fresh parsley
2   tablespoons drained capers
1½ tablespoons chopped fresh basil leaves
1½ tablespoons cider vinegar
⅛   teaspoon salt

1. Cut artichoke quarters in half lengthwise, if desired, and place in a large zip-top plastic bag. Add tomatoes and remaining ingredients. Seal bag; toss to coat. Chill 2 hours. YIELD: 6 servings (serving size: ¾ cup).

Per serving: CAL 66 (33% from fat); FAT 2.4g (sat 1.5g); PRO 5.1g; CARB 6g; FIB 0.9g; CHOL 8mg; IRON 1mg; SOD 433mg; CALC 105mg

WARM FINGERLING POTATO SALAD

POINTS value: 3

prep: 10 minutes • cook: 20 minutes

Fingerling potatoes are not a specific variety of potato. Instead, they are immature potatoes with a long, thin shape. They can be white, red-skinned, or yellow-fleshed and vary in texture from waxy to starchy. In this recipe, you can substitute small red potatoes.

10 fingerling potatoes, cut into ⅛-inch slices (about 3 cups)
½   cup fat-free balsamic vinaigrette
1   tablespoon chopped fresh basil
2   teaspoons whole-grain mustard
¼   teaspoon salt
¼   teaspoon freshly ground black pepper
½   cup (4 ounces) goat cheese

1. Preheat broiler.
2. Place potato in a medium saucepan; cover with an inch of water. Bring to a boil. Reduce heat; simmer 5 minutes or until tender. Drain.
3. While potato cooks, combine balsamic vinaigrette and next 4 ingredients in a small bowl, stirring with a whisk.
4. Pour mixture over hot potato, tossing to coat. Spoon potato mixture into an 11 x 7–inch baking dish; sprinkle evenly with goat cheese.
5. Broil 5 minutes or until cheese is lightly browned. YIELD: 6 servings (serving size: ½ cup).

Per serving: CAL 146 (35% from fat); FAT 5.7g (sat 3.9g); PRO 5.7g; CARB 18g; FIB 1.2g; CHOL 15mg; IRON 0.9mg; SOD 487mg; CALC 63mg

PASTA SALAD WITH BLACK BEANS AND TOMATOES

POINTS value: 2

prep: 10 minutes • cook: 12 minutes
other: 1 hour

Black beans add protein and fiber to pasta salad, and sharp feta cheese contributes extra flavor. You can make this salad a day ahead and sprinkle the cheese on top just before serving.

4   ounces uncooked rotini
2   cups diced plum tomato (about 4)
½   cup chopped English cucumber
3   tablespoons chopped fresh cilantro
1   (15-ounce) can black beans, rinsed and drained
¾   cup fat-free balsamic vinaigrette
¼   teaspoon kosher salt
¼   cup (1 ounce) crumbled reduced-fat feta cheese

1. Cook pasta according to package directions, omitting salt and fat. Drain; rinse with cold water. Drain.
2. Combine pasta, tomato, and next 3 ingredients. Add vinaigrette and salt; toss well. Cover; chill at least 1 hour.

3. Spoon salad onto plates; sprinkle with feta cheese. YIELD: 6 servings (serving size: ¾ cup salad and 2 teaspoons cheese).

Per serving: CAL 154 (8% from fat); FAT 1.4g (sat 0.5g); PRO 6.6g; CARB 28.5g; FIB 3.9g; CHOL 2mg; IRON 1.8mg; SOD 639mg; CALC 38mg

ORZO SALAD WITH WHITE BEANS

POINTS value: 3

prep: 6 minutes • cook: 18 minutes

*You can double the serving size and serve this Greek-style pasta and bean salad as a main dish for a **POINTS** value of 6.*

⅔   cup uncooked orzo
1   cup diced cucumber (about 1 small)
½   cup (2 ounces) crumbled feta cheese
2   tablespoons chopped fresh parsley
1   (15.8-ounce) can Great Northern beans, rinsed and drained
⅓   cup reduced-fat olive oil vinaigrette
1   tablespoon lemon juice
¼   teaspoon kosher salt
¼   teaspoon coarsely ground black pepper

1. Cook orzo according to package directions, omitting salt and fat; drain and rinse with cold water. Drain.
2. Combine pasta, cucumber, and next 3 ingredients in a large bowl, tossing gently. Combine vinaigrette and next 3 ingredients, stirring with

a whisk. Add vinaigrette mixture to pasta mixture, tossing gently to combine. YIELD: 6 servings (serving size: about ⅔ cup).

Per serving: CAL 151 (30% from fat); FAT 5.1g (sat 1.6g); PRO 6g; CARB 22.7g; FIB 3g; CHOL 8mg; IRON 0.7mg; SOD 396mg; CALC 66mg

WARM TORTELLINI SALAD WITH ZUCCHINI AND TOMATOES

POINTS value: 4

prep: 5 minutes • cook: 16 minutes

Reserve some pasta water and add it to the salad to keep the pasta moist without having to add oil.

1   (9-ounce) package fresh three-cheese tortellini
1   cup cherry tomatoes, halved
1   cup diced zucchini
¼   cup finely chopped fresh flat-leaf parsley
¼   cup fat-free Italian dressing
¼   teaspoon kosher salt
⅛   teaspoon coarsely ground black pepper

1. Cook tortellini according to package directions; drain in a colander over a bowl. Reserve 2 tablespoons pasta water.
2. Combine tortellini, 2 tablespoons pasta water, tomatoes, and remaining ingredients in a large bowl, tossing gently to coat. YIELD: 4 servings (serving size: 1 cup).

Per serving: CAL 220 (18% from fat); FAT 4.3g (sat 1.7g); PRO 8.9g; CARB 36.9g; FIB 2.6g; CHOL 20mg; IRON 0.5mg; SOD 592mg; CALC 21mg

☑ TEX-MEX RICE SALAD

POINTS value: 3

prep: 12 minutes • cook: 9 minutes

Turn instant brown rice into a colorful Tex-Mex salad by adding avocado, black beans, tomato, cilantro, and cumin.

1   cup uncooked instant brown rice
⅓   cup fat-free balsamic vinaigrette
1   teaspoon ground cumin
¼   teaspoon salt
¼   teaspoon freshly ground black pepper
½   cup diced peeled avocado
1   cup chopped plum tomato
2   tablespoons sliced green onions
2   tablespoons chopped fresh cilantro
1   (15-ounce) can black beans, rinsed and drained

1. Cook rice according to package directions, omitting salt and fat.
2. Combine vinaigrette and next 3 ingredients in a medium bowl, stirring well with a whisk.
3. Combine rice, avocado, and next 4 ingredients in a large bowl. Add vinaigrette mixture, and toss gently. YIELD: 6 servings (serving size: ⅔ cup).

Per serving: CAL 196 (15% from fat); FAT 3.3g (sat 0.5g); PRO 5.6g; CARB 35.9g; FIB 4.9g; CHOL 0mg; IRON 2mg; SOD 371mg; CALC 33mg

GREEK GRAIN SALAD

POINTS value: 5

prep: 15 minutes
other: 1 hour and 30 minutes

Although tabbouleh is a traditional Middle Eastern salad, we've added some Greek flavor with feta cheese. Serve with pita wedges and fresh fruit.

1   (5.25-ounce) package tabbouleh mix (such as Near East)
1   cup boiling water
1½ teaspoons grated fresh lemon rind
3   tablespoons fresh lemon juice
1   tablespoon extravirgin olive oil
½   teaspoon minced garlic
2   cups chopped romaine lettuce
1   cup (4 ounces) crumbled feta cheese with basil and sun-dried tomatoes
¾   cup chopped plum tomato (about 2)
¼   cup chopped fresh mint
⅛   teaspoon crushed red pepper
1   (16-ounce) can navy beans, rinsed and drained

1. Combine tabbouleh mix (bulgur wheat and spice packet) and boiling water in a large bowl. Cover and let stand in refrigerator 30 minutes or until water is absorbed.
2. Add lemon rind and next 3 ingredients to tabbouleh mixture; toss well. Add lettuce and remaining ingredients, and toss gently. Cover and chill at least 1 hour. YIELD: 5 servings (serving size: about 1⅓ cups).

Per serving: CAL 246 (32% from fat); FAT 8.6g (sat 3.5g); PRO 11.8g; CARB 36.5g; FIB 8.9g; CHOL 17mg; IRON 2.6mg; SOD 673mg; CALC 112mg

TACO SALAD

POINTS value: 6

prep: 10 minutes • cook: 23 minutes

1   (3.5-ounce) package boil-in-bag brown rice
1   teaspoon olive oil
¼   cup chopped onion
3   garlic cloves, minced
1   (15-ounce) can black beans or kidney beans, rinsed and drained
1½ teaspoons Mexican seasoning
4   cups shredded iceberg lettuce
1½ cups chopped tomato
½   cup reduced-fat shredded Cheddar cheese
1   (4-ounce) can chopped green chiles
1   (3.8-ounce) can sliced black olives
3   ounces light tortilla chips
6   tablespoons light ranch dressing

1. Cook rice according to package directions, omitting salt and fat.
2. Heat oil in a large nonstick skillet over medium heat. Add onion and garlic, and sauté 2 minutes or until tender. Add cooked rice, beans, and Mexican seasoning; cook 5 minutes or until thoroughly heated. Set aside.
3. Combine lettuce and next 4 ingredients in a large bowl. To serve, place 5 chips on each of 6 plates; top with salad mixture and bean mixture. Drizzle dressing over salads. YIELD: 6 servings (serving size: 5 chips, 1 cup lettuce mixture, ½ cup bean mixture, and 1 tablespoon dressing).

Per serving: CAL 291 (35% from fat); FAT 11.3g (sat 2.5g); PRO 8.8g; CARB 38.1g; FIB 6.8g; CHOL 11mg; IRON 2.4mg; SOD 749mg; CALC 161mg

TUNA-EGG SALAD

POINTS value: 3

prep: 11 minutes • cook: 1½ minutes

*You can also serve this salad as an open-faced sandwich on a slice of lightly toasted high-fiber whole wheat bread for a **POINTS** value of 4.*

1   (6-ounce) can albacore tuna in water
¼   cup light mayonnaise
1   tablespoon fat-free milk
¾   cup thinly sliced celery
3   tablespoons sweet pickle relish
1   tablespoon Dijon mustard
¼   teaspoon salt
2   hard-cooked eggs, chopped
4   cups mixed salad greens

1. Place tuna in a fine mesh strainer, and rinse under cold water. Using the back of a spoon, press down firmly to release excess liquid.
2. Combine tuna, mayonnaise, and next 5 ingredients in a medium bowl; stir well. Add egg, and stir gently.
3. Divide greens evenly among plates; top with tuna salad. YIELD: 4 servings (serving size: ½ cup tuna salad and 1 cup greens).

Per serving: CAL 151 (51% from fat); FAT 8.5g (sat 1.8g); PRO 12.5g; CARB 6.6g; FIB 1.7g; CHOL 124mg; IRON 1.1mg; SOD 450mg; CALC 57mg

GRILLED SALMON SALADE NIÇOISE

POINTS value: 8
(pictured on page 138)

prep: 19 minutes • cook: 35 minutes
other: 10 minutes

Classic salade Niçoise features tuna alongside potato, green beans, tomato, and olives. Here we've used heart-healthy salmon.

3   tablespoons stone-ground mustard
3   tablespoons white wine vinegar
2   tablespoons honey
4   teaspoons olive oil, divided
⅛   teaspoon salt
2   tablespoons fresh lemon juice
1   teaspoon kosher salt
1   teaspoon black pepper
4   (6-ounce) salmon fillets
1   pound small red potatoes, quartered
2   large eggs
½   pound green beans, trimmed
Cooking spray
4   cups fresh baby spinach
¼   cup niçoise or pitted kalamata olives, halved
1   large tomato, cut into wedges (about 2 cups)
½   red onion, thinly sliced

1. Combine mustard, vinegar, honey, 1 teaspoon oil, and ⅛ teaspoon salt in a small bowl; stir with a whisk. Set aside.
2. Combine remaining 1 tablespoon olive oil, lemon juice, kosher salt, and pepper in a large zip-top plastic bag. Add fish to bag; seal. Marinate in refrigerator 10 minutes.
3. While fish marinates, place potato and whole unbroken eggs in a large

saucepan or Dutch oven; cover with water. Bring to a boil. Reduce heat, and simmer 10 minutes. Remove eggs and plunge into cold water. Cook potato 5 minutes; add green beans. Simmer 5 minutes or until vegetables are tender. Remove potato and beans, and plunge into cold water; drain. Peel eggs, and slice each into 6 wedges; set aside.
4. Prepare grill.
5. Place fish, skin sides down, on grill rack coated with cooking spray, and grill, covered, 10 to 12 minutes or until fish flakes easily when tested with a fork. Remove skin from fish, and cut fish into chunks.
6. Combine spinach, olives, tomato, and onion in a large bowl; add vinaigrette, potato, and beans, and toss to combine. Arrange salad evenly on plates, and top evenly with fish and eggs. YIELD: 6 servings (serving size: 2 cups salad mixture, 3 ounces fish, and 2 egg wedges).

Per serving: CAL 353 (39% from fat); FAT 15.2g (sat 3.2g); PRO 29g; CARB 25.3g; FIB 4.1g; CHOL 128mg; IRON 2.1mg; SOD 665mg; CALC 69mg

microwave hard-cooked eggs

To quickly hard-cook eggs, lightly coat 2 (10-ounce) custard cups with cooking spray. Break and slip 1 egg into each cup, and gently prick the yolks with the tip of a knife or a wooden pick. Cover with plastic wrap. Microwave at medium (50% power) 1½ minutes until eggs are almost at desired doneness. Cool long enough to handle comfortably, and then chop.

GREEK SHRIMP SALAD

POINTS value: 5

prep: 30 minutes • cook: 8 minutes

Serve this colorful salad in a large glass bowl, spooned on a lettuce leaf or tomato slices, or even wrapped up in a flour tortilla.

6   cups water
1½   pounds large shrimp, peeled
     and deveined
¼   cup white wine vinegar
3   tablespoons olive oil
½   teaspoon sugar
¼   teaspoon freshly ground black
     pepper
¼   teaspoon salt
1   small garlic clove, minced
1½   cups chopped yellow bell pepper
1   cup halved grape tomatoes
1   cup chopped English cucumber
½   cup chopped red onion
⅓   cup (1.3 ounces) crumbled
     reduced-fat feta cheese
¼   cup pitted kalamata olives,
     chopped

1. Bring 6 cups water to a boil in a Dutch oven. Add shrimp; cook 3 minutes or until done. Drain and rinse with cold water. Chop; set aside.
2. Combine vinegar and next 5 ingredients in a small bowl, stirring with a whisk.
3. Combine shrimp, bell pepper, and next 5 ingredients in a large bowl. Pour vinegar mixture over shrimp mixture, and toss gently. YIELD: 6 servings (serving size: 1⅓ cups).

Per serving: CAL 235 (44% from fat); FAT 11.6g (sat 2.1g); PRO 25.4g; CARB 7.5g; FIB 1.2g; CHOL 175mg; IRON 3.1mg; SOD 453mg; CALC 93mg

CHICKEN SALAD WITH FRESH PEACHES AND BLUE CHEESE

POINTS value: 6

prep: 22 minutes

Make the most of summer produce by creating a hearty salad with fresh, sweet peaches; roasted chicken; smoky almonds; and sharp blue cheese. It's a great way to use leftover cooked or rotisserie chicken.

3   tablespoons white wine vinegar
3   tablespoons orange juice
1   tablespoon honey
¼   teaspoon kosher salt
¼   teaspoon freshly ground black
     pepper
2   tablespoons extravirgin olive oil
6   cups chopped romaine lettuce
½   cup (2 ounces) crumbled blue
     cheese
3   cups coarsely chopped cooked
     chicken breast
2   cups chopped peeled peaches
     (about 2 medium)
¼   cup chopped smoked almonds

1. Combine first 5 ingredients in a small bowl. Add olive oil, and stir with a whisk.
2. Combine lettuce and next 4 ingredients in a large bowl, and toss gently. Drizzle with vinaigrette; toss to coat. YIELD: 6 servings (serving size: 1¾ cups).

Per serving: CAL 260 (46% from fat); FAT 13.2g (sat 3.4g); PRO 26.1g; CARB 10g; FIB 2.4g; CHOL 67mg; IRON 1.7mg; SOD 286mg; CALC 97mg

CHICKEN AND EDAMAME ASIAN SALAD

POINTS value: 3
(pictured on page 137)

prep: 8 minutes • cook: 3 minutes

Asian-style salads are all the rage at fast-food restaurants these days. Now you can make your own at home.

1   cup snow peas, trimmed
1   (10-ounce) package leaf lettuce
     and romaine blend salad greens
2   (6-ounce) packages refrigerated
     grilled chicken strips, coarsely
     chopped
1⅓ cups frozen shelled edamame
     (green soybeans), thawed
1   (11-ounce) can mandarin
     oranges in light syrup, drained
1   (8-ounce) can diced water
     chestnuts, drained
½   cup low-fat sesame-ginger
     dressing (such as Newman's
     Own)
1   cup crispy chow mein noodles

1. Steam snow peas, covered, 3 to 4 minutes or until crisp-tender. Plunge into ice water until cool; drain well.
2. Combine snow peas, salad greens, and next 5 ingredients in a large bowl; toss well. Sprinkle with chow mein noodles. YIELD: 8 servings (serving size: 1½ cups).

Per serving: CAL 174 (27% from fat); FAT 5.3g (sat 0.9g); PRO 13.6g; CARB 17.3g; FIB 3.3g; CHOL 28mg; IRON 2.1mg; SOD 656mg; CALC 29mg

CHICKEN AND CHICKPEA FATTOUSH

POINTS value: 7

prep: 16 minutes

Fattoush means "moistened bread," and in this case, it's pita bread. The addition of chicken and chickpeas transforms this cool Lebanese salad into a complete summer meal.

½   cup fresh lemon juice
¼   cup olive oil
2   teaspoons Dijon mustard
½   teaspoon salt
½   teaspoon black pepper
2   garlic cloves, crushed
6   cups chopped romaine lettuce
1½   cups shredded rotisserie chicken breast
1   cup chopped English cucumber
1   cup halved cherry tomatoes
¼   cup chopped red onion
¼   cup chopped fresh mint
¼   cup chopped fresh flat-leaf parsley
2   (6-inch) multigrain pitas, torn into bite-sized pieces
1   (16-ounce) can chickpeas (garbanzo beans), rinsed and drained

1. Combine first 6 ingredients in a large bowl, stirring with a whisk. Add romaine lettuce and remaining ingredients; toss gently. YIELD: 5 servings (serving size: 2 cups).

Per serving: CAL 327 (37% from fat); FAT 13.7g (sat 2.2g); PRO 20.1g; CARB 34g; FIB 6.4g; CHOL 36mg; IRON 3.6mg; SOD 588mg; CALC 89mg

☑ PORTOBELLO AND FLANK STEAK OVER GREENS

POINTS value: 6

prep: 19 minutes • cook: 20 minutes
other: 2 hours and 35 minutes

Allowing the steak to stand before cutting it preserves the juices and makes for easier slicing. To enhance the steak's tenderness, cut the meat diagonally across the grain.

½   cup balsamic vinegar
⅓   cup olive oil
1   tablespoon Worcestershire sauce
½   teaspoon kosher salt
½   teaspoon freshly ground black pepper
2   garlic cloves, minced
1   (1½-pound) flank steak, trimmed
6   large portobello mushroom caps
1   large red onion, cut into ½-inch-thick slices
     Cooking spray
6   cups mixed salad greens
1   cup halved cherry tomatoes

1. Combine first 6 ingredients in a small bowl, stirring with a whisk until blended.
2. Combine steak, mushrooms, and onion in a large zip-top plastic bag. Add ½ cup vinegar mixture to bag; seal. Marinate in refrigerator 2½ hours, turning occasionally. Reserve remaining 6 tablespoons vinegar mixture.
3. Prepare grill.
4. Remove steak and onion from bag, and place on grill rack coated with cooking spray. Grill 6 to 8 minutes on each side or until steak is

desired degree of doneness and onion is tender. Remove mushrooms from bag; discard marinade. Place mushrooms on grill rack; grill 4 to 5 minutes on each side or until tender. Cut mushrooms into ½-inch-thick slices. Let steak stand 5 minutes. Cut steak diagonally across grain into thin slices.
5. Chop onion; combine onion and mushrooms in a medium bowl. Combine mixed greens and tomatoes, and arrange evenly on plates. Top evenly with mushroom mixture. Arrange steak evenly over mushroom mixture; drizzle each serving evenly with reserved vinegar mixture. Serve immediately. YIELD: 6 servings (serving size: 1 cup salad, about ¾ cup mushroom mixture, 3 ounces steak, and 1 tablespoon dressing).

Per serving: CAL 283 (43% from fat); FAT 13.6g (sat 3.4g); PRO 28g; CARB 11.8g; FIB 3.2g; CHOL 38mg; IRON 3.3mg; SOD 223mg; CALC 77mg

portobello mushrooms

Portobello mushroom caps, with their meaty texture and intense flavor, are great for grilling. They often measure from 3 to 6 inches across, so they won't fall through the grill rack. The portobello stands up to bold flavors, such as acidic marinades, and pairs well with steak.

sandwiches ▶▶

GOAT CHEESE SANDWICH WITH CUCUMBER AND ALFALFA SPROUTS

POINTS value: 4

prep: 5 minutes • cook: 3 minutes

Serve with a bowl of Two-Bean Soup (page 158) for a light lunch.

2   tablespoons goat cheese
1   (2-ounce) whole-grain English muffin, split and toasted
⅛   teaspoon freshly ground black pepper
6   (⅛-inch-thick) slices cucumber
2   tablespoons alfalfa sprouts

1. Spread 1 tablespoon goat cheese on each half of warm English muffin. Sprinkle evenly with pepper. Top with cucumber slices and alfalfa sprouts. YIELD: 1 serving (serving size: 2 halves).

Per serving: CAL 223 (39% from fat); FAT 9.7g (sat 6.1g); PRO 11.5g; CARB 24.5g; FIB 4.1g; CHOL 22mg; IRON 2mg; SOD 508mg; CALC 240mg

sodium and sandwiches

According to the *Dietary Guidelines for Americans, 2005,* we should eat less than 2,300 milligrams of sodium per day. People with hypertension should try to eat no more than 1,500 milligrams of sodium per day.

Because breads, cheeses, lunch meats, and condiments are generally high in sodium, sandwiches are a challenge to work into a low-sodium eating plan. If you have a sandwich, try to include plenty of low-sodium foods during the rest of the day.

GREEK SALAD–STUFFED PITAS

POINTS value: 6

prep: 20 minutes

Create a portable lunch by spooning tangy Greek salad into pita-bread pockets.

2   cups chopped plum tomato (about 5)
1   cup chopped peeled cucumber (about 1 small)
¼   cup chopped pitted kalamata olives
2   tablespoons chopped fresh dill
1   tablespoon fresh lemon juice
2   teaspoons extravirgin olive oil
½   teaspoon freshly ground black pepper
¼   teaspoon salt
4   (6-inch) onion pitas, cut in half
8   small curly leaf lettuce leaves
½   cup (2 ounces) crumbled feta cheese

1. Combine first 8 ingredients in a large bowl; toss to combine. Line each pita half with a lettuce leaf. Spoon about ⅓ cup tomato mixture into each pita half, and sprinkle with 1 tablespoon cheese. YIELD: 4 servings (serving size: 2 pita halves).

Per serving: CAL 280 (29% from fat); FAT 9g (sat 3.5g); PRO 11g; CARB 40g; FIB 2.5g; CHOL 17mg; IRON 3.5mg; SOD 672mg; CALC 153mg

the perfect hard-cooked egg

Place the egg in a saucepan with enough cool water to cover the egg by at least 1 inch. Cover the pan, and bring water just to a boil; immediately turn off the heat. Let the egg stand, covered, for 15 minutes. Run the egg under cold water until completely cooled. Gently crack the shell, and peel under running water, starting with the large end.

NIÇOISE SANDWICHES

POINTS value: 5

prep: 13 minutes • cook: 3 minutes
other: 15 minutes

Salade Niçoise is a classic French salad composed of tuna, vegetables, hard-cooked eggs, olives, and tomato. In this sandwich version, a tuna mixture is spooned into a hollowed-out baguette.

¼   cup thinly sliced red onion
¼   cup chopped pitted kalamata olives
8   slices plum tomato (about 2 tomatoes)
4   green leaf lettuce leaves, chopped
1   (6-ounce) can albacore tuna in water, drained
1   hard-cooked large egg, sliced
2   tablespoons red wine vinegar
1   tablespoon olive oil
½   teaspoon salt
½   teaspoon freshly ground black pepper
1   (8-ounce) honey-wheat baguette

1. Combine first 6 ingredients in a medium bowl. Combine vinegar and next 3 ingredients, stirring well with a whisk. Add vinegar mixture to tuna mixture, tossing to coat.

2. Cut a "V"-shaped pocket in top of baguette; remove cut portion, and hollow out inside of bread, leaving a ½-inch border. Reserve cut portion and torn bread for another use.

3. Spoon tuna mixture into hollowed-out baguette, mounding slightly. Cut filled baguette crosswise into 4 equal portions. YIELD: 4 servings (serving size: ¼ of loaf).

Per serving: CAL 233 (36% from fat); FAT 9.2g (sat 1.4g); PRO 13.3g; CARB 24.1g; FIB 2.1g; CHOL 66mg; IRON 2mg; SOD 773mg; CALC 78mg

lunch bag safety

Keep the contents of your lunch bag safe as well as nutritious with these simple tips.

■ Pack your lunch in an insulated lunch bag. The bag will keep your food fresh and at the proper temperature longer than a brown bag.

■ If you don't have access to a refrigerator, put an ice pack or a frozen drink in the bag to keep your food cold.

■ Keep hot foods hot. Seal hot liquids, such as soup, tightly in a clean thermos. If you rinse the thermos with boiling water and immediately pour the soup into the thermos, the soup should stay warm until lunchtime.

■ If you reuse packaging materials, such as plastic containers or zip-top plastic bags, be sure to wash them thoroughly after each use.

CHICKEN PAN BAGNA

POINTS value: 8

prep: 19 minutes

To make ahead, wrap the sandwich tightly in plastic wrap and refrigerate.

2   cups sliced skinless, boneless rotisserie chicken breast
1   cup thinly sliced zucchini
½   cup thinly sliced red onion
2   tablespoons coarsely chopped pitted kalamata olives
¼   teaspoon grated fresh lemon rind
1½ tablespoons fresh lemon juice
1½ tablespoons olive oil
1   teaspoon capers, drained and coarsely chopped
½   teaspoon freshly ground black pepper
¼   teaspoon salt
¼   teaspoon chopped fresh rosemary
1   (8-ounce) French bread baguette
4   small curly leaf lettuce leaves
8   thin slices tomato

1. Combine first 11 ingredients in a medium bowl; toss well. Set aside.

2. Cut baguette in half horizontally. Hollow out top and bottom halves of loaf, leaving a ½-inch border. Reserve torn bread for another use.

3. Arrange lettuce and tomato on bottom half of loaf. Spoon chicken mixture evenly over lettuce and tomato. Replace top half of loaf; cut crosswise into 4 equal portions. YIELD: 4 servings (serving size: ¼ of loaf).

Per serving: CAL 369 (32% from fat); FAT 13.2g (sat 2.3g); PRO 26.4g; CARB 36.1g; FIB 3.7g; CHOL 60mg; IRON 1.9mg; SOD 750mg; CALC 35mg

CURRIED CHICKEN SALAD SANDWICHES

POINTS value: 7
(pictured on page 133)

prep: 19 minutes • cook: 3 minutes

*If you don't want to make all eight sandwiches at once, simply keep the chicken salad in the refrigerator and assemble the sandwiches as desired. Or if you prefer to eat chicken salad without the bread, a ½-cup portion has a **POINTS** value of 6.*

½   cup light mayonnaise
¼   cup plain low-fat yogurt
1   teaspoon curry powder
1   teaspoon lemon juice
½   teaspoon salt
4   cups shredded cooked chicken breast
½   cup seedless red grapes, halved
½   cup chopped walnuts, toasted
1   (8-ounce) can pineapple tidbits in juice, drained
⅓   cup diced red onion
16 slices whole wheat double-fiber bread (such as Nature's Own)
8   lettuce leaves

1. Combine first 5 ingredients in a large bowl. Add chicken and next 4 ingredients; stir well to combine.

2. Top each of 8 bread slices with ½ cup chicken salad. Top each with a lettuce leaf and a bread slice. YIELD: 8 servings (serving size: 1 sandwich).

Per serving: CAL 321 (40% from fat); FAT 14.1g (sat 2.1g); PRO 32.4g; CARB 28.4g; FIB 10.9g; CHOL 65mg; IRON 4.1mg; SOD 626mg; CALC 339mg

BACON AND SWISS WRAPS WITH ADOBO SPREAD

POINTS value: 5

prep: 21 minutes

Wrap up a Southwestern-style BLT sandwich for an out-of-the-ordinary lunchtime treat.

1   (7-ounce) can chipotle chiles in adobo sauce
¼   cup reduced-fat sour cream
½   teaspoon minced garlic
4   (1.9-ounce) multigrain sandwich wraps (such as Flatout)
6   precooked bacon slices, cut in half
4   (¾-ounce) slices reduced-fat Swiss cheese
½   cup thinly vertically sliced red onion
1   medium tomato, chopped
4   cups shredded romaine lettuce

1. Remove 1 teaspoon adobo sauce from can. Reserve chiles and remaining adobo sauce for another use. Combine 1 teaspoon adobo sauce, sour cream, and garlic in a small bowl, stirring until blended.
2. Spread adobo sauce mixture evenly over sandwich wraps. Arrange 3 bacon halves crosswise down center of each wrap. Top each with a cheese slice. Top evenly with onion, tomato, and lettuce. Starting at short end, roll up wraps; cut in half. YIELD: 4 servings (serving size: 2 halves).

Per serving: CAL 240 (38% from fat); FAT 10.2g (sat 4.1g); PRO 20.6g; CARB 22.4g; FIB 10g; CHOL 25mg; IRON 2.2mg; SOD 573mg; CALC 287mg

HAM, PEAR, AND ARUGULA SANDWICHES

POINTS value: 7

prep: 15 minutes

Coarse, slightly sour pumpernickel bread is the perfect base for maple-flavored ham, fresh pear slices, and a sweet cream cheese spread. Toast the bread before assembling the sandwiches, if desired. Baby spinach may be substituted for the arugula.

⅓   cup (2.6 ounces) ⅓-less-fat cream cheese
2   tablespoons mango chutney
1½   tablespoons finely chopped pecans
8   (1.1-ounce) slices pumpernickel bread
6   ounces thinly sliced maple-flavored ham
2   cups baby arugula
1   small ripe pear, thinly sliced

1. Combine first 3 ingredients in a small bowl, stirring well. Spread cheese mixture evenly over each bread slice. Top 4 bread slices evenly with ham, arugula, and pear slices. Top with remaining bread slices, cheese-mixture side down. YIELD: 4 servings (serving size: 1 sandwich).

Per serving: CAL 332 (25% from fat); FAT 9.3g (sat 3.5g); PRO 16.4g; CARB 48.2g; FIB 6.1g; CHOL 29mg; IRON 2.6mg; SOD 985mg; CALC 81mg

ROAST BEEF AND SUN-DRIED TOMATO SANDWICHES

POINTS value: 4

prep: 7 minutes • cook: 10 minutes

Soaking the roast beef briefly in Worcestershire sauce and balsamic vinegar adds a delightful tang to the meat that complements the robust flavors of the blue cheese and sun-dried tomatoes.

2   tablespoons low-sodium Worcestershire sauce
2   tablespoons balsamic vinegar
½   pound shaved deli roast beef
⅓   cup fat-free mayonnaise
2   tablespoons chopped drained oil-packed sun-dried tomato halves
4   teaspoons crumbled blue cheese
8   (0.7-ounce) slices Italian bread, toasted
4   lettuce leaves
1   large tomato, thinly sliced

1. Combine Worcestershire sauce and vinegar in a medium bowl. Add roast beef, and toss to combine.
2. Combine mayonnaise, chopped sun-dried tomato, and blue cheese in a small bowl; stir well. Spread about 1½ tablespoons mayonnaise mixture on each of 4 bread slices. Top evenly with roast beef, lettuce, tomato, and remaining bread slices. YIELD: 4 servings (serving size: 1 sandwich).

Per serving: CAL 220 (18% from fat); FAT 4.4g (sat 1.6g); PRO 14.9g; CARB 29.6g; FIB 2.4g; CHOL 24mg; IRON 2.3mg; SOD 886mg; CALC 59mg

VEGGIE PATTY PITAS

POINTS value: 7

prep: 10 minutes • cook: 8 minutes

Use any extra hummus as a dip for pita chips or fresh vegetables.

1   (10-ounce) package veggie patties (such as Gardenburger)
Cooking spray
½   cup prepared roasted red bell pepper hummus
4   (6-inch) whole wheat pitas, cut in half
2   cups shredded lettuce
8   (¼-inch-thick) slices tomato
16   (¼-inch-thick) slices cucumber

1. Heat a large nonstick skillet over medium heat. Coat veggie patties with cooking spray; place patties in pan, and cook 4 to 5 minutes on each side or until thoroughly heated and lightly browned. Cut each patty in half.
2. Spread 1 tablespoon hummus inside each pita half. Fill each pita half with a veggie patty half, ¼ cup lettuce, 1 slice tomato, and 2 slices cucumber. Serve immediately. YIELD: 4 servings (serving size: 2 pita halves).

Per serving: CAL 357 (21% from fat); FAT 8.4g (sat 1.3g); PRO 21g; CARB 52.7g; FIB 11.6g; CHOL 1mg; IRON 4.3mg; SOD 865mg; CALC 84mg

MARINATED PORTOBELLO PANINI

POINTS value: 6
(pictured on page 130)

prep: 8 minutes • cook: 3 minutes
other: 15 minutes

Fill a small loaf of bread with "meaty" portobellos, flavorful cheeses, and olives for a hearty lunch.

1   (6-ounce) package presliced portobello mushrooms
2   tablespoons reduced-fat olive oil vinaigrette
1   (12-ounce) loaf Italian or ciabatta bread
⅓   cup light garlic-and-herbs spreadable cheese (such as Alouette Light)
¼   cup (1 ounce) crumbled blue cheese
¼   cup pitted kalamata olives, coarsely chopped
2   teaspoons Dijon mustard
½   teaspoon minced garlic
12   fresh basil leaves
1   medium tomato, cut into 8 slices
Cooking spray

1. Place mushrooms in a quart-size zip-top plastic bag. Add vinaigrette; seal bag, and gently toss to coat. Let stand 15 minutes.
2. While mushrooms marinate, cut bread loaf in half horizontally. Hollow out top and bottom halves of loaf, leaving a ½-inch border. Reserve torn bread for another use.
3. Combine cheeses in a small microwave-safe bowl; microwave at HIGH 15 seconds or until soft. Add olives, mustard, and garlic; stir well. Spread mixture on bottom half of loaf; top with basil, tomato, and mushrooms. Top with remaining half of loaf. Coat both sides of sandwich with cooking spray.
4. Heat a large nonstick skillet over medium heat; place sandwich in pan. Place a piece of foil over sandwich; top with a heavy skillet. Cook 2 minutes. Turn sandwich; replace foil and heavy skillet. Cook 1 to 2 minutes or until golden brown. Cut into 4 equal portions. YIELD: 4 servings (serving size: ¼ of loaf).

Per serving: CAL 279 (36% from fat); FAT 11.3g (sat 4.2g); PRO 9.7g; CARB 34.9g; FIB 2.8g; CHOL 16mg; IRON 2.2mg; SOD 753mg; CALC 117mg

GRILLED SHRIMP PO'BOY

POINTS value: 7

(pictured on page 138)

prep: 22 minutes • cook: 6 minutes
other: 3 hours

Po'boys are Louisiana's version of a submarine sandwich. They're typically made with fried seafood, but ours features shrimp that's marinated in a spicy seasoning mixture and grilled.

1   pound jumbo shrimp, peeled
    and deveined
1   tablespoon olive oil
2   teaspoons lemon juice
½   teaspoon Old Bay seasoning
1   (11.5-ounce) loaf unsliced
    French bread
Olive oil–flavored cooking spray
¼   cup fat-free mayonnaise
3   tablespoons chopped drained
    oil-packed sun-dried tomatoes
2   tablespoons Dijon mustard
⅛   teaspoon ground red pepper
1   garlic clove, pressed
2   cups thinly sliced romaine lettuce
½   cup sliced red onion

1. Combine first 4 ingredients in a large zip-top freezer bag; seal bag, and toss to coat. Marinate in refrigerator 3 hours, turning bag occasionally.
2. Cut bread loaf in half horizontally. Hollow out top half of loaf, leaving a ½-inch border; reserve torn bread for another use. Coat cut sides of both loaf halves with cooking spray.
3. Prepare grill.
4. Thread shrimp evenly onto 4 (12-inch) metal skewers, leaving ¼ inch between each shrimp. Place skewers on a grill rack coated with cooking spray; grill 2 to 3 minutes

on each side or until done. Place bread, cut sides down, on grill rack; grill 2 minutes or until lightly toasted.
5. Combine mayonnaise and next 4 ingredients, stirring well. Spread mayonnaise mixture evenly over cut sides of loaf. Arrange lettuce, shrimp, and onion evenly over bottom half. Replace top half of loaf. Cut sandwich crosswise into 4 equal portions. YIELD: 4 servings (serving size: ¼ of loaf).

Per serving: CAL 332 (21% from fat); FAT 7.6g (sat 0.9g); PRO 26g; CARB 41.3g; FIB 2.8g; CHOL 170mg; IRON 5.3mg; SOD 989mg; CALC 168mg

GREEK GRILLED CHICKEN WRAPS

POINTS value: 6

prep: 22 minutes • cook: 10 minutes
other: 2 hours

Wrap a Greek salad with grilled chicken in a whole wheat tortilla for a satisfying meal.

¾   pound skinless, boneless
    chicken breast halves
¾   cup fat-free Greek dressing,
    divided
1   (14-ounce) can artichoke
    hearts, drained and coarsely
    chopped
1   large red bell pepper
Cooking spray
1   cup shredded romaine lettuce
½   cup grape tomatoes, halved
¼   cup thinly sliced red onion
½   cup prepared artichoke and
    garlic hummus
4   (8-inch) whole wheat tortillas
¼   cup (1 ounce) crumbled feta
    cheese

1. Combine chicken and ½ cup dressing in a large zip-top plastic bag. Seal bag; marinate in refrigerator at least 2 hours, turning bag occasionally.
2. While chicken marinates, combine artichoke and remaining ¼ cup dressing in a small bowl; cover and refrigerate.
3. Prepare grill.
4. Cut bell pepper in half lengthwise. Discard seeds and membranes. Flatten pepper halves with palm of hand.
5. Remove chicken from bag; discard marinade. Place chicken and pepper halves on grill rack coated with cooking spray. Cook chicken 5 to 6 minutes on each side or until done. Cook pepper halves, skin sides down, 10 to 11 minutes or until charred. Discard charred skins. Slice chicken and bell pepper into strips.
6. Add lettuce, tomato, and onion to artichoke mixture; toss gently.
7. Spread 2 tablespoons hummus over each tortilla; arrange chicken and bell pepper evenly over hummus. Top evenly with artichoke mixture; sprinkle evenly with feta cheese. Fold top and bottom of each tortilla toward center; roll up burrito-style (wrap will be full). Secure with wooden picks, if necessary. Serve immediately. YIELD: 4 servings (serving size: 1 wrap).

Per serving: CAL 294 (30% from fat); FAT 9.8g (sat 1.7g); PRO 29.3g; CARB 23.3g; FIB 7.9g; CHOL 58mg; IRON 2.6mg; SOD 925mg; CALC 127mg

SESAME-GINGER CHICKEN WRAPS WITH PEANUT SAUCE

POINTS value: 6

prep: 23 minutes • cook: 10 minutes

Soak the cucumbers in vinegar while you prep the rest of the wraps to add a pickled punch to each bite.

2 cups thinly sliced cucumber (about 1 large)
½ cup rice wine vinegar
2 (6-ounce) skinless boneless chicken breast halves, cut in half horizontally
2 teaspoons canola oil
1 teaspoon ground ginger
¼ teaspoon salt
1½ tablespoons sesame seeds
Cooking spray
2 cups shredded napa (Chinese) cabbage
4 (1.9-ounce) multigrain sandwich wraps (such as Flatout)
Peanut Sauce

1. Combine cucumber slices and vinegar in a medium bowl; let stand, stirring often.
2. While cucumber stands, brush chicken with oil; sprinkle evenly with ginger, salt, and sesame seeds, pressing to adhere. Heat a large non-stick skillet over medium–high heat. Coat pan with cooking spray. Add chicken; cook 3 minutes on each side or until done. Remove from heat; keep warm.
3. Place ½ cup cabbage and ½ cup cucumber slices on each wrap. Cut chicken into strips, and toss with Peanut Sauce. Arrange chicken over cucumber. Roll up; secure with wooden picks, if necessary. **YIELD:** 4 servings (serving size: 1 wrap).

Per serving: CAL 307 (34% from fat); FAT 11.7g (sat 1.2g); PRO 32g; CARB 24.8g; FIB 10.3g; CHOL 49mg; IRON 3.1mg; SOD 664mg; CALC 87mg

PEANUT SAUCE
POINTS value: 1

2 tablespoons water
2 tablespoons natural-style creamy peanut butter
1 teaspoon light brown sugar
1 teaspoon rice wine vinegar
1 teaspoon low-sodium soy sauce
1 garlic clove, minced
Dash of ground red pepper

1. Combine all ingredients in a small saucepan, stirring with a whisk. Bring to a boil over medium heat, and cook 1 minute. **YIELD:** about ¼ cup.

Per tablespoon: CAL 56 (64% from fat); FAT 4g (sat 0.5g); PRO 1.9g; CARB 3.3g; FIB 0.5g; CHOL 0mg; IRON 0.2mg; SOD 75mg; CALC 3mg

---

napa cabbage

Napa cabbage is similar in appearance to romaine lettuce and is thin and delicate with a mild flavor. Like other cruciferous vegetables, it contains compounds that, according to some studies, may help prevent certain types of cancer. In stores, napa cabbage may also be found under the names "celery cabbage" or "Chinese cabbage." Look for heads that seem heavy for their size and are free of cracks. Use a chef's knife to thinly slice the cabbage into shreds.

ROASTED CHICKEN–PROVOLONE GRILLED CHEESE SANDWICHES

POINTS value: 8

prep: 11 minutes • cook: 10 minutes

The Chicago-style Italian bread makes this sandwich great. Look for an oval-shaped loaf in the deli or bakery section of the supermarket. Roasted chicken is also available in the deli.

¼ cup light mayonnaise
8 (¾-ounce) slices crusty Chicago-style Italian bread (about ½ inch thick)
8 (⅔-ounce) slices reduced-fat provolone cheese (such as Sargento)
2 cups fresh baby arugula
8 ounces very thinly sliced roasted skinless, boneless chicken breast
Olive oil–flavored cooking spray

1. Spread ½ tablespoon mayonnaise over each of 8 bread slices. Layer each of 4 bread slices with 1 cheese slice, ½ cup arugula, 2 ounces chicken, a second cheese slice, and a bread slice.
2. Heat a large nonstick skillet over medium heat. Coat sandwiches with cooking spray; add to pan. Cook 5 to 7 minutes on each side or until cheese melts and bread is toasted. **YIELD:** 4 servings (serving size: 1 sandwich).

Per serving: CAL 357 (36% from fat); FAT 14.4g (sat 4.8g); PRO 32.9g; CARB 22.6g; FIB 1.3g; CHOL 63mg; IRON 2mg; SOD 834mg; CALC 339mg

TURKEY REUBENS

POINTS value: 6

prep: 4 minutes • cook: 8 minutes

A traditional deli-style Reuben sandwich is high in fat and sodium because of the generous layers of corned beef, Swiss cheese, and sauerkraut. We've reduced the fat by using turkey, reduced-fat cheese, and reduced-fat dressing. Although it's still fairly high in sodium, our version has about half the sodium of a traditional sandwich.

8   ounces thinly sliced smoked turkey breast
8   (1-ounce) slices rye bread (such as Cobblestone Mill)
¼   cup reduced-fat Thousand Island dressing
¾   cup canned Bavarian-style sauerkraut, drained
4   (1-ounce) slices reduced-fat, reduced-sodium Swiss cheese (such as Boar's Head Lacey Swiss)
Cooking spray

1. Divide turkey evenly among 4 bread slices, and spread 1 tablespoon dressing over turkey on each sandwich. Top each with 3 tablespoons sauerkraut, 1 cheese slice, and a bread slice. Coat tops of sandwiches with cooking spray.
2. Heat a large nonstick skillet over medium heat. Place 2 sandwiches, coated side down, in pan. Cook 2 to 3 minutes or until bread is golden and cheese begins to melt. Coat tops of sandwiches with cooking spray; turn sandwiches. Cook an additional 2 to 3 minutes or until bread is golden and cheese melts. Repeat procedure with remaining sandwiches. Serve immediately. YIELD: 4 servings (serving: 1 sandwich).

Per serving: CAL 327 (28% from fat); FAT 10g (sat 4.5g); PRO 22.8g; CARB 35.8g; FIB 4.4g; CHOL 32mg; IRON 2.5mg; SOD 1,237mg; CALC 297mg

THAI TURKEY BURGERS WITH MANGO MAYONNAISE

POINTS value: 9
(pictured opposite page)

prep: 16 minutes • cook: 16 minutes
other: 5 minutes

Green curry paste, made from green chiles, lemongrass, and spices, is milder than red curry paste but still gives these burgers an exotic kick.

2   tablespoons green curry paste
1   tablespoon light mayonnaise
1   large egg white, beaten
1¼   pounds ground turkey breast
½   cup minced green onions
⅓   cup fresh breadcrumbs
¼   teaspoon salt
Olive oil–flavored cooking spray
Mango Mayonnaise
5   (2-ounce) whole grain hamburger buns
5   romaine lettuce leaves
10   slices tomato
15   slices cucumber

1. Prepare grill.
2. Combine first 3 ingredients in a large bowl, stirring well with a whisk. Add turkey and next 3 ingredients; stir just until blended. Divide mixture into 5 equal portions, shaping each into a ½-inch-thick patty.
3. Coat both sides of patties with cooking spray. Place patties on grill rack coated with cooking spray. Grill 8 minutes on each side or until done. Spread 1 tablespoon Mango Mayonnaise on bottom half of each bun; top with 1 lettuce leaf, 2 tomato slices, 1 patty, 3 cucumber slices, and top half of bun. YIELD: 5 servings (serving size: 1 burger).

Per serving: CAL 409 (35% from fat); FAT 16g (sat 3.5g); PRO 28g; CARB 39.1g; FIB 5.7g; CHOL 101mg; IRON 3.4mg; SOD 850mg; CALC 127mg

MANGO MAYONNAISE
POINTS value: 1

¼   cup light mayonnaise
1½   tablespoons mango chutney
½   tablespoon minced fresh cilantro

1. Combine all ingredients. Let stand 5 minutes before serving. YIELD: ⅓ cup.

Per tablespoon: CAL 54 (67% from fat); FAT 4g (sat 0.8g); PRO 0g; CARB 4.1g; FIB 0g; CHOL 4mg; IRON 0.1mg; SOD 172mg; CALC 0.1mg

ground turkey

Ground turkey can be a lean substitute for ground beef, but be sure to read the labels carefully at the store because the fat content varies. "Ground turkey breast" is the leanest, with about 3% fat. It contains white meat only and no skin. Regular ground turkey contains white and dark meat and some skin and is about 10% fat (similar to ground sirloin). Frozen ground turkey is usually all dark meat and skin and is 15% fat (similar to ground round).

Thai Turkey Burgers with Mango Mayonnaise, *opposite page*

Marinated Portobello Panini, *page 125*

Carrot-Coriander Soup with
Cilantro Cream, *page 156*

Pork Stir-Fry with Orange Sauce,
page 94

Curried Chicken Salad
Sandwiches, *page 123*

Broccoli Slaw Salad, *page 112*

Chilled Tomatillo-Avocado Soup
with Tomato Salsa,
page 156

Ginger-Apple Salad,
page 112

Hunter's-Style Beef Pie, *page 90*

Chicken, Broccoli, and Gnocchi
with Parsley Pesto, *page 98*

Greek Isle Chicken, *page 104*

Chicken and Edamame Asian Salad, *page 119*

Grilled Salmon
Salade Niçoise,
page 118

Grilled Shrimp
Po'boy, *page 126*

Chile-Rubbed Pork Tenderloin
with Quick Mole Sauce, *page 96*

139

Chicken Thighs with Tomatoes and Olives, *page 108*

Zucchini, Parmesan, and Mâche Salad, *page 115*

Moroccan Butternut Soup, page 157

Orange-Sesame Snow Peas,
page 148

Middle Eastern Roasted Cauliflower, *page 147*

side dishes ▶▶

POINTS value: 0
☑ Oven-Roasted Zucchini, *page 149*

POINTS value: 1
Balsamic Asparagus, *page 146*
Broccoli with Garlic-Herb Butter, *page 146*
Cauliflower with Green Onions and Parmesan, *page 147*
Green Peas with Pimiento, *page 147*
Orange-Sesame Snow Peas, *page 148*
☑ Herb-Roasted Acorn Squash, *page 148*
Zucchini with Pine Nuts and Lemon, *page 148*

POINTS value: 2
Roasted Green Beans with Bacon and Shallots, *page 146*
Middle Eastern Roasted Cauliflower, *page 147*
Roasted Root Vegetables, *page 149*
Edamame Mashed Potatoes, *page 150*
Garlic-Herbed Spaetzle, *page 154*

POINTS value: 3
Cranberry-Orange Sweet Potatoes, *page 150*
Mashed Potatoes with Caramelized Onions and Goat
  Cheese, *page 150*
Potato, Parsnip, and Gorgonzola Mash, *page 151*
Curried Rice with Onions and Cashews, *page 152*
Caramelized Onion Rice, *page 153*
Baked Butternut Squash Risotto, *page 154*

POINTS value: 4
Roasted Sweet Potatoes with Bacon, Apple, and Thyme,
  page 149
Peanut Butter–Banana Oatmeal, *page 152*
Cumin-Scented Rice with Black Beans, *page 153*

POINTS value: 5
Bacon-Cheddar Potatoes, *page 152*

BALSAMIC ASPARAGUS

POINTS value: 1

prep: 4 minutes • cook: 4 minutes

Slightly sweet balsamic vinegar and sharp Parmesan cheese are tasty partners for tender asparagus spears.

1	pound asparagus, trimmed
1	tablespoon balsamic vinegar
1	teaspoon extravirgin olive oil
¼	teaspoon salt
¼	teaspoon freshly ground black pepper
¼	cup preshredded fresh Parmesan cheese

1. Place asparagus in a microwave-safe dish; cover with plastic wrap. Microwave at HIGH 4 to 5 minutes or until crisp-tender. Drizzle with vinegar and oil. Sprinkle with salt, pepper, and cheese. YIELD: 4 servings (serving size: ¼ of asparagus).

Per serving: CAL 52 (55% from fat); FAT 3.2g (sat 1.3g); PRO 3.6g; CARB 3.2g; FIB 1.3g; CHOL 6mg; IRON 1.3mg; SOD 248mg; CALC 90mg

ROASTED GREEN BEANS WITH BACON AND SHALLOTS

POINTS value: 2

prep: 5 minutes • cook: 30 minutes

For the best browning of the beans, place the oven rack in the top third of the oven. Use a large jelly-roll pan so you can spread the beans out in a single layer. Also, the rim of the pan will help contain the bacon drippings.

2	bacon slices
2	small shallots, sliced
1	(12-ounce) package trimmed thin green beans
¼	teaspoon kosher salt

1. Preheat oven to 450°.
2. Place bacon on a large jelly-roll pan. Bake at 450° for 8 to 10 minutes or until crisp.
3. Drain bacon on paper towels, reserving 2 teaspoons drippings in pan. Discard remaining drippings.
4. Add shallots and beans to drippings in pan; toss to coat. Arrange beans in a single layer on pan, and sprinkle with salt. Bake at 450° for 15 minutes; stir and bake an additional 7 minutes or until lightly browned and tender. Crumble bacon; sprinkle over beans. YIELD: 3 servings (serving size: about ½ cup).

Per serving: CAL 102 (46% from fat); FAT 5.2g (sat 1.9g); PRO 4g; CARB 11.4g; FIB 4.3g; CHOL 9mg; IRON 0.9mg; SOD 283mg; CALC 65mg

BROCCOLI WITH GARLIC-HERB BUTTER

POINTS value: 1

prep: 4 minutes • cook: 4 minutes

Buy a package of broccoli florets so you don't have to spend time chopping broccoli. A 12-ounce package contains about 4½ cups of florets. You can have any leftover raw broccoli with a little light ranch dressing for a snack on another day.

2	tablespoons light stick butter
2	tablespoons chopped fresh parsley
2	garlic cloves, minced
4	cups broccoli florets
2	tablespoons water
¼	teaspoon salt
¼	teaspoon freshly ground black pepper

1. Place butter in a small microwave-safe dish. Microwave at HIGH 15 seconds or until melted. Stir in parsley and garlic.
2. Place broccoli florets in a large microwave-safe bowl. Add 2 tablespoons water, and cover with wax paper. Microwave at HIGH 4 minutes or until crisp-tender. Drain well. Add butter mixture, salt, and pepper; toss gently to coat. YIELD: 4 servings (serving size: 1 cup).

Per serving: CAL 48 (62% from fat); FAT 3.3g (sat 1.8g); PRO 2.3g; CARB 4.9g; FIB 2.2g; CHOL 8mg; IRON 0.8mg; SOD 213mg; CALC 40mg

CAULIFLOWER WITH GREEN ONIONS AND PARMESAN

POINTS value: 1

prep: 6 minutes • cook: 7 minutes

If the florets in the package are large, cut them into bite-sized pieces using a sharp paring knife. The smaller pieces will steam faster.

1   (10⅜-ounce) package cauliflower florets (about 3½ cups)
3   tablespoons thinly sliced green onions
2   tablespoons grated Parmesan cheese
2   teaspoons butter
¼   teaspoon kosher salt
⅛   teaspoon coarsely ground black pepper

1. Steam cauliflower, covered, 4 minutes or until tender.
2. Transfer cauliflower to a medium bowl; add green onions and remaining ingredients. Toss well to combine. YIELD: 4 servings (serving size: ¾ cup).

Per serving: CAL 48 (51% from fat); FAT 2.7g (sat 1.7g); PRO 2.5g; CARB 4.4g; FIB 2g; CHOL 7mg; IRON 0.4mg; SOD 192mg; CALC 48mg

cruciferous vegetables

Vegetables in the cruciferous family, including broccoli, Brussels sprouts, cauliflower, and cabbage, contain phytochemicals that have been shown to reduce the risk of certain types of cancer.

MIDDLE EASTERN ROASTED CAULIFLOWER

POINTS value: 2
(pictured on page 144)

prep: 8 minutes • cook: 12 minutes

Combine mild cauliflower with the aromatic spices of the Middle East for a distinctive side dish. Instead of cutting a head of cauliflower into florets, you can use 2 (10⅜-ounce) packages of florets.

6   cups cauliflower florets (about 1 medium head)
1   tablespoon olive oil
½   teaspoon salt
½   teaspoon freshly ground black pepper
½   teaspoon ground cumin
¼   teaspoon curry powder
⅛   teaspoon ground cinnamon
½   cup canned petite diced tomatoes, drained
¼   cup raisins
1   tablespoon chopped fresh parsley

1. Preheat oven to 500°.
2. Combine first 7 ingredients in a large bowl; toss well. Place cauliflower on a foil-lined jelly-roll pan. Bake at 500° for 12 minutes or until lightly browned, stirring once after 5 minutes.
3. Combine tomatoes, raisins, and parsley in a large bowl. Stir in cauliflower. Serve warm or at room temperature. YIELD: 4 servings (serving size: ¾ cup).

Per serving: CAL 107 (30% from fat); FAT 3.6g (sat 0.5g); PRO 3.6g; CARB 17.5g; FIB 4.1g; CHOL 0mg; IRON 1mg; SOD 377mg; CALC 46mg

GREEN PEAS WITH PIMIENTO

POINTS value: 1

prep: 1 minute • cook: 5 minutes

There's no need to thaw the peas before you start the recipe. Just put the frozen peas directly into the hot pan with the other ingredients.

1   tablespoon light stick butter
2   tablespoons slivered almonds
2¼ cups frozen petite green peas
1   (4-ounce) jar diced pimiento, drained
¼   teaspoon salt
⅛   teaspoon freshly ground black pepper

1. Melt butter in a nonstick skillet over medium heat. Add almonds; cook 2 minutes or until toasted, stirring frequently. Add peas and remaining ingredients; cook 2 minutes or until thoroughly heated. YIELD: 4 servings (serving size: ½ cup).

Per serving: CAL 79 (38% from fat); FAT 3.3g (sat 1g); PRO 4.3g; CARB 11.2g; FIB 4.2g; CHOL 3.8mg; IRON 1.4mg; SOD 291mg; CALC 27mg

Orange juice concentrate is a great way to add intense citrus flavor to sauces, dressings, and sides. But you rarely need to use a whole container for those recipes. Instead of thawing the whole container, allow it to stand at room temperature for about 15 minutes—it will be soft enough to scoop out what you need. Then seal the container inside a zip-top plastic freezer bag, and return it to the freezer. The remainder will then be on hand for another recipe whenever you need it.

ORANGE-SESAME SNOW PEAS

POINTS value: 1
(pictured on page 143)

prep: 8 minutes • cook: 3 minutes

Snow peas are best and will keep their fresh crunch when you cook them just enough to bring out the bright green color.

3   tablespoons thawed orange juice concentrate
1   tablespoon low-sodium soy sauce
1   teaspoon toasted sesame seeds
½   teaspoon grated fresh orange rind
1½   teaspoons dark sesame oil
⅛   teaspoon crushed red pepper
3   cups snow peas, trimmed (about ¾ pound)

1. Combine first 6 ingredients in a small bowl.
2. Heat a large nonstick skillet over medium–high heat; add orange juice mixture and snow peas. Cook 3 minutes, stirring often. Serve immediately. YIELD: 4 servings (serving size: ½ cup).

Per serving: CAL 96 (23% from fat); FAT 2.4g (sat 0.3g); PRO 4.1g; CARB 15.1g; FIB 3.4g; CHOL 0mg; IRON 3.8mg; SOD 139mg; CALC 59mg

☑ HERB-ROASTED ACORN SQUASH

POINTS value: 1

prep: 11 minutes • cook: 24 minutes

Acorn squash is a winter squash that's ribbed and shaped like a giant acorn. It has dark green skin and orange flesh. The sweetness of the squash pairs well with savory fresh herbs.

2   tablespoons chopped fresh parsley
2   teaspoons chopped fresh oregano
2   teaspoons chopped fresh thyme
¼   teaspoon kosher salt
⅛   teaspoon freshly ground black pepper
1   acorn squash (about 1½ pounds)
Olive oil–flavored cooking spray

1. Preheat oven to 450°.
2. Combine parsley and next 4 ingredients in a small bowl.
3. Cut squash in half lengthwise. Discard seeds and membranes. Cut each half lengthwise into 4 wedges. Place wedges, cut sides up, in a large roasting pan. Coat squash with cooking spray; top with parsley mixture. Bake at 450° for 24 minutes, turning squash after 12 minutes. YIELD: 4 servings (serving size: 2 wedges).

Per serving: CAL 70 (3% from fat); FAT 0.2g (sat 0g); PRO 1.5g; CARB 18.1g; FIB 2.7g; CHOL 0mg; IRON 1.4mg; SOD 124mg; CALC 64mg

ZUCCHINI WITH PINE NUTS AND LEMON

POINTS value: 1

prep: 6 minutes • cook: 12 minutes

Fresh lemon juice is a great way to perk up the flavor of fresh vegetables. If you microwave the lemon for about 30 seconds before squeezing it, you'll get more juice. One medium lemon will generally yield about 2 to 3 tablespoons of juice.

2   teaspoons extravirgin olive oil
Cooking spray
3   medium zucchini, cut into ½-inch cubes
1   tablespoon pine nuts, toasted
2   teaspoons fresh lemon juice
½   teaspoon kosher salt
¼   teaspoon dried thyme
⅛   teaspoon coarsely ground black pepper

1. Heat oil in a large nonstick skillet coated with cooking spray over medium heat. Add zucchini; sauté 11 minutes or until tender. Stir in pine nuts and remaining ingredients. YIELD: 5 servings (serving size: ½ cup).

Per serving: CAL 47 (61% from fat); FAT 3.2g (sat 0.4g); PRO 1.7g; CARB 4.4g; FIB 1.4g; CHOL 0mg; IRON 0.5mg; SOD 200mg; CALC 19mg

☑ OVEN-ROASTED ZUCCHINI

POINTS value: 0

prep: 4 minutes • cook: 25 minutes

Although summer is the peak season for zucchini, it's usually available year-round in most supermarkets. Choose small zucchini because they have thinner skins and are more tender than the large ones.

2 pounds zucchini (about 6 small), halved lengthwise and cut into 1½-inch pieces
Olive oil–flavored cooking spray
½ teaspoon salt
¼ teaspoon freshly ground black pepper

1. Preheat oven to 475°.
2. Arrange zucchini in a single layer on a jelly-roll pan coated with cooking spray. Coat zucchini lightly with cooking spray. Bake at 475° for 25 minutes. Sprinkle with salt and pepper, and serve immediately. YIELD: 4 servings (serving size: 1 cup).

Per serving: CAL 38 (14% from fat); FAT 0.6g (sat 0.1g); PRO 2.8g; CARB 7.7g; FIB 2.5g; CHOL 0mg; IRON 0.8mg; SOD 313mg; CALC 35mg

root vegetables

Root vegetables are at their flavor peak during the cooler months.

Select roots by weight, looking for ones that are not too large but are heavy for their size. Avoid those with hairy rootlets that indicate age.

ROASTED ROOT VEGETABLES

POINTS value: 2

prep: 13 minutes • cook: 25 minutes

To store beets and carrots, trim the stems to about 1 inch and keep the roots in plastic bags in the refrigerator about 2 weeks. Peel the beets under cold running water to prevent them from staining your fingers.

½ pound beets (about 3 medium), trimmed and peeled
3 medium carrots, peeled
1 medium onion
1 tablespoon extravirgin olive oil
2 teaspoons balsamic vinegar
1 teaspoon sugar
⅛ teaspoon salt
⅛ teaspoon crushed red pepper

1. Preheat oven to 450°.
2. Line a large baking sheet with foil.
3. Cut beets into 8 wedges each. Cut carrots in half lengthwise; cut halves into 3-inch pieces. Remove skin from onion; cut into large wedges, leaving root intact.
4. Place beets, carrot, and onion in a medium bowl; drizzle with oil, and toss well. Arrange vegetables in a single layer on prepared pan. Bake at 450° for 15 minutes; stir and bake an additional 10 minutes or until tender.
5. Return vegetables to bowl; add vinegar and remaining ingredients. Toss gently to coat. YIELD: 4 servings (serving size: ½ cup).

Per serving: CAL 93 (36% from fat); FAT 3.7g (sat 0.5g); PRO 1.6g; CARB 14.7g; FIB 2.2g; CHOL 0mg; IRON 0.8mg; SOD 150mg; CALC 31mg

ROASTED SWEET POTATOES WITH BACON, APPLE, AND THYME

POINTS value: 4

prep: 13 minutes • cook: 38 minutes

Smoky bacon and onion add a savory note to the tender roasted sweet potato and tart Granny Smith apple. Serve with roasted pork or turkey for a hearty meal featuring the flavors of autumn.

2 bacon slices
1 pound sweet potato (about 1 large), cubed
1 large onion, cut into wedges
2 tablespoons cider vinegar
1 tablespoon chopped fresh thyme
½ teaspoon kosher salt
¼ teaspoon freshly ground black pepper
1 Granny Smith apple, cut into chunks

1. Preheat oven to 450°.
2. Place bacon slices on a jelly-roll pan. Bake at 450° for 8 minutes or until crisp.
3. Remove bacon from pan, reserving 1 tablespoon drippings. Crumble bacon, and set aside.
4. Toss potato and onion with bacon drippings, vinegar, and next 3 ingredients; spoon into pan. Bake at 450° for 20 minutes. Add apple; bake an additional 10 minutes or until tender. Transfer potato mixture to a large bowl. Toss with bacon. YIELD: 4 servings (serving size: 1 cup).

Per serving: CAL 204 (23% from fat); FAT 5.3g (sat 1.8g); PRO 3.8g; CARB 36g; FIB 2.3g; CHOL 7mg; IRON 1mg; SOD 346mg; CALC 39mg

CRANBERRY-ORANGE SWEET POTATOES

POINTS value: 3

prep: 10 minutes
cook: 1 hour and 29 minutes

Nothing says "Thanksgiving" like sweet potatoes and cranberries. This tangy, sweet casserole is great with either ham or roasted turkey.

2¼ pounds sweet potatoes
     (about 4 medium)
1   cup fresh cranberries
⅓   cup water
¾   cup orange marmalade
½   teaspoon ground
     cinnamon
½   teaspoon vanilla extract
¼   teaspoon salt
⅛   teaspoon ground cloves
Cooking spray

1. Preheat oven to 400°.
2. Wrap each sweet potato in foil, and place on a baking sheet. Bake at 400° for 1 hour and 10 minutes or until very tender.
3. Combine cranberries and water in a medium saucepan. Bring to a boil; reduce heat, and simmer, uncovered, 4 minutes or until most cranberries pop. Remove from heat; add marmalade, and stir until marmalade melts. Stir in cinnamon and next 3 ingredients.
4. Scoop out pulp from potatoes; place pulp in a large mixing bowl. Discard potato skins. Mash pulp with a potato masher until smooth. Stir in cranberry mixture, and spoon into a 2-quart baking dish coated with cooking spray. Cover and bake at 400° for 15 minutes or until

thoroughly heated. YIELD: 8 servings (serving size: ½ cup).

Per serving: CAL 174 (1% from fat); FAT 0.2g (sat 0.1g); PRO 1.8g; CARB 43.3g; FIB 3.9g; CHOL 0mg; IRON 1mg; SOD 123mg; CALC 48mg

EDAMAME MASHED POTATOES

POINTS value: 2

prep: 10 minutes • cook: 27 minutes

The secret ingredient in these home-style, chunky mashed potatoes is edamame. The pureed beans add not only a nutty, buttery flavor, but also the health benefits of soy protein.

1½ cups frozen shelled edamame
     (green soybeans)
2   cups cubed peeled Yukon gold
     potato (about 1 pound)
⅓   cup warm 1% low-fat milk
3   tablespoons reduced-fat sour
     cream
1   tablespoon butter
½   teaspoon salt
¼   teaspoon freshly ground black
     pepper

1. Place edamame in a medium saucepan. Add water to cover 2 inches above edamame; bring to a boil. Cook 7 to 8 minutes or until soft; drain and set aside.
2. Place potato in same pan; add water to cover. Bring to a boil; reduce heat, and simmer, uncovered, 8 minutes or until tender. Drain, reserving ¼ cup cooking liquid.
3. Place edamame and reserved cooking liquid in a food processor or blender; process until smooth.

Combine pureed edamame, potato, milk, and remaining ingredients in a large bowl. Mash with a potato masher until desired consistency. YIELD: 6 servings (serving size: ½ cup).

Per serving: CAL 131 (31% from fat); FAT 4.5g (sat 1.9g); PRO 6.2g; CARB 15.7g; FIB 2.7g; CHOL 9mg; IRON 1.3mg; SOD 237mg; CALC 55mg

MASHED POTATOES WITH CARAMELIZED ONIONS AND GOAT CHEESE

POINTS value: 3

prep: 6 minutes • cook: 23 minutes

The additions of sweet, rich caramelized onion and sharp goat cheese take these mashed potatoes from satisfactory to spectacular. We loved them with a grilled beef tenderloin steak. *Turn to page 153 for tips on caramelizing onions.*

1   teaspoon olive oil
1   cup chopped onion (about 1
     large)
¾   teaspoon salt, divided
2   tablespoons water
2½ pounds Yukon gold potatoes,
     peeled and cubed (about 5
     medium)
⅓   cup fat-free milk
1   (4-ounce) package goat cheese,
     cut into cubes
¼   teaspoon freshly ground black
     pepper

1. Heat oil in a medium nonstick skillet over medium heat. Add onion and ¼ teaspoon salt, and cook 22 minutes or until golden brown, stirring frequently. Add 2 tablespoons water, 1 tablespoon at a time, as liquid evaporates, scraping pan to loosen browned bits after each addition. Remove from heat, and set aside.

2. While onion cooks, place potato in a Dutch oven, and add water to cover. Bring to a boil; reduce heat, and simmer, uncovered, 15 minutes or until tender. Drain and return to pan.

3. Place milk in a 1-cup glass measure. Microwave at MEDIUM (50% power) 30 seconds or until warm.

4. Add cheese to potato in pan. Mash potato mixture with a potato masher 3 or 4 times or until cheese melts. Add milk, remaining ½ teaspoon salt, and pepper; mash to desired consistency. Stir in reserved onion, and serve immediately. YIELD: 10 servings (serving size: ½ cup).

Per serving: CAL 133 (31% from fat); FAT 4.6g (sat 2.9g); PRO 5.4g; CARB 18g; FIB 1.6g; CHOL 12mg; IRON 0.5mg; SOD 222mg; CALC 118mg

yukon gold potatoes

Yukon gold is one of the most common varieties of yellow-fleshed potatoes. Yukon gold potatoes have a good balance of starchiness and waxiness, so they're quite versatile. However, they're not good for baking or roasting because the flesh has too much moisture and starch, so the skins don't get crisp, and the insides get mushy.

how to mash potatoes

Potato mashers give you a multitude of texture options. They're your best bet if you like the texture of the skin in your mashed potatoes.

Use a hand mixer instead of a food processor to whip potatoes. A food processor is so powerful that it will over-mix the potatoes and make them gummy.

POTATO, PARSNIP, AND GORGONZOLA MASH

POINTS value: 3

prep: 11 minutes • cook: 18 minutes

Parsnips add a touch of sweetness to the mashed potatoes, but the sweetness is balanced by the strong-flavored cheese. This is an ideal side dish for your favorite beef or pork entrée.

1	pound Yukon gold potatoes, peeled and cut into 1-inch chunks (about 2 medium)
½	pound parsnips, peeled and cut into 1-inch chunks (about 2 medium)
½	cup fat-free evaporated milk
¼	cup (1 ounce) crumbled Gorgonzola cheese
1½	tablespoons butter
¾	teaspoon salt
¼	teaspoon minced garlic
¼	teaspoon freshly ground black pepper

1. Place potato and parsnip in a large saucepan; add water to cover. Bring to a boil; reduce heat, cover, and simmer 13 minutes or until vegetables are tender. Drain and place in a large bowl.

2. Add milk and remaining ingredients to potato mixture in bowl. Beat with a mixer at medium speed until smooth. YIELD: 6 servings (serving size: about ½ cup).

Per serving: CAL 144 (28% from fat); FAT 4.5g (sat 2.8g); PRO 4g; CARB 22.8g; FIB 2g; CHOL 12mg; IRON 0.4mg; SOD 409mg; CALC 97mg

BACON-CHEDDAR POTATOES

POINTS value: 5

prep: 7 minutes • cook: 20 minutes
other: 2 minutes

Our stovetop version of a bacon and Cheddar–topped baked potato is perfect for a weeknight side dish. To keep it superquick, cook the bacon in the microwave.

¾   cup water
3½ cups diced peeled baking
      potato (about 1½ pounds)
1   cup chopped green bell pepper
¼   teaspoon salt, divided
⅛   teaspoon black pepper
½   cup chopped green onions
¼   cup chopped fresh parsley
¾   cup (3 ounces) reduced-fat
      shredded sharp Cheddar cheese
6   bacon slices, cooked and
      crumbled

1. Bring ¾ cup water to a boil in a medium saucepan. Add potato, bell pepper, ⅛ teaspoon salt, and black pepper; cook 15 minutes or until potato is tender, stirring once.
2. Remove potato mixture from heat; stir in remaining ⅛ teaspoon salt, green onions, parsley, and cheese. Let stand 2 minutes or until cheese melts. Sprinkle with bacon. YIELD: 4 servings (serving size: ¾ cup).

Per serving: CAL 250 (32% from fat); FAT 8.8g (sat 4.4g); PRO 11.8g; CARB 30.4g; FIB 3.6g; CHOL 26mg; IRON 1.1mg; SOD 559mg; CALC 182mg

PEANUT BUTTER–BANANA OATMEAL

POINTS value: 4

prep: 3 minutes • cook: 3 minutes

This fiber-filled breakfast treat is slightly chewy, yet it's creamy because of the milk. If you like softer oats, cook them up to 1 minute longer before adding the sugar and peanut butter. Serve alongside scrambled eggs and mixed fresh fruit for a hearty breakfast.

½   cup regular oats
½   cup water
½   cup fat-free milk
⅛   teaspoon salt
⅛   teaspoon ground cinnamon
⅓   cup chopped banana
1½ tablespoons light brown sugar
1   tablespoon chunky natural-style
      peanut butter

1. Combine first 6 ingredients in a 3-cup microwave-safe bowl; stir well. Microwave at HIGH 3 minutes.
2. Add sugar and peanut butter to oats mixture. Stir until thick and creamy. Serve immediately. YIELD: 2 servings (serving size: about ⅔ cup).

Per serving: CAL 206 (24% from fat); FAT 5.6g (sat 0.7g); PRO 7g; CARB 34g; FIB 3g; CHOL 1mg; IRON 1.3mg; SOD 215mg; CALC 84mg

CURRIED RICE WITH ONIONS AND CASHEWS

POINTS value: 3

prep: 12 minutes • cook: 42 minutes

Basmati rice has a nutlike flavor and aroma. Toasting the mustard seeds, curry, and turmeric releases their flavors, infusing the rice with a warm spiciness.

⅔   cup uncooked basmati rice
1   tablespoon canola oil
½   teaspoon mustard seeds
½   teaspoon ground turmeric
½   teaspoon curry powder
2   cups sliced onion
1   tablespoon grated peeled fresh
      ginger
1   jalapeño pepper, minced
½   teaspoon salt
½   teaspoon sugar
2   tablespoons fresh lime juice
¼   cup chopped dry-roasted
      cashews, salted

1. Cook rice according to package directions, omitting salt and fat.
2. Heat oil in a medium saucepan over medium-high heat. Add mustard seeds; cover and cook 1 minute or until seeds pop. Reduce heat to medium, and stir in turmeric and curry. Add onion, ginger, and jalapeño; cook 13 minutes or until onion is tender and lightly browned, stirring frequently.
3. Add salt, sugar, and cooked rice to onion mixture, stirring well. Cook 3 minutes or until thoroughly heated. Stir in lime juice, and top with cashews. YIELD: 5 servings (serving size: ½ cup).

Per serving: CAL 134 (42% from fat); FAT 6.2g (sat 0.9g); PRO 2.5g; CARB 18.2g; FIB 1.3g; CHOL 0mg; IRON 0.8mg; SOD 278mg; CALC 18mg

how to caramelize onions

1. Slice the onion in half vertically. Place halves, cut sides down, on cutting board, and slice into thin slivers.

2. Cook over medium heat, stirring often. After about 10 minutes, the onions begin to soften and release their liquid.

3. After cooking 15 minutes, the onions begin to take on a golden color but are not quite done. Keep stirring frequently.

4. At 20 minutes, the onions are a deep golden brown and are done.

CARAMELIZED ONION RICE

POINTS value: 3

prep: 7 minutes • cook: 42 minutes

This has a flavor similar to an herbed risotto, but the texture is fluffy.

1   teaspoon olive oil
1   large onion, thinly sliced
1   teaspoon fresh thyme, divided
½   teaspoon salt
½   teaspoon freshly ground black pepper
1½   cups fat-free, less-sodium chicken broth
¾   cup uncooked long-grain rice
1   tablespoon shredded fresh Parmesan cheese

1. Heat oil in a large nonstick skillet over medium heat; add onion. Cook 20 to 22 minutes or until onion is golden brown, stirring frequently.
2. Add ½ teaspoon fresh thyme and next 3 ingredients to onion; bring to a boil. Add rice. Cover, reduce heat to medium-low, and simmer 18 to 20 minutes or until liquid is absorbed and rice is tender.
3. Remove from heat, and fluff rice with a fork. Stir in remaining ½ teaspoon thyme and Parmesan cheese. **YIELD:** 4 servings (serving size: ¾ cup).

Per serving: CAL 166 (10% from fat); FAT 1.9g (sat 0.5g); PRO 4.6g; CARB 32.2g; FIB 1.1g; CHOL 2mg; IRON 1.6mg; SOD 532mg; CALC 39mg

CUMIN-SCENTED RICE WITH BLACK BEANS

POINTS value: 4

prep: 8 minutes • cook: 22 minutes
other: 1 minute

Complement your favorite Southwestern-style entrée with this filling side dish, which gets its distinct flavor from cumin, cilantro, and green chiles.

1   teaspoon canola oil
1   garlic clove, minced
¼   cup chopped onion
¾   cup uncooked long-grain rice
½   teaspoon ground cumin
¼   teaspoon salt
¼   teaspoon freshly ground black pepper
1½   cups fat-free, less-sodium chicken broth
1   (15-ounce) can black beans, rinsed and drained
2   tablespoons canned chopped green chiles
¼   cup chopped fresh cilantro

1. Heat oil in a medium saucepan over medium-high heat. Add garlic and onion; sauté 2 to 3 minutes or until tender. Add rice, cumin, salt, and pepper; sauté 30 seconds. Add broth, and bring to a boil. Cover, reduce heat, and simmer 15 minutes or until liquid is absorbed and rice is tender. Remove from heat.
2. Add black beans, chiles, and cilantro to rice mixture; fluff gently with a fork. Cover and let stand 1 minute before serving. **YIELD:** 4 servings (serving size: 1 cup).

Per serving: CAL 214 (8% from fat); FAT 2g (sat 0.2g); PRO 7.9g; CARB 39.6g; FIB 4.8g; CHOL 0mg; IRON 3.2mg; SOD 502mg; CALC 39mg

BAKED BUTTERNUT SQUASH RISOTTO

POINTS value: 3

prep: 10 minutes • cook: 46 minutes

The traditional method for making creamy risotto involves adding the stock or broth to the rice ½ cup at a time and stirring constantly. This "hands-off" version calls for baking the rice mixture in a Dutch oven instead of cooking it on the stovetop. We got great results using a cast-iron Dutch oven, but you can use any type of ovenproof Dutch oven. It needs to be one that does not have plastic handles.

2 teaspoons olive oil
1 cup diced onion (about 1 medium)
2 garlic cloves, minced
1 cup uncooked Arborio rice
½ cup dry white wine
3 cups fat-free, less-sodium chicken broth
1 small butternut squash, peeled and chopped (about 2 cups)
½ cup (2 ounces) grated fresh Parmesan cheese
2 teaspoons chopped fresh rosemary
¼ teaspoon salt
¼ teaspoon black pepper

1. Preheat oven to 400°.
2. Heat oil in an ovenproof Dutch oven over medium heat. Add onion and garlic; sauté 5 minutes or until tender. Stir in rice. Add wine; cook 2 minutes or until wine evaporates, stirring constantly. Add broth and squash to pan, and bring to a boil. Cover, reduce heat, and simmer 5 minutes.

3. Remove rice mixture from heat; stir in cheese and remaining ingredients. Cover and bake at 400° for 30 minutes or until liquid is almost completely absorbed. Stir gently before serving. YIELD: 8 servings (serving size: about ⅔ cup).

Per serving: CAL 152 (21% from fat); FAT 3.5g (sat 1.2g); PRO 6.7g; CARB 24.5g; FIB 2g; CHOL 5mg; IRON 0.4mg; SOD 416mg; CALC 119mg

GARLIC-HERBED SPAETZLE

POINTS value: 2

prep: 5 minutes • cook: 19 minutes

Spaetzle are little noodle-like dumplings and are a great alternative to potatoes or rice. Treat your family to a German-style meal by serving this spaetzle with Chicken Schnitzel (page 102).

2 quarts water
1¾ cups all-purpose flour
1 teaspoon salt
½ teaspoon black pepper
2 large eggs
¾ cup fat-free milk
2 tablespoons butter
1 garlic clove, minced
2 tablespoons chopped fresh parsley
2 tablespoons chopped fresh chives

1. Bring 2 quarts water to a boil in a Dutch oven.
2. While water comes to a boil, lightly spoon flour into dry measuring cups; level with a knife. Combine flour, salt, and pepper in a large bowl. Combine eggs and milk in a medium bowl, stirring with a whisk.

Add milk mixture to flour mixture, stirring with a whisk until smooth. Fill cup of a spaetzle maker with batter. Working quickly, place maker over Dutch oven, and press dough into boiling water. Quickly repeat procedure until all batter has been pressed into water. Cook 2 minutes. Drain well.
3. Melt butter in a large nonstick skillet with deep sides over medium-high heat; add garlic, and sauté 30 seconds. Add spaetzle; cook 7 minutes or until golden, turning with a large spatula every 2 minutes. Stir in herbs, and serve immediately. YIELD: 10 servings (serving size: about ½ cup).

Per serving: CAL 113 (26% from fat); FAT 3.3g (sat 1.8g); PRO 4.1g; CARB 17.4g; FIB 0.6g; CHOL 49mg; IRON 1.3mg; SOD 273mg; CALC 27mg

making spaetzle

A spaetzle maker is a small, inexpensive kitchen gadget that resembles a handheld grater. It comes in handy if you're planning to make German-style dumplings often. Spaetzle makers are available at kitchen stores as well as in the kitchen sections of many discount retail stores. You can also order them online.

If you don't have a spaetzle maker, just spoon your batter in batches into a clean, empty 14.5-ounce diced-tomato can. Place a flat cheese grater with large holes, cutting side up, over top of can. Invert grater and can over boiling water, pressing can tightly to grater. Slide can back and forth over grater to force batter through holes into water.

soups & stews ▶▶

☑ CHILLED TOMATILLO-AVOCADO SOUP WITH TOMATO SALSA

POINTS value: 3

(pictured on page 134)

prep: 19 minutes • cook: 34 minutes
other: 1 hour and 30 minutes

Cooking tomatillos not only brings out their flavor but also softens their thick skin. Choose darker poblano chiles because they have the richest flavor.

2	teaspoons olive oil
1¼	cups chopped onion (1 medium)
4	garlic cloves, chopped
2	poblano chiles, chopped
1	jalapeño pepper, seeded and chopped
1	pound tomatillos, quartered
3	cups fat-free, less-sodium chicken broth
¾	teaspoon salt
¾	teaspoon ground cumin
1	ripe peeled avocado, chopped
¼	cup fresh cilantro leaves
¼	cup fresh lime juice
	Tomato Salsa

1. Heat oil in a large Dutch oven over medium-high heat. Add onion and next 3 ingredients; sauté 5 minutes or until tender.

2. Add tomatillos and next 3 ingredients to pan; bring to a boil. Cover, reduce heat, and simmer 23 minutes, stirring occasionally. Remove from heat; cover and chill 1½ hours.

3. Place avocado and half of soup in a blender; process until smooth. Transfer to a large bowl. Place remaining soup and cilantro in blender; process until smooth, and add to bowl. Stir in lime juice.

Ladle soup into bowls; top with Tomato Salsa. YIELD: 5 servings (serving size: 1 cup soup and about ⅓ cup salsa).

Per serving: CAL 134 (60% from fat); FAT 9g (sat 0.9g); PRO 4.7g; CARB 14.9g; FIB 4.1g; CHOL 0mg; IRON 1mg; SOD 754mg; CALC 27mg

TOMATO SALSA
POINTS value: 0

1½	cups chopped tomato (1 large)
2	tablespoons diced onion
2	tablespoons chopped fresh cilantro
1	tablespoon fresh lime juice
⅛	teaspoon salt
1	jalapeño pepper, seeded and diced

1. Combine all ingredients, tossing gently. YIELD: 1½ cups.

Per ⅓ cup: CAL 10 (9% from fat); FAT 0.1g (sat 0g); PRO 0.4g; CARB 2.3g; FIB 0.6g; CHOL 0mg; IRON 0.1mg; SOD 60mg; CALC 6mg

---

how to prepare avocado

1. Cut the avocado in half lengthwise by cutting around the pit with a sharp knife. Twist the two sides away from each other to separate.

2. Using the knife, whack the seed; pull out the seed, which will be stuck on the knife.

3. After you've removed the seed, use the knife's tip to cut the flesh in horizontal and vertical rows. Don't cut through the skin. Remove the flesh gently with a spoon.

CARROT-CORIANDER SOUP WITH CILANTRO CREAM

POINTS value: 2

(pictured on page 131)

prep: 20 minutes • cook: 26 minutes

2	teaspoons olive oil
1	small onion, chopped
2	garlic cloves, minced
1	tablespoon plus ⅛ teaspoon ground coriander, divided
4	cups fat-free, less-sodium chicken broth
1	pound carrots, peeled and cut into 1-inch slices
2	tablespoons plus 1 teaspoon fresh lime juice, divided
⅛	teaspoon salt
¼	cup reduced-fat sour cream
1	tablespoon chopped fresh cilantro

1. Heat oil in a large saucepan over medium heat. Add onion and garlic; sauté 5 minutes. Stir in 1 tablespoon coriander. Add chicken broth and carrot; bring to a boil. Cover, reduce heat, and simmer 15 minutes or until carrot is tender. Let cool slightly.

2. Transfer mixture in batches to a blender or food processor, and process 1 minute or until very smooth. Stir in 2 tablespoons lime juice and salt. Set aside.

3. Combine sour cream, cilantro, remaining 1 teaspoon lime juice, and remaining ⅛ teaspoon coriander in a small bowl. Ladle soup into bowls, and top with sour cream mixture. YIELD: 4 servings (serving size: 1 cup soup and 1 tablespoon sour cream mixture).

Per serving: CAL 109 (36% from fat); FAT 4.3g (sat 1.5g); PRO 4.7g; CARB 14.4g; FIB 3.2g; CHOL 6mg; IRON 0.4mg; SOD 721mg; CALC 58mg

☑ GINGERED BUTTERNUT SQUASH AND APPLE SOUP

POINTS value: 1

prep: 17 minutes • cook: 47 minutes

Bring the flavors of fall to your table by combining apples and winter squash. A dollop of crème fraîche or sour cream is a great finish for this creamy soup.

1   (2-pound) butternut squash
1   tablespoon olive oil
1   cup minced onion
½   cup minced celery
½   teaspoon salt
¼   teaspoon freshly ground black pepper
1   tablespoon minced peeled fresh ginger
2   McIntosh apples, peeled, cored, and cut into 1-inch chunks (about 1 pound)
5   cups fat-free, less-sodium chicken broth
1   (3-inch) cinnamon stick
2   teaspoons fresh lemon juice

1. Pierce squash several times with the tip of a sharp knife. Microwave at HIGH 1 minute. Cut squash in half lengthwise; remove seeds and membrane with a spoon. Peel squash, and cut into 1-inch chunks.
2. Heat oil in a Dutch oven over medium heat. Add onion and next 3 ingredients; sauté 5 minutes. Add ginger, squash, and apple to pan; sauté 3 minutes. Add broth and cinnamon stick; bring to a boil. Cover, reduce heat, and simmer 30 minutes. Discard cinnamon stick.
3. Place half of soup in a blender, and process until smooth. Transfer to a large bowl. Repeat with remaining soup. Return soup to pan. Stir in lemon juice, and cook over low heat 2 minutes or until thoroughly heated, stirring frequently. YIELD: 9 servings (servings size: 1 cup).

Per serving: CAL 83 (18% from fat); FAT 1.7g (sat 0.3g); PRO 2.8g; CARB 16.3g; FIB 2.4g; CHOL 0mg; IRON 0.7mg; SOD 457mg; CALC 49mg

MOROCCAN BUTTERNUT SOUP

POINTS value: 2
(pictured on page 142)

prep: 7 minutes
cook: 1 hour and 3 minutes

Curry powder, cumin, and coriander give this creamy squash soup a warm exotic flavor that's characteristic of Moroccan dishes.

1   (2-pound) butternut squash
3   large garlic cloves, unpeeled
Cooking spray
1   teaspoon curry powder
½   teaspoon ground cumin
¼   teaspoon ground coriander
⅛   teaspoon ground red pepper
2½ cups fat-free, less-sodium chicken broth, divided
½   cup 1% low-fat milk
¼   teaspoon salt
5   tablespoons reduced-fat sour cream
Fresh chopped cilantro (optional)

1. Preheat oven to 375°.
2. Pierce squash several times with the tip of a sharp knife. Microwave at HIGH 1 minute. Cut squash in half lengthwise; remove seeds and membrane with a spoon. Place butternut squash, cut sides down, and garlic cloves in a 13 x 9–inch baking dish coated with cooking spray. Pierce squash multiple times with a fork. Bake at 375° for 1 hour or until squash is very tender.
3. While squash bakes, place curry powder and next 3 ingredients in a small nonstick skillet over medium heat; toast 1 minute or until fragrant. Set aside.
4. Peel cooked squash, and place in a food processor or blender. Remove and discard skins from garlic; add garlic to food processor. Add 1½ cups chicken broth, and process until smooth.
5. Transfer squash mixture to a large saucepan. Stir in remaining 1 cup broth, milk, salt, and toasted spices. Cook over low heat 2 minutes or until thoroughly heated, stirring frequently.
6. Ladle soup into bowls. Top with sour cream and, if desired, cilantro. YIELD: 5 servings (serving size: 1 cup soup and 1 tablespoon sour cream).

Per serving: CAL 113 (19% from fat); FAT 2.4g (sat 1.3g); PRO 4.7g; CARB 21.3g; FIB 3.3g; CHOL 7mg; IRON 1.3mg; SOD 430mg; CALC 131mg

test kitchen tip

Winter squash such as acorn, butternut, and spaghetti are difficult to cut in half. Try microwaving the whole squash 1 minute at HIGH to make cutting easier.

☑ WHITE BEAN SOUP WITH KALE AND WINTER SQUASH

POINTS value: 1

prep: 30 minutes • cook: 36 minutes

This is the quintessential healthy soup. It's chock-full of antioxidants and fiber from colorful veggies, beans, and dark leafy greens. If you're on a reduced-sodium diet, omit the salt for a sodium value of 391 milligrams. You can freeze this soup in an airtight container for up to 1 month.

1   pound kale
2   teaspoons olive oil
1   cup chopped onion
      (1 medium)
½   cup chopped celery
      (1 large stalk)
2   garlic cloves, minced
6   cups fat-free, less-sodium
      chicken broth
3¼ cups peeled, seeded, and
      chopped butternut squash
      (1 small)
1   cup chopped carrot (2 large)
⅓   cup no-salt-added tomato paste
½   teaspoon salt
½   teaspoon dried thyme leaves
1   (15.5-ounce) can cannellini
      beans, rinsed and drained
1   (14.5-ounce) can no-salt-added
      diced tomatoes, undrained
¼   teaspoon freshly ground black
      pepper

1. Remove and discard stems from kale. Coarsely chop leaves to equal 6 cups, reserving any remaining kale for another use. Wash chopped kale thoroughly in cold water. Drain well, and set aside.
2. Heat olive oil in a large Dutch oven over medium-high heat. Add onion, celery, and garlic; sauté 5 minutes or until vegetables begin to soften. Add chopped kale, broth, and next 7 ingredients. Bring to a boil. Cover, reduce heat, and simmer 25 minutes or until vegetables are tender. Stir in pepper. YIELD: 11 servings (serving size: 1 cup).

Per serving: CAL 107 (11% from fat); FAT 1.3g (sat 0.2g); PRO 5.1g; CARB 21.2g; FIB 4.5g; CHOL 0mg; IRON 1.8mg; SOD 499mg; CALC 96mg

☑ TWO-BEAN SOUP

POINTS value: 2

prep: 5 minutes • cook: 26 minutes

This "from-the-pantry" soup gets its hot and spicy Tex-Mex flavor from taco seasoning, green chiles, and cilantro.

Cooking spray
1½ cups frozen vegetable seasoning
      blend (such as McKenzie's)
2   tablespoons 40%-less-sodium
      taco seasoning
1   cup fat-free, less-sodium beef
      broth
1   (16-ounce) can pinto beans,
      rinsed and drained
1   (15-ounce) can black beans,
      rinsed and drained
1   (14½-ounce) can diced
      tomatoes and green chiles,
      undrained
⅛   teaspoon hot sauce
4   teaspoons fat-free sour cream
¼   cup chopped fresh cilantro

1. Heat a large saucepan over medium-high heat. Coat pan with cooking spray, and add vegetable seasoning blend; cook 5 minutes or until tender. Stir in taco seasoning; cook 1 minute, stirring constantly.
2. Add broth and next 4 ingredients; bring to a boil. Cover, reduce heat, and simmer 15 minutes, stirring occasionally. Ladle into bowls, and top with sour cream and cilantro. YIELD: 4 servings (serving size: 1¼ cups soup, 1 teaspoon sour cream, and 1 tablespoon cilantro).

Per serving: CAL 145 (0% from fat); FAT 0g (sat 0g); PRO 7g; CARB 26.7g; FIB 7.6g; CHOL 1mg; IRON 2.1mg; SOD 744mg; CALC 63mg

SPICY VEGETARIAN BLACK BEAN SOUP

POINTS value: 2

prep: 5 minutes • cook: 15 minutes

Although it only simmers for 10 minutes, this spicy meatless soup boasts the big flavor that usually comes from a long simmer on the stovetop.

2   (15-ounce) cans black beans,
      rinsed and drained
1   (16-ounce) package frozen
      pepper stir-fry, slightly thawed
1   (12-ounce) package frozen
      meatless burger crumbles (such
      as Morningstar Farms or Boca)
1   (16-ounce) bottle chunky salsa
1   (14-ounce) can organic
      vegetable broth (such as
      Swanson Certified Organic)
2   teaspoons salt-free Mexican
      seasoning
½   cup (2 ounces) shredded 50%
      reduced-fat Cheddar cheese
      with jalapeño peppers (such as
      Cabot)

1. Mash half of beans with a fork. Combine mashed beans and remaining beans in a Dutch oven. Add pepper stir-fry and next 4 ingredients; bring to a boil. Reduce heat, and simmer, uncovered, 10 minutes. Ladle soup into bowls; top with cheese. YIELD: 8 servings (serving size: 1 cup soup and 1 tablespoon cheese).

Per serving: CAL 117 (14% from fat); FAT 1.8g (sat 0.8g); PRO 13.5g; CARB 16.2g; FIB 5.3g; CHOL 4mg; IRON 2mg; SOD 803mg; CALC 111mg

ITALIAN PASTA-BEAN STEW

POINTS value: 5

prep: 14 minutes • cook: 41 minutes
other: 2 minutes

1   teaspoon extravirgin olive oil
1½ cups chopped green bell pepper
1   cup chopped onion
1   medium zucchini, sliced
⅛   teaspoon crushed red pepper
1   (14.5-ounce) can stewed tomatoes, undrained
1   (14-ounce) can fat-free, less-sodium chicken broth
3   ounces uncooked multigrain rotini (such as Barilla Plus)
1   (15-ounce) can navy beans, rinsed and drained
1   cup packed fresh spinach
2   tablespoons chopped fresh basil
2   teaspoons red wine vinegar
⅛   teaspoon salt
¼   cup (1 ounce) grated Asiago cheese

1. Heat oil in a large Dutch oven over medium-high heat. Add bell pepper and next 3 ingredients; sauté 5 minutes or until tender. Add tomatoes and broth. Bring to a boil; cover, reduce heat, and simmer 20 minutes.
2. Using a fork, break up larger pieces of tomato. Add pasta; cover and cook 12 minutes or until pasta is done. Remove from heat.
3. Add beans and next 4 ingredients; cover and let stand 2 minutes or until spinach wilts. Ladle into bowls, and top with Asiago cheese. YIELD: 4 servings (serving size: 1½ cups stew and 1 tablespoon cheese).

Per serving: CAL 258 (14% from fat); FAT 4.1g (sat 1.5g); PRO 14.9g; CARB 43.3g; FIB 7.9g; CHOL 6mg; IRON 4.1mg; SOD 818mg; CALC 172mg

☑ MUSHROOM-BARLEY SOUP

POINTS value: 2

prep: 12 minutes • cook: 55 minutes
other: 10 minutes

The combination of barley and two types of mushrooms gives this soup a rich, earthy flavor.

1½ cups boiling water
1   ounce dried shiitake mushrooms (about ⅔ cup)
1   tablespoon olive oil
2   cups finely chopped onion (about 1 medium)
1   (12-ounce) package presliced button mushrooms
½   teaspoon salt
½   teaspoon freshly ground black pepper
½   cup uncooked pearl barley
2   garlic cloves, minced
5½ cups fat-free, less-sodium chicken broth
3   tablespoons minced fresh chives

1. Pour boiling water over shiitake mushrooms; let stand 10 minutes. Drain shiitake mushrooms, reserving liquid. Remove and discard stems, and slice shiitake mushrooms. Set shiitake mushrooms aside.
2. Heat oil in a Dutch oven over medium heat 1 minute. Add onion; cook 9 minutes, stirring often. Add button mushrooms, salt, and pepper. Cook 5 minutes, stirring often. Add barley, garlic, and shiitake mushrooms. Cook 2 minutes, stirring constantly. Add chicken broth and reserved mushroom soaking liquid, discarding sediment, if necessary. Cover and bring to a boil. Reduce heat to medium-low; simmer 30 minutes or until barley is tender. Sprinkle with chives. YIELD: 8 servings (serving size 1 cup).

Per serving: CAL 108 (17% from fat); FAT 2g (sat 0.3g); PRO 5.2g; CARB 19.3g; FIB 3.3g; CHOL 0mg; IRON 0.7mg; SOD 545mg; CALC 23mg

shiitake mushrooms

Shiitakes are Asian mushrooms that boast a strong smoky flavor. When dried, these mushrooms have a chewier texture and an even more intense flavor. The dried stems are too tough to be eaten, but they can be used to add wonderful flavor to stocks and broths. After rehydrating dried shiitake mushrooms, be sure to discard the stems and any sediment that may settle in the bottom of your dish before using the broth.

TURKEY CHOWDER

POINTS value: 4

prep: 10 minutes • cook: 34 minutes

Deli-style turkey makes the soup too salty, so we suggest using leftover roasted turkey or baking your own. Start with about ⅔ pound of turkey tenderloins and bake them at 350° for 22 minutes to get 2 cups of diced cooked turkey.

1 tablespoon olive oil
1 cup thinly sliced celery
¾ cup chopped onion (1 small)
2 garlic cloves, minced
1 (10-ounce) package frozen whole-kernel corn, thawed
½ teaspoon freshly ground black pepper
¼ teaspoon salt
¼ cup all-purpose flour
4 cups fat-free, less-sodium chicken broth
1 tablespoon minced fresh thyme
2 cups diced cooked turkey breast
1 cup 1% low-fat milk
1 tablespoon fresh lemon juice
⅓ cup reduced-fat sour cream
3 tablespoons minced fresh parsley (optional)

1. Heat oil in a Dutch oven over medium heat. Add celery, onion, and garlic. Sauté 3 minutes. Add corn, pepper, and salt. Sauté 1 minute. Lightly spoon flour into a dry measuring cup; level with a knife. Add flour to pan; cook 1 minute, stirring constantly. Stir in chicken broth and thyme; bring to a boil. Cover, reduce heat, and simmer 20 minutes, stirring occasionally.

2. Add turkey, milk, and lemon juice to pan, stirring well. Cook 3 minutes or until thoroughly heated. Remove from heat, and stir in sour cream. Sprinkle with parsley, if desired. **YIELD:** 8 servings (serving size: 1 cup).

Per serving: CAL 171 (34% from fat); FAT 6.5g (sat 2.1g); PRO 14.5g; CARB 14.6g; FIB 1.5g; CHOL 32mg; IRON 1mg; SOD 415mg; CALC 68mg

CORN AND SALMON CHOWDER

POINTS value: 4

prep: 13 minutes • cook: 37 minutes

Canned sockeye salmon has a brighter color and a deeper flavor than pink salmon. We've found that rinsing the salmon after draining it freshens its flavor.

1 teaspoon olive oil
½ cup diced celery
½ cup diced onion
3 cups fat-free, less-sodium chicken broth
1 baking potato, peeled and diced
1 cup frozen whole-kernel corn
¼ teaspoon dried dill
2½ tablespoons all-purpose flour
1 cup 1% low-fat milk
1 (14¾-ounce) can boneless, skinless sockeye red salmon in water, rinsed and drained
1 tablespoon dry white wine
½ teaspoon freshly ground black pepper
¼ teaspoon salt

1. Heat oil in a large saucepan over medium-high heat; add celery and onion. Sauté 3 to 4 minutes or until tender. Add chicken broth and potato;

bring to a boil. Cover, reduce heat, and simmer 15 minutes or until potato is tender. Stir in corn and dill.
2. Combine flour and milk, stirring with a whisk. Add flour mixture to potato mixture. Bring to a boil; cover, reduce heat, and simmer 10 minutes or until thickened. Stir in salmon and remaining ingredients. Cook 3 minutes or until thoroughly heated. **YIELD:** 6 servings (serving size: 1 cup).

Per serving: CAL 202 (25% from fat); FAT 5.7g (sat 1.4g); PRO 16.9g; CARB 21.6g; FIB 2g; CHOL 27mg; IRON 1.2mg; SOD 723mg; CALC 206mg

SMOKY BACON-CLAM CHOWDER

POINTS value: 4

prep: 5 minutes • cook: 36 minutes

Fresh clams and smoky bacon give this New England–style chowder a savory, rich flavor.

3 slices reduced-fat center-cut bacon
½ cup chopped onion
2 cups refrigerated diced potato with onions (such as Simply Potatoes)
⅓ cup flour
1 (8-ounce) bottle clam juice
4 cups 1% low-fat milk
1 (16-ounce) container fresh shucked chopped clams, undrained
3 tablespoons chopped fresh parsley
½ teaspoon freshly ground black pepper
¼ teaspoon salt

1. Cook bacon in a large Dutch oven over medium heat 6 minutes or until crisp. Drain bacon on a paper towel, and crumble.

2. Add onion to pan, and sauté 3 minutes. Add potato; sauté 2 minutes or until lightly browned. Lightly spoon flour into a dry measuring cup; level with a knife. Stir flour into potato mixture, and cook 1 minute. Add clam juice, and stir well. Stir in milk; cook over medium-low heat 11 minutes or until thick and bubbly. Cover, reduce heat, and simmer 11 minutes or until potato is tender.

3. Drain clams, reserving 2 cups liquid. Stir in clams and reserved clam liquid, and cook 2 minutes or until thoroughly heated. Stir in parsley, pepper, and salt. Ladle into bowls; top with crumbled bacon. YIELD: 8 cups (servings size: 1 cup).

Per serving: CAL 172 (19% from fat); FAT 3.6g (sat 1.6g); PRO 15.6g; CARB 20g; FIB 1.1g; CHOL 53mg; IRON 15mg; SOD 612mg; CALC 227mg

cellophane noodles

Translucent cellophane noodles are known by a variety of names, including bean threads, Chinese vermicelli, glass noodles, and *bai fun*. Unlike most "pastas," cellophane noodles are made from the starch of mung beans rather than wheat. Instead of boiling, soak them briefly in warm water before serving.

HOT AND SOUR HALIBUT SOUP POT

POINTS value: 7

prep: 5 minutes • cook: 14 minutes
other: 12 minutes

The lime wedges are more than just a garnish for this soup. The lime juice adds a brightness that accentuates the other Asian flavors.

1   (3.75-ounce) package bean threads (cellophane noodles)
2   tablespoons low-sodium soy sauce
4   (6-ounce) skinless halibut fillets (about 1½ inches thick)
3   cups fat-free, less-sodium chicken broth
2½ tablespoons ketchup
2   tablespoons cider vinegar
2   teaspoons sugar
¼   teaspoon ground red pepper
1   (½-inch) piece peeled fresh ginger, thinly sliced
¾   cup diced carrot (about 2 large)
¼   cup thinly sliced green onions
¼   cup chopped fresh cilantro
4   teaspoons sesame seeds, toasted
4   lime wedges

1. Soak bean threads in warm water 10 minutes; drain.

2. Drizzle soy sauce over fish, and set aside.

3. Combine broth and next 5 ingredients in a deep 12-inch skillet. Bring to a simmer over medium heat, stirring until sugar melts. Add carrot; cover and simmer 5 minutes.

4. Add fish; cover, reduce heat to low, and simmer 5 minutes or until fish is firm and centers of fillets are almost opaque (fish should not be

completely cooked). Remove from heat; let stand, covered, 2 minutes to allow fish to finish cooking.

5. To serve, divide bean threads among shallow bowls. Place fish over bean threads; ladle soup over fish. Sprinkle with green onions, cilantro, and sesame seeds. Serve immediately with lime wedges. YIELD: 4 servings (serving size: ¾ cup bean threads, 1 fillet, ¾ cup soup, 1 tablespoon green onions, 1 tablespoon cilantro, 1 teaspoon sesame seeds, and 1 lime wedge).

Per serving: CAL 352 (14% from fat); FAT 5.5g (sat 0.6g); PRO 39.1g; CARB 33.5g; FIB 1.3g; CHOL 54mg; IRON 6.7mg; SOD 913mg; CALC 106mg

soup serving suggestions

■ To keep the soup from cooling too quickly, rinse the serving bowls with hot water just before ladling. For chilled soups, place the empty bowls in the refrigerator about 30 minutes before filling.

■ Use simple garnishes, such as fresh herbs; lemon or lime wedges; or grated, shredded, or shaved cheeses. Sometimes the ingredients used in the recipe can be used to garnish the soup as well as enhance the flavor and texture.

■ For cream or pureed soups, garnish with whole, thinly sliced, or chopped vegetables.

■ For stews served with rice or pasta, mound the rice or pasta in the center of a bowl, and ladle the stew around it, taking care not to completely cover the rice or pasta.

☑ BEEFY VEGETABLE SOUP

POINTS value: 5

prep: 7 minutes • cook: 44 minutes

When the weather turns cold and blustery, there's nothing more cozy than a bowl of steaming vegetable soup—especially one that takes only 7 minutes to assemble. You can chop the tomatoes directly in the can with kitchen shears.

1   pound ground sirloin
1   cup chopped green bell pepper
     (about 1 medium)
2   (14.5-ounce) cans Mexican-
     style stewed tomatoes with
     jalapeño peppers and spices,
     undrained and chopped
1   (8-ounce) can no-salt-added
     tomato sauce
¾   cup fat-free, less-sodium beef
     broth
1   (16-ounce) package frozen
     soup vegetables
⅛   teaspoon salt

1. Combine beef and bell pepper in a large Dutch oven; cook over medium-high heat until beef is browned, stirring to crumble beef. Drain, if necessary.
2. Add tomatoes, tomato sauce, and broth to pan; bring to a boil. Add vegetables and salt; cover, reduce heat, and simmer 30 minutes or until vegetables are tender. **YIELD:** 6 servings (serving size: 1½ cups).

Per serving: CAL 237 (30% from fat); FAT 7.8g; (sat 3.1g); PRO 19.3g; CARB 23.3g; FIB 6.4g; CHOL 49mg; IRON 3.1mg; SOD 620mg; CALC 57mg

HEARTY RED WINE AND BEEF STEW

POINTS value: 7

prep: 22 minutes
cook: 2 hours and 27 minutes

Roasted red bell peppers, mushrooms, and red wine give traditional beef stew a sophisticated slant. We recommend using cabernet sauvignon or merlot in this recipe. Serve over pasta, couscous, polenta, or rice.

1½   pounds top sirloin steak,
     trimmed and cut into 1-inch
     cubes
½   teaspoon salt, divided
¼   teaspoon black pepper
¼   cup all-purpose flour
6   teaspoons olive oil, divided
2   carrots, chopped
1   cup chopped onion
4   garlic cloves, minced
1   (8-ounce) package mushrooms,
     quartered
1   tablespoon no-salt-added
     tomato paste
1   (12-ounce) jar roasted red bell
     peppers, drained and chopped
1   cup water
¾   cup dry red wine
½   cup less-sodium beef broth

1. Sprinkle beef with ¼ teaspoon salt and black pepper. Place beef and flour in a large zip-top plastic bag; seal and shake to coat. Heat 2 teaspoons oil in a large Dutch oven over medium-high heat. Add half of beef; cook 5 minutes or until browned, stirring frequently. Repeat with 2 teaspoons oil and remaining beef. Remove from pan; set aside.
2. Add remaining 2 teaspoons oil to

pan. Add carrot, onion, and garlic; cook 5 minutes, stirring occasionally. Add mushrooms; cook 5 minutes, stirring occasionally. Stir in tomato paste; cook 1 minute. Add beef, remaining ¼ teaspoon salt, bell pepper, and remaining ingredients to pan; bring to a boil. Cover, reduce heat to low, and simmer 2 hours. **YIELD:** 6 cups (serving size: 1 cup).

Per serving: CAL 312 (27% from fat); FAT 9.4g (sat 2.4g); PRO 29.6g; CARB 21.3g; FIB 1.7g; CHOL 48mg; IRON 3mg; SOD 865mg; CALC 71mg

AFRICAN LAMB AND PEANUT STEW

POINTS value: 6

prep: 14 minutes • cook: 1 hour

2   teaspoons canola oil
Cooking spray
¾   pound boneless leg of lamb,
     trimmed and cut into 1-inch
     cubes
2   teaspoons garam masala
1   large onion, thinly sliced
2   garlic cloves, minced
2   tablespoons tomato paste
2   cups water, divided
2   cups chopped tomato
½   cup sliced carrot
2   small sweet potatoes, peeled
     and cut into 1-inch cubes
1½   cups frozen cut okra
¼   cup natural-style chunky
     peanut butter
1   jalapeño pepper, finely chopped
1½   teaspoons salt
¼   teaspoon freshly ground black
     pepper
1   (10-ounce) package couscous

1. Heat oil in a medium Dutch oven coated with cooking spray over medium-high heat. Add lamb, and cook 8 to 10 minutes or until browned, stirring frequently. Add garam masala, onion, and garlic; cook 3 to 4 minutes or until onion is tender, stirring frequently.

2. Combine tomato paste and 1 cup water in a small bowl. Add tomato paste mixture and tomato to Dutch oven. Stir in remaining 1 cup water; bring mixture to a boil over medium-high heat. Add carrot and sweet potato; cover, reduce heat, and simmer 25 minutes or until vegetables are tender. Add okra; cook 5 minutes.

3. Remove ¼ cup cooking liquid from pan; place in a small bowl. Add peanut butter, and stir with a whisk. Add peanut butter mixture to pan; stir in jalapeño pepper, salt, and black pepper. Cook over medium-low heat 15 minutes or until thickened.

4. While stew simmers, prepare couscous according to package directions, omitting salt and fat. Serve stew over hot cooked couscous. YIELD: 8 servings

garam masala

If you can't find a garam masala spice blend at your supermarket, you can make your own. Combine 3 tablespoons cumin seeds, 2 tablespoons coriander seeds, 1 tablespoon black peppercorns, 8 cardamom pods, and 6 whole cloves in a spice or coffee grinder; process until finely ground. Store in an airtight container for up to two weeks.

(serving size: about ⅔ cup couscous and 1 cup stew).

Per serving: CAL 309 (20% from fat); FAT 6.8g (sat 1.4g); PRO 17.2g; CARB 44.8g; FIB 5g; CHOL 28mg; IRON 2.1mg; SOD 543mg; CALC 70mg

VIETNAMESE PORK–RICE NOODLE SOUP

POINTS value: 7

prep: 13 minutes • cook: 36 minutes
other: 20 minutes

Aromatic star anise, fish sauce, and a Thai chile infuse the broth with an intense flavor. When you slice the pork, hold the knife at a slant and cut the pork diagonally into very thin pieces—the meat will be more tender and will cook more quickly.

8	ounces flat rice stick noodles (banh pho)
1	pound pork tenderloin, trimmed
1	tablespoon dark sesame oil divided
⅛	teaspoon ground red pepper
2	garlic cloves, minced
1	(1-inch) piece peeled fresh ginger, thinly sliced
½	medium onion, sliced
4	cups less-sodium beef broth
2	cups water
2	whole star anise
1	(3-inch) cinnamon stick
1½	tablespoons fish sauce
1	small red Thai chile, seeded
1¼	cups fresh bean sprouts
½	cup fresh basil leaves, coarsely chopped
10	lime wedges

1. Place noodles in a large bowl. Add boiling water to cover; let stand 20 minutes. Drain.

2. While noodles soak, cut tenderloin in half lengthwise. Cut each strip into thin slices. Heat 2 teaspoons oil in a Dutch oven over medium-high heat. Add pork, red pepper, and garlic; sauté 3 to 4 minutes on each side or until pork is lightly browned. Remove pork mixture from pan, and set aside.

3. Heat remaining 1 teaspoon oil in pan over medium-high heat. Add ginger and onion; sauté 3 minutes or until onion is tender. Add broth and next 5 ingredients; bring to a boil. Reduce heat, and simmer, uncovered, 15 minutes or until liquid is reduced by one-third to about 3¾ cups. Strain broth through a metal sieve into a large bowl; discard solids. Keep broth warm.

4. Divide bean sprouts among bowls; top with noodles. Place pork evenly over noodles. Ladle broth over pork; top evenly with basil. Squeeze 1 lime wedge over each serving. Serve with remaining lime wedges. YIELD: 5 servings (serving size: ¼ cup bean sprouts, 1 cup noodles, about 3 ounces pork, ¾ cup broth, and about 1½ tablespoons basil).

Per serving: CAL 351 (21% from fat); FAT 8g (sat 2.2g); PRO 23.2g; CARB 45g; FIB 1.6g; CHOL 60mg; IRON 1.9mg; SOD 899mg; CALC 31mg

Holiday Brunch

Serves 8 • Total **POINTS** value: 14

Cranberry-Orange Spritzers • **English Muffin Breakfast Strata**
Creamy Cheese Grits • **Spiced Pumpkin Bread** • **Spirited Fruit Salad**

▶▶ GAME PLAN

1. One day in advance, prepare **English Muffin Breakfast Strata.** Cover and chill.

2. One day in advance, prepare and bake **Spiced Pumpkin Bread.** Cool and store in an airtight container.

3. One hour before the meal, preheat oven to 350°. Prepare **Spirited Fruit Salad.** Cover and chill.

4. Combine juices for **Cranberry-Orange Spritzers;** cover and chill.

5. Bake strata. Halfway through the baking time for the strata, prepare **Creamy Cheese Grits.**

6. Sprinkle **Spirited Fruit Salad** with toasted coconut. Add lemon-lime beverage to spritzers just before serving.

ENGLISH MUFFIN BREAKFAST STRATA

POINTS value: 8

prep: 6 minutes • cook: 55 minutes • other: 8 hours and 10 minutes

A strata is ideal for holiday entertaining because you can make the dish a day in advance. On the morning of the brunch, all you'll have to do is put it in the oven.

Cooking spray
1   (16-ounce) package turkey breakfast sausage
¾   cup chopped green bell pepper
¾   cup bottled roasted red bell pepper, drained
½   cup chopped onion
1   (13-ounce) package whole wheat English muffins, split and toasted
2   cups (8 ounces) reduced-fat shredded sharp Cheddar cheese, divided
4   large eggs
4   large egg whites
1½ cups 1% low-fat milk
1   teaspoon dry mustard
¼   teaspoon ground red pepper

1. Heat a large nonstick skillet over medium-high heat. Coat pan with cooking spray. Add sausage and next 3 ingredients; sauté 9 minutes or until sausage is browned and vegetables are tender. Drain and set aside.

2. Cut muffin halves into quarters, and arrange in an 11 x 7–inch baking dish coated with cooking spray. Sprinkle half of sausage mixture and 1 cup cheese over muffins.

3. Combine eggs, egg whites, and next 3 ingredients in a large bowl; stir well with a whisk. Pour evenly over mixture in baking dish. Top with remaining sausage mixture and remaining 1 cup cheese. Cover and chill at least 8 hours.

4. Preheat oven to 350°.

5. Bake, uncovered, at 350° for 45 minutes. Let stand 10 minutes before serving. YIELD: 8 servings (serving size: ⅛ of strata).

Per serving: CAL 356 (38% from fat); FAT 14.9g (sat 7.2g); PRO 28.4g; CARB 24.5g; FIB 2.7g; CHOL 172mg; IRON 2.6mg; SOD 900mg; CALC 363mg

CRANBERRY-ORANGE SPRITZERS

POINTS value: 1

prep: 2 minutes

Begin the brunch with this tangy sparkling beverage and a toast to good times and good friends.

4½ cups reduced-calorie cranberry juice cocktail, chilled
3 tablespoons orange juice
3½ cups lemon-lime carbonated beverage (such as Sprite Zero), chilled

1. Combine juices in a large pitcher. Cover and chill. Stir in lemon-lime beverage just before serving. Serve over crushed ice. YIELD: 8 servings (serving size: 1 cup).

Per serving: CAL 29 (0% from fat); FAT 0g (sat 0g); PRO 0.1g; CARB 6.7g; FIB 0g; CHOL 0mg; IRON 0.1mg; SOD 4mg; CALC 13mg

SPIRITED FRUIT SALAD

POINTS value: 1

prep: 21 minutes • cook: 6 minutes

Brighten up your table with this colorful rum-splashed version of classic holiday ambrosia.

3 ruby red grapefruit
2 cups halved strawberries (about 7 large)
3 kiwifruit, peeled and cut into wedges
3 tablespoons light brown sugar
3 tablespoons dark rum
¼ cup flaked sweetened coconut, toasted

1. Peel and section grapefruit over a bowl; discard membranes.
2. Combine grapefruit sections, strawberries, and kiwifruit in bowl.
3. Combine brown sugar and rum in a small bowl, stirring well. Add rum mixture to fruit, tossing gently to combine. Cover and chill until ready to serve. Sprinkle with toasted coconut. YIELD: 8 servings (serving size: ¾ cup).

Per serving: CAL 89 (10% from fat); FAT 1g (sat 0.7g); PRO 1.1g; CARB 17.6g; FIB 2.3g; CHOL 0mg; IRON 0.4mg; SOD 8.3mg; CALC 27mg

CREAMY CHEESE GRITS

POINTS value: 2

prep: 5 minutes • cook: 23 minutes

2½ cups fat-free, less-sodium chicken broth
1⅓ cups water
1 cup uncooked stone-ground yellow grits
1 garlic clove, pressed
⅓ cup (1.3 ounces) reduced-fat shredded sharp Cheddar cheese
⅓ cup (2.6 ounces) ⅓-less-fat cream cheese

1. Combine first 4 ingredients in a 4-quart saucepan. Bring to a boil; partially cover, reduce heat, and simmer 19 minutes or until thick, stirring occasionally.
2. Add cheeses to pan, stirring until cheeses melt. YIELD: 8 servings (serving size: ½ cup).

Per serving: CAL 110 (25% from fat); FAT 3.1g (sat 2.1g); PRO 4.7g; CARB 15.8g; FIB 0.5g; CHOL 10mg; IRON 0.2mg; SOD 262mg; CALC 41mg

SPICED PUMPKIN BREAD

POINTS value: 2

prep: 6 minutes • cook: 45 minutes

The "batter" for this moist bread is the consistency of a soft dough. You'll need to stir a little more than for most quick breads to make sure all the flour is moistened.

1½ cups all-purpose flour
1 teaspoon baking soda
½ teaspoon baking powder
½ teaspoon ground cinnamon
¼ teaspoon salt
⅛ teaspoon ground cloves
⅛ teaspoon ground nutmeg
1 cup canned pumpkin
¾ cup sugar
3 tablespoons canola oil
1 large egg, lightly beaten
Cooking spray

1. Preheat oven to 350°.
2. Lightly spoon flour into dry measuring cups; level with a knife. Combine flour and next 6 ingredients in a large bowl; make a well in center of mixture. Combine pumpkin, sugar, oil, and egg in a medium bowl; stir with a whisk until well blended. Add to flour mixture, stirring just until moist. Turn batter into an 8 x 4–inch loaf pan coated with cooking spray.
3. Bake at 350° for 45 minutes or until a wooden pick inserted in center comes out clean. Remove from pan; cool completely on a wire rack. YIELD: 16 servings (serving size: 1 slice).

Per serving: CAL 112 (25% from fat); FAT 3.1g (sat 0.3g); PRO 1.8g; CARB 19.7g; FIB 0.8g; CHOL 13mg; IRON 0.8mg; SOD 133mg; CALC 16mg

Casual Patio Gathering

Serves 4 • Total **POINTS** value: 13

Cilantro-Lemon Grilled Chicken • Grilled Polenta with Fresh Tomato Salad
Asparagus Gremolata • Grilled Peaches with Honeyed Yogurt

▶▶ GAME PLAN

1. One day in advance, prepare Step 1 of **Cilantro-Lemon Grilled Chicken.**

2. About 1 hour before the meal, prepare Step 1 of **Grilled Peaches with Honeyed Yogurt.**

3. Prepare Steps 2 and 3 of **Grilled Peaches with Honeyed Yogurt,** and let oat mixture cool on parchment paper.

4. Preheat grill. Prepare Step 2 of **Grilled Polenta with Fresh Tomato Salad** and **Asparagus Gremolata.**

5. Place chicken and polenta on grill first. Grill asparagus and peaches after chicken and polenta are done.

6. Assemble **Grilled Peaches with Honeyed Yogurt** just before serving.

☑ CILANTRO-LEMON GRILLED CHICKEN

POINTS value: 5

prep: 10 minutes • cook: 12 minutes • other: 8 hours

Marinating the chicken overnight infuses it with the tangy flavor of the citrus-yogurt marinade.

⅓   cup plain fat-free yogurt
¼   cup chopped fresh cilantro
3   garlic cloves, minced
1   tablespoon olive oil
1   teaspoon grated fresh lemon rind
2   teaspoons fresh lemon juice
4   (6-ounce) skinless, boneless chicken breast halves
½   teaspoon salt
¼   teaspoon black pepper
⅛   teaspoon ground cumin
Cooking spray

1. Combine first 6 ingredients in a large zip-top plastic bag; add chicken, and seal. Marinate in refrigerator at least 8 hours or overnight, turning bag occasionally.
2. Preheat grill.
3. Remove chicken from bag; discard marinade. Sprinkle chicken evenly with salt, pepper, and cumin. Place chicken on grill rack coated with cooking spray; grill 6 minutes on each side or until done. YIELD: 4 servings (serving size: 1 chicken breast half).

Per serving: CAL 211 (27% from fat); FAT 6.3g (sat 1.5g); PRO 35g; CARB 1.6g; FIB 0.1g; CHOL 95mg; IRON 1.2mg; SOD 385mg; CALC 42mg

Core Plan® option

This menu is easy to adapt if you or one of your guests is following the Core Plan.

Simply omit the polenta and feta cheese from the **Grilled Polenta with Fresh Tomato Salad,** and double the remaining ingredients. The yield will be about 2 cups **Fresh Tomato Salad** or 4 (½-cup) servings. Serve sweet, juicy peaches by themselves for dessert.

GRILLED POLENTA WITH FRESH TOMATO SALAD

POINTS value: 3

prep: 9 minutes • cook: 14 minutes

Look for precooked polenta in the produce section of the supermarket. To get the polenta slices nicely browned, grill over medium-high heat.

1   tablespoon olive oil
2   teaspoons balsamic vinegar
¼   teaspoon salt
⅛   teaspoon black pepper
½   cup diced tomato
¼   cup diced red onion
¼   cup diced English cucumber
1   tablespoon chopped pitted
    kalamata olives
1   (16-ounce) tube of polenta, cut
    into 12 (½-inch-thick) slices
Cooking spray
¼   cup (1 ounce) crumbled feta
    cheese

1. Prepare grill.
2. Combine first 4 ingredients in a medium bowl, stirring with a whisk. Add tomato and next 3 ingredients, and toss gently.
3. Coat polenta slices with cooking spray. Place slices on grill rack coated with cooking spray; grill 7 to 8 minutes on each side or until lightly browned. Top polenta evenly with tomato mixture and feta cheese. YIELD: 4 servings (serving size: 3 slices polenta, ¼ cup tomato mixture, and 1 tablespoon cheese).

Per serving: CAL 146 (34% from fat); FAT 5.5g (sat 1.6g); PRO 3.4g; CARB 19g; FIB 2.5g; CHOL 6mg; IRON 0.9mg; SOD 460mg; CALC 42mg

☑ ASPARAGUS GREMOLATA

POINTS value: 1

prep: 4 minutes • cook: 6 minutes

Because asparagus spears don't really have "sides," simply roll them around with tongs while grilling to guarantee even cooking.

1   tablespoon olive oil, divided
1   tablespoon chopped fresh
    flat-leaf parsley
½   teaspoon grated fresh lemon
    rind
2   teaspoons fresh lemon juice
½   teaspoon minced garlic
1   pound asparagus, trimmed
Cooking spray
¼   teaspoon salt
⅛   teaspoon black pepper

1. Prepare grill.
2. Combine 2 teaspoons olive oil and next 4 ingredients in a small bowl; stir well with a whisk, and set aside.
3. Drizzle remaining 1 teaspoon olive oil over asparagus. Place asparagus on grill rack coated with cooking spray; grill 6 minutes or until crisp-tender. Place asparagus on a serving platter, and sprinkle evenly with salt and pepper. Drizzle lemon-parsley mixture over asparagus. YIELD: 4 servings (serving size: about 5 spears).

Per serving: CAL 45 (72% from fat); FAT 3.6g (sat 0.5g); PRO 1.4g; CARB 2.8g; FIB 1.3g; CHOL 0mg; IRON 1.4mg; SOD 149mg; CALC 16mg

GRILLED PEACHES WITH HONEYED YOGURT

POINTS value: 4

prep: 3 minutes • cook: 12 minutes
other: 10 minutes

½   cup plain low-fat yogurt
1   tablespoon honey
½   teaspoon vanilla extract
2   tablespoons brown sugar
1½ tablespoons butter
½   teaspoon ground cinnamon
2   large unpeeled ripe peaches,
    halved and pitted
¼   cup regular oats
2   tablespoons chopped walnuts,
    toasted

1. Combine yogurt, honey, and vanilla in a bowl; cover and chill.
2. Combine brown sugar, butter, and cinnamon in a large skillet; cook over medium heat until butter melts, stirring constantly. Remove from heat, and dip peach halves in mixture; set peach halves aside.
3. Return pan with butter mixture to heat; cook over medium-low heat 1 minute or until syrupy and bubbly, stirring often. Remove from heat; stir in oats. Spread mixture onto parchment paper, and cool 10 to 15 minutes. Break into pieces.
4. Prepare grill.
5. Place peach halves on grill rack; grill, cut sides down, 2 minutes. Turn and grill 3 minutes or until tender. Place peach halves on plates; top evenly with yogurt mixture, oat mixture, and walnuts. YIELD: 4 servings (serving size: 1 stuffed peach half).

Per serving: CAL 165 (41% from fat); FAT 7.5g (sat 3.2g); PRO 4.1g; CARB 22.5g; FIB 2g; CHOL 13mg; IRON 0.8mg; SOD 54mg; CALC 75mg

Italian-Style Dinner

Serves 6 • Total **POINTS** value: 11 to 16

Chicken, Artichoke, and Mushroom Fettuccine • **Spinach Salad with Pears and Walnuts** • **Caramelized Onion and Rosemary Focaccia**
Fudgy Chocolate-Cherry Bites *(page 47)* *or* **Layered Amaretti–Ice Cream Loaf**

▶▶ GAME PLAN

1. Up to 1 week ahead, prepare **Layered Amaretti–Ice Cream Loaf**. Cover and freeze. Or prepare **Fudgy Chocolate-Cherry Bites** *(page 47)* 1 day ahead. Store in an airtight container.

2. About 45 minutes before the meal, prepare **Caramelized Onion and Rosemary Focaccia**.

3. While focaccia bakes, prepare **Chicken, Artichoke, and Mushroom Fettuccine** and Step 1 of **Spinach Salad with Pears and Walnuts**.

4. Assemble salads just before serving.

CHICKEN, ARTICHOKE, AND MUSHROOM FETTUCCINE

POINTS value: 5

prep: 5 minutes • cook: 15 minutes

This creamy pasta is jam-packed with veggies and roasted chicken. The shaved fresh Parmesan is optional, but it adds extra richness to the dish.

1   (9-ounce) package fresh fettuccine
Cooking spray
1   (8-ounce) package presliced mushrooms
2   tablespoons light stick butter
1   tablespoon all-purpose flour
1   cup fat-free milk
⅛   teaspoon salt
¼   teaspoon freshly ground black pepper
2   cups chopped skinless rotisserie chicken breast
1   (14-ounce) can quartered artichoke hearts, drained
2   tablespoons fresh lemon juice
¼   cup chopped green onions (optional)
Shaved fresh Parmesan cheese (optional)

1. Cook pasta according to package directions, omitting salt and fat. Drain and keep warm.

2. While pasta cooks, heat a large nonstick skillet over medium heat. Coat pan with cooking spray. Add mushrooms, and sauté 5 minutes or until mushrooms are tender and liquid evaporates, stirring frequently. Remove from pan, and keep warm.

3. Add butter to pan, and cook over medium heat 1 minute or until butter melts. Add flour, and stir with a whisk; cook 1 minute or until bubbly. Add milk, salt, and pepper; cook 3 minutes or until thick, stirring constantly.

4. Add reserved mushrooms, chicken, and artichokes to pan, stirring gently. Cook 3 minutes or until thoroughly heated. Add lemon juice and, if desired, green onions. Toss chicken mixture with pasta. Sprinkle with Parmesan cheese, if desired. YIELD: 6 servings (serving size: 1⅓ cups).

Per serving: CAL 259 (16% from fat); FAT 4.6g (sat 1.7g); PRO 23.2g; CARB 30g; FIB 2.2g; CHOL 45mg; IRON 1.3mg; SOD 473mg; CALC 59mg

SPINACH SALAD WITH PEARS AND WALNUTS

POINTS value: 3

prep: 6 minutes • cook: 1 minute

Pears are one of the few fruits that improve in flavor and texture after they're picked. The sweetness of the pear slices balances the tangy vinaigrette and sharp cheese in this colorful salad.

2 tablespoons olive oil
2 tablespoons balsamic vinegar
1 garlic clove, minced
⅛ teaspoon salt
⅛ teaspoon freshly ground black pepper
6 cups fresh baby spinach
1 small ripe red Bartlett pear, thinly sliced
¼ cup (1 ounce) crumbled goat cheese
3 tablespoons chopped walnuts, toasted

1. Combine first 5 ingredients in a small bowl; stir well with a whisk.
2. Combine spinach and pear in a large bowl. Pour vinaigrette over spinach mixture; toss gently to combine. Arrange spinach mixture evenly on plates. Top evenly with goat cheese and walnuts. YIELD: 6 servings (serving size: about 1 cup salad, 2 teaspoons goat cheese, and 1½ teaspoons walnuts).

Per serving: CAL 115 (67% from fat); FAT 8.6g (sat 2g); PRO 3.1g; CARB 8.3g; FIB 2.2g; CHOL 5mg; IRON 1mg; SOD 106mg; CALC 65mg

CARAMELIZED ONION AND ROSEMARY FOCACCIA

POINTS value: 2

prep: 5 minutes • cook: 38 minutes

Olive oil–flavored cooking spray
1 large onion, halved and thinly sliced
¼ teaspoon freshly ground black pepper
1 to 2 tablespoons water
1 (13.8-ounce) can refrigerated pizza crust dough
2 teaspoons olive oil
1 tablespoon chopped fresh rosemary
1 teaspoon kosher salt

1. Heat a large nonstick skillet over medium-high heat. Coat pan with cooking spray. Add onion and pepper. Cover and cook 10 minutes or until onion is lightly browned, stirring occasionally. Uncover and cook 10 minutes or until golden brown, stirring frequently. While onion cooks, add 1 to 2 tablespoons water to prevent onion from sticking to pan. Remove from heat; set aside.
2. Preheat oven to 375°.
3. Unroll dough into a jelly-roll pan, and flatten slightly. Press handle of a wooden spoon into dough to make indentations at 1-inch intervals. Drizzle with oil; sprinkle with rosemary and salt. Bake at 375° for 15 minutes or until lightly browned; top with onion, and bake an additional 3 minutes or until golden. Cut bread into rectangles, and serve warm. YIELD: 12 servings (serving size: 1 piece).

Per serving: CAL 93 (18% from fat); FAT 1.9g (sat 0.4g); PRO 2.6g; CARB 16.9g; FIB 0.2g; CHOL 0mg; IRON 0.9mg; SOD 393mg; CALC 3mg

LAYERED AMARETTI–ICE CREAM LOAF

POINTS value: 6

prep: 10 minutes • cook: 2 minutes
other: 8 hours

Our Test Kitchens staff raved over this layered ice cream dessert, and your guests will too.

⅓ cup sliced almonds, toasted
2 cups chocolate fat-free ice cream, softened
1 cup crushed amaretti cookies, divided (about 14 cookies)
2 cups caramel praline light frozen yogurt (such as Edy's), softened
2 cups coffee light ice cream, softened
10 tablespoons fat-free fudge topping

1. Line an 8 x 4–inch loaf pan with plastic wrap, letting plastic wrap extend over sides of pan. Sprinkle toasted almonds evenly in pan. Carefully spoon chocolate ice cream over almonds, and spread evenly. Top chocolate ice cream with ½ cup crushed cookies. Spoon frozen yogurt over cookies, and spread. Top frozen yogurt evenly with remaining ½ cup cookies. Spoon coffee ice cream over cookies, and spread.
2. Cover with plastic wrap, and freeze 8 hours or until firm.
3. Invert pan onto a serving plate, and remove plastic wrap. Cut into vertical slices; serve with fudge topping. YIELD: 10 servings (serving size: 1 slice and 1 tablespoon topping).

Per serving: CAL 271 (23% from fat); FAT 6.8g (sat 3.3g); PRO 6.2g; CARB 47.5g; FIB 2.2g; CHOL 10mg; IRON 0.3mg; SOD 164mg; CALC 67mg

Thai Night

Serves 6 • Total **POINTS** value: 13

Basil Spring Rolls with Asian Dipping Sauce
Thai Red Curry Chicken and Vegetables • Pineapple-Orange Sherbet

▶▶ GAME PLAN

1. One day in advance, prepare **Pineapple-Orange Sherbet,** and freeze.

2. Two hours before the meal, prepare ingredients for **Thai Red Curry Chicken and Vegetables** (except rice).

3. One hour before the meal, prepare **Asian Dipping Sauce** and **Basil Spring Rolls.** Cover spring rolls to keep them from drying out.

4. Prepare jasmine rice according to package directions, omitting salt and fat. You'll need 1 cup uncooked jasmine rice to yield 3 cups cooked rice.

5. While rice cooks, prepare Steps 1 through 3 of **Thai Red Curry Chicken and Vegetables.**

THAI RED CURRY CHICKEN AND VEGETABLES

POINTS value: 8

prep: 25 minutes • cook: 18 minutes

2½ tablespoons cornstarch
2   tablespoons water
2⅓ cups light coconut milk
½   cup fat-free, less-sodium chicken broth
2   tablespoons fish sauce
1½ tablespoons minced fresh ginger
1   tablespoon red curry paste
1   tablespoon honey
1½ teaspoons grated fresh lime rind (about 2 limes)
2   large garlic cloves, minced
1   jalapeño pepper, seeded and minced
1   tablespoon peanut oil, divided
1½ pounds skinless, boneless chicken breast, cut diagonally into thin strips
3   cups sugar snap peas, trimmed
2   cups thin red bell pepper strips
1   cup thinly diagonally sliced carrot (2 large)
½   cup chopped onion
⅓   cup chopped unsalted, dry-roasted peanuts
¼   cup chopped fresh cilantro
6   lime wedges
3   cups hot cooked jasmine rice

1. Combine cornstarch and water in a medium bowl, stirring until smooth. Add coconut milk and next 8 ingredients, stirring well. Set aside.

2. Heat ½ tablespoon oil in a large, deep nonstick skillet over medium-high heat. Add chicken to pan; sauté 5 minutes or until done. Remove chicken from pan, and set aside. Add remaining ½ tablespoon oil to pan.

3. Add peas and next 3 ingredients to pan; sauté 3 minutes or just until crisp-tender. Stir in coconut milk mixture. Bring to a boil over medium-high heat; cook 3 to 4 minutes or until thick. Return chicken to pan; cook 1 to 2 minutes or until chicken is thoroughly heated.

4. Spoon chicken mixture into bowls; top with peanuts, cilantro, and lime wedges. Serve immediately with rice.

YIELD: 6 servings (serving size: 1⅔ cups chicken mixture, about 1 tablespoon peanuts, 2 teaspoons cilantro, 1 lime wedge, and ½ cup rice).

Per serving: CAL 379 (30% from fat); FAT 12.8g (sat 5.9g); PRO 32.8g; CARB 34.8g; FIB 3.7g; CHOL 66mg; IRON 2.5mg; SOD 677mg; CALC 64mg

BASIL SPRING ROLLS WITH ASIAN DIPPING SAUCE

POINTS value: 2

prep: 33 minutes • cook: 5 minutes
other: 4 minutes

This is an authentic appetizer for a Thai-style meal. Make sure to roll the spring rolls tightly so you'll experience every layer of flavor in each bite.

1   ounce uncooked rice noodles
¼   cup julienne-cut English cucumber
¼   cup julienne-cut carrot
2   tablespoons rice wine vinegar, divided
¼   cup julienne-cut yellow bell pepper
¼   cup fresh bean sprouts
6   (8-inch) round sheets rice paper
12 basil leaves
12 medium cooked shrimp, peeled, deveined, and halved lengthwise (about ¼ pound)
¼   cup chopped fresh cilantro
¼   cup chopped fresh mint
½   cup shredded romaine lettuce
Asian Dipping Sauce

1. Place noodles in a small bowl; cover with boiling water. Let stand 1 minute, and drain.
2. Place cucumber and carrot in separate small bowls; add 1 tablespoon rice wine vinegar to each bowl, and let stand while cutting and measuring remaining ingredients.
3. Combine cucumber, carrot, bell pepper, and bean sprouts. Divide into 6 piles.
4. Place 1 inch hot water in a large shallow dish. Add 1 sheet rice paper

to dish; let stand 30 seconds or until soft. Remove rice paper from dish, and place 2 basil leaves in center of paper. Top with about 2 tablespoons cooked rice noodles and 4 shrimp halves. Sprinkle with 2 teaspoons cilantro and 2 teaspoons mint. Pack 1 pile of bell pepper mixture tightly, and place on top of herbs. Place about 1 tablespoon shredded lettuce next to bell pepper mixture.
5. Fold sides of rice paper over filling; roll up tightly, jelly-roll fashion. Gently press seam to seal. Place spring roll, seam side down, on a serving platter (cover to keep from drying). Repeat procedure 5 times. Serve with Asian Dipping Sauce.
YIELD: 6 servings (serving size: 1 spring roll and about 1 tablespoon sauce).

Per serving: CAL 95 (8% from fat); FAT 0.8g (sat 0.1g); PRO 5.5g; CARB 16.5g; FIB 1.1g; CHOL 37mg; IRON 1.4mg; SOD 248mg; CALC 37mg

ASIAN DIPPING SAUCE
POINTS value: 0

3   tablespoons rice wine vinegar
2   tablespoons low-sodium soy sauce
1   teaspoon minced fresh ginger
½   teaspoon brown sugar
½   teaspoon dark sesame oil
½   teaspoon chile paste with garlic (such as Sambal Oelek)

1. Combine all ingredients in a small bowl; stir well with a whisk. YIELD: about ⅓ cup.

Per tablespoon: CAL 8 (56% from fat); FAT 0.5g (sat 0.1g); PRO 0.3g; CARB 1g; FIB 0.1g; CHOL 0mg; IRON 0.1mg; SOD 214mg; CALC 1mg

PINEAPPLE-ORANGE SHERBET

POINTS value: 3

prep: 20 minutes • cook: 7 minutes
other: 2 hours and 20 minutes

If you're in a hurry, set the saucepan in an ice-water bath for 5 to 10 minutes, stirring often. This will quickly chill the sherbet mixture before freezing.

2   navel oranges
1   lemon
1½ cups water
2   cups fresh orange juice
6   tablespoons fresh lemon juice
2   (6-ounce) cans unsweetened pineapple juice
1   (14-ounce) can fat-free sweetened condensed milk

1. Carefully remove rind from oranges and lemon using a vegetable peeler, making sure to avoid white pithy part of the rind. Combine water and citrus strips in a saucepan; bring to a boil, reduce heat, and simmer, uncovered, 3 minutes. Remove from heat, and cool 15 minutes.
2. Remove citrus strips from water; discard strips. Combine juices in a bowl. Stir in citrus water and milk. Cover and chill 30 minutes.
3. Pour mixture into the freezer can of an ice-cream freezer; freeze according to manufacturer's instructions. Spoon sherbet into a freezer-safe container; cover and freeze 1 hour or until firm. YIELD: 13 servings (serving size: ½ cup).

Per serving: CAL 153 (1% from fat); FAT 0.1g (sat 0g); PRO 3.6g; CARB 34.1g; FIB 0.2g; CHOL 5mg; IRON 0.2mg; SOD 44mg; CALC 116mg

Classic Thanksgiving

Serves 12 • Total **POINTS** value: 16

Herb-Roasted Turkey Breast • **Cranberry-Pecan Corn Bread Dressing**
Brussels Sprouts with Caramelized Onions and Almonds
Cranberry-Pear Relish • **Pecan Pie Squares** *(page 48)*

GAME PLAN

1. Up to 3 days in advance, prepare the corn bread for **Cranberry-Pecan Corn Bread Dressing** (Steps 1 and 2). Prepare **Cranberry-Pear Relish;** cover and chill.

2. One day ahead, prepare **Pecan Pie Squares** *(page 48)*. Store in an airtight container.

3. Two and a half hours before the meal, prepare **Herb-Roasted Turkey Breast.**

4. Twenty minutes before turkey is done, prepare **Cranberry-Pecan Corn Bread Dressing.**

5. Remove turkey from oven, and keep warm. Increase oven temperature, and bake dressing. Prepare **Brussels Sprouts with Caramelized Onions and Almonds** on stovetop.

CRANBERRY-PECAN CORN BREAD DRESSING

POINTS value: 3

prep: 27 minutes • cook: 50 minutes

½   cup all-purpose flour
½   cup yellow cornmeal
1   teaspoon baking powder
½   teaspoon salt
1   teaspoon sugar
½   cup 1% low-fat milk
1   large egg, lightly beaten
Cooking spray
1   tablespoon butter
¾   cup chopped onion
    (½ medium)
½   cup chopped celery (1 stalk)
2   teaspoons chopped fresh sage
1   teaspoon chopped fresh thyme
¼   teaspoon black pepper
½   cup chopped pecans, toasted
½   cup dried cranberries
1   (14-ounce) can fat-free, less-sodium chicken broth
¼   cup 1% low-fat milk
1   large egg
1   large egg white

1. Preheat oven to 425°.
2. Combine first 5 ingredients in a medium bowl. Combine ½ cup milk and 1 egg in a small bowl, stirring well.

Add milk mixture to dry ingredients, stirring just until moist. Pour batter into an 8-inch square pan coated with cooking spray. Bake at 425° for 13 minutes or until golden. Cool in pan.
3. Reduce oven temperature to 350°.
4. Crumble corn bread into small pieces in a large bowl.
5. Melt butter over medium heat in a medium nonstick skillet. Add onion and celery, and sauté 4 minutes or until tender. Stir in sage, thyme, and pepper. Add celery mixture, pecans, and cranberries to crumbled corn bread, and stir.
6. Combine chicken broth, ¼ cup milk, egg, and egg white. Add chicken broth mixture to corn bread mixture, stirring gently to combine. Spoon mixture into an 8-inch square pan coated with cooking spray. Bake at 350° for 30 minutes or until set and lightly browned. YIELD: 12 servings (serving size: ⅓ cup).

Per serving: CAL 131 (39% from fat); FAT 5.7g (sat 1.3g); PRO 4g; CARB 16.3g; FIB 1.3g; CHOL 38mg; IRON 0.8mg; SOD 218mg; CALC 36mg

HERB-ROASTED TURKEY BREAST

POINTS value: 5

prep: 7 minutes
cook: 1 hour and 20 minutes

You can bake a turkey breast in much less time than it takes to prepare and roast a whole bird. And a turkey breast will still feed a crowd of twelve.

1 teaspoon chopped fresh sage
1 teaspoon chopped fresh rosemary
1 teaspoon chopped fresh thyme
1 teaspoon black pepper
½ teaspoon salt
2 garlic cloves, minced
2 tablespoons olive oil
1 (6-pound) bone-in turkey breast
Cooking spray

1. Preheat oven to 325°.
2. Combine first 6 ingredients in a small bowl; add olive oil, and stir with a whisk.
3. Pat turkey dry with paper towels. Loosen skin from breast by inserting fingers, gently pushing between skin and meat. Rub olive oil mixture under loosened skin. Coat turkey with cooking spray. Place turkey on a rack in a small roasting pan. Cover loosely with foil. Bake at 325° for 1 hour and 20 minutes or until a thermometer inserted in thickest portion of breast registers 165°. Remove turkey skin before serving. YIELD: 12 servings (serving size: about 4 ounces).

Per serving: CAL 213 (14% from fat); FAT 3.4g (sat 0.7g); PRO 42.6g; CARB 0.3g; FIB 0.1g; CHOL 118mg; IRON 2.2mg; SOD 172mg; CALC 19mg

BRUSSELS SPROUTS WITH CARAMELIZED ONIONS AND ALMONDS

POINTS value: 1

prep: 8 minutes • cook: 21 minutes

2 tablespoons butter
2 cups sliced onion
2 garlic cloves, minced
2 pounds Brussels sprouts, trimmed and sliced
2 tablespoons balsamic vinegar
4 teaspoons sugar
1 teaspoon salt
½ teaspoon black pepper
¼ cup slivered almonds, toasted

1. Melt butter in a large, deep non-stick skillet over medium heat. Add onion; cover and cook 3 minutes. Uncover and cook 10 minutes, stirring frequently. Add garlic; sauté 1 minute. Add Brussels sprouts; cover and cook 5 minutes or until crisp-tender. Remove from heat.
2. Combine vinegar and next 3 ingredients; add to Brussels sprouts mixture, tossing gently. Top with almonds. YIELD: 12 servings (serving size: about ½ cup).

Per serving: CAL 75 (40% from fat); FAT 3.3g (sat 1.3g); PRO 3.1g; CARB 10.4g; FIB 3.2g; CHOL 5mg; IRON 1.1mg; SOD 229mg; CALC 41mg

CRANBERRY-PEAR RELISH

POINTS value: 2

prep: 11 minutes • cook: 15 minutes
other: 2 hours

The aroma of orange, cranberry, and cinnamon simmering together lets you know that the holidays are here.

1 (12-ounce) package fresh cranberries
1½ cups diced peeled pear (about 3)
2 teaspoons grated fresh orange rind
1 cup fresh orange juice
¾ cup packed brown sugar
¼ teaspoon salt
⅛ teaspoon ground allspice
2 (3-inch) cinnamon sticks
⅓ cup chopped pecans, toasted

1. Combine first 8 ingredients in a large saucepan. Bring to a boil over medium-high heat, stirring frequently. Reduce heat; simmer, uncovered, 10 minutes or until berries pop. Cool to room temperature (about 2 hours).
2. Remove and discard cinnamon sticks. Stir in pecans. Cover and chill. YIELD: 3¾ cups (serving size: ¼ cup).

Per serving: CAL 90 (20% from fat); FAT 2g (sat 0.2g); PRO 0.4g; CARB 18.4g; FIB 1.7g; CHOL 0mg; IRON 0.3mg; SOD 44mg; CALC 15mg

a toast to nuts

You can toast nuts quickly in a skillet or in the microwave oven. Place the nuts in a dry skillet, and cook them over medium heat 1 to 2 minutes or until they're toasted, stirring frequently. To toast in the microwave oven, place the nuts in a shallow microwave-safe dish, and microwave at HIGH 1 to 3 minutes, stirring every 30 seconds. The nuts won't turn golden, but they'll have a toasted flavor.

One day's menu provides at least two servings of dairy and at least five servings of fruits and/or vegetables.

	MONDAY	TUESDAY	WEDNESDAY	THURSDAY
BREAKFAST	**1% low-fat cottage cheese**, ½ cup **fresh peach slices**, ½ cup (1 medium) ✓	**Weight Watchers English muffin**, 1 **all-fruit spread**, 2 tablespoons **light stick butter**, 2 teaspoons **strawberry light nonfat yogurt**, 1 (6-ounce) carton **light orange juice**, 1 cup	**whole-grain puffed cereal**, 1 cup ✓ **blueberries**, 1 cup ✓ **fat-free milk**, 1 cup ✓ **light orange juice**, 1 cup	**Breakfast Muffinwich** (Whisk together 1 large egg, 3 large egg whites, and a dash each of salt and black pepper. Scramble in a small skillet over medium heat. Place a [¾-ounce] slice Cheddar cheese over eggs. Gently spoon mixture between cut sides of a toasted Weight Watchers English muffin - **POINTS value: 6**.) **peach**, 1 medium ✓
LUNCH	**Chicken and Edamame Asian Salad, page 119**, 2 servings **grapes**, 1 cup ✓ **lemon cream pie light nonfat yogurt**, 1 (6-ounce) carton	**canned hearty vegetable and pasta soup**, 1 cup **Minted Melon Toss** (Combine ½ cup each of cubed honeydew melon and watermelon. Whisk together ½ teaspoon chopped fresh mint and 2 tablespoons light orange juice. Pour over melon, and toss - **POINTS value: 1**.) **low-fat whole wheat crackers**, 6 **fat-free milk**, 1 cup ✓	**Sweet and Spicy Turkey Melt** (Place 2 ounces smoked honey turkey breast and 1 [¾-ounce] pepper Jack cheese slice on a slice of reduced-calorie wheat bread; broil 1 to 2 minutes or until melted. Top with 2 lettuce leaves, 2 tomato slices, and additional bread slice - **POINTS value: 5**.) **cantaloupe**, 1 cup ✓ **fat-free milk**, 1 cup ✓	**bean burrito**, 1 fast-food **carrot sticks**, 10 baby ✓ **black cherry light nonfat yogurt**, 1 (6-ounce) carton
DINNER	**Pork Chops with Apricot Sauce, page 93**, 1 serving **roasted new potatoes**, 5 ounces cooked ✓ **Balsamic Asparagus, page 146**, 1 serving	**grilled tuna steak**, 6 ounces cooked ✓ **Cumin-Scented Rice with Black Beans, page 153**, 1 serving **sautéed yellow squash and zucchini**, 1 cup ✓	**hamburger**, 1 (3-ounce) cooked patty made with 10%-fat ground beef **light wheat hamburger bun**, 1 **lettuce and tomato slice**, 1 each ✓ **corn on the cob**, 1 medium ✓ **light stick butter**, 2 teaspoons **Blue Cheese Slaw, page 113**, 1 serving	**Chicken with Mushrooms and Green Onions, page 104**, 1 serving **mashed potatoes**, ½ cup **steamed green beans**, 1 cup ✓ **fat-free milk**, 1 cup ✓
SNACK	**Raspberry–Chocolate Truffle Cheesecake, page 46**, 1 serving **fat-free milk**, 1 cup ✓	**94% fat-free popcorn**, 4 cups ✓ **Weight Watchers giant cookies-and-cream ice cream bar**, 1	**apple**, 1 medium ✓ **mozzarella string cheese**, 1	**vanilla light ice cream**, ½ cup **light chocolate syrup**, 2 tablespoons **raspberries**, 1 cup ✓
POINTS VALUE	*POINTS* value for the day: 27	*POINTS* value for the day: 25	*POINTS* value for the day: 25	*POINTS* value for the day: 28

	FRIDAY	SATURDAY	SUNDAY
BREAKFAST	**whole-grain puffed cereal,** 1 cup ✓ **banana slices,** 1 small ✓ **fat-free milk,** 1 cup ✓ **light orange juice,** 1 cup	**mixed berry light smoothie,** 1 (7-ounce) container **fruit and nut granola bar,** 1 **cantaloupe,** 1 cup ✓	**Open-Faced PB&J Muffin** (Top each cut half of a toasted Weight Watchers English muffin with 1 tablespoon each of peanut butter and all-fruit spread - *POINTS* value: **7.**) **fat-free milk,** 1 cup ✓
LUNCH	**Chicken Parmesan,** 1 light frozen entrée **Strawberries and Cream** (Stir together 1 cup sliced strawberries and 1 [6-ounce] carton of vanilla light nonfat yogurt - *POINTS* value: **2.**) **carrot sticks,** 10 baby ✓	**Roast Beef and Swiss Sandwich** (Spread 2 teaspoons each of fat-free mayonnaise and Dijon mustard over 2 slices reduced-calorie bread. Place 2 ounces sliced deli lean roast beef, 1 [¾-ounce] Swiss cheese slice, 2 lettuce leaves, and 2 tomato slices on 1 bread slice; top with remaining bread slice - *POINTS* value: **5.**) **coleslaw,** ½ cup **fat-free milk,** 1 cup ✓	**Fruit and Cheese Plate** (Arrange lettuce leaves on plate; top with ½ cup each of 1% low-fat cottage cheese, peach slices, and blueberries. Garnish with 6 low-fat whole wheat crackers - *POINTS* value: **5.**) **strawberry banana light nonfat yogurt,** 1 (6-ounce) carton
DINNER	**Shrimp and White Beans, page 75,** 1 serving **Tender Bibb, Orange, and Bacon Salad, page 113,** 1 serving	**Slow-Cooker Chicken-Sausage Paella, page 99,** 1 serving **mixed fruit salad,** 1 cup ✓	**teriyaki-flavored pork tenderloin,** 4 ounces cooked **baked sweet potato,** 1 medium (4 ounces cooked) ✓ **light stick butter,** 2 teaspoons **Broccoli with Garlic-Herb Butter, page 146,** 2 servings
SNACK	**Layered Bean Dip, page 19,** 2 servings **baked bite-size tortilla chips,** 20 **carrot sticks,** 10 baby ✓	**Key Lime–Berry Parfait** (Layer ½ of a 6-ounce carton of key lime pie light nonfat yogurt; ½ cup sliced strawberries; and ½ low-fat graham cracker sheet, crumbled, in a parfait glass; repeat layers once - *POINTS* value: **4.**)	**94% fat-free popcorn,** 4 cups ✓ **apple,** 1 medium ✓
POINTS VALUE	*POINTS* value for the day: **25**	*POINTS* value for the day: **28**	*POINTS* value for the day: **27**

One day's menu provides at least two servings of dairy and at least five servings of fruits and/or vegetables.

	MONDAY	TUESDAY	WEDNESDAY	THURSDAY
BREAKFAST	**instant grits**, 1 packet ✓ **light stick butter**, 2 teaspoons **turkey bacon**, 3 slices	**wheat bran flakes cereal with raisins**, 1 cup **banana**, 1 small ✓ **fat-free milk**, 1 cup ✓	**scrambled eggs**, 1 large egg and 3 large egg whites ✓ **reduced-calorie whole wheat toast**, 2 slices **light stick butter**, 2 teaspoons **grapefruit sections**, 1 cup ✓	**Garlic Cheese Grits** (Prepare 1 packet instant grits according to package directions. Add ¼ cup reduced-fat shredded sharp Cheddar cheese and a dash of garlic salt; stir until cheese melts - *POINTS* value: **4**.) **peach light nonfat yogurt**, 1 (6-ounce) carton
LUNCH	**cheeseburger**, 1 small fast-food **side salad**, 1 fast-food ✓ **low-fat Italian dressing**, 1 packet **fat-free milk**, 1 cup ✓	**Pasta Salad with Black Beans and Tomatoes, page 116**, 2 servings over 1 cup **romaine lettuce** **pineapple cubes**, 1 cup ✓ **lemon cream pie light nonfat yogurt**, 1 (6-ounce) carton	**Mexican Chicken Spud** (Cut a large baked potato [7 ounces cooked] in half; top with ½ cup shredded chicken breast and ¼ cup each shredded 2% reduced-fat Mexican cheese and salsa. Dollop with 2 tablespoons fat-free sour cream and 1 tablespoon chopped green onions - *POINTS* value: **8**.) **grapes**, 1 cup ✓ **fat-free milk**, 1 cup ✓	**Turkey Club** (Spread 2 teaspoons fat-free mayonnaise over 2 slices toasted reduced-calorie bread. Place 1 ounce each of sliced lean deli ham and turkey; 1 [¾-ounce] Swiss cheese slice; 2 lettuce leaves; 2 tomato slices; and 1 turkey bacon slice, halved, on 1 bread slice; top with remaining bread slice - *POINTS* value: **6**.) **Cranberry Salad, page 112**, 1 serving
DINNER	**baked skinless, boneless chicken breast**, 4 ounces cooked ✓ **Roasted Sweet Potatoes with Bacon, Apple, and Thyme, page 149**, 1 serving **steamed green beans**, 1 cup ✓	**Pork Medallions with Dried Cherries, page 95**, 1 serving **wild rice**, 1 cup ✓ **steamed sugar snap peas**, 1 cup ✓	**grilled grouper**, 6 ounces cooked ✓ **Tomato Fettuccine** (Toss 1 cup hot cooked whole wheat fettuccine with 1 teaspoon olive oil and ⅛ teaspoon salt; gently stir in ½ diced ripe tomato and 1 tablespoon chopped fresh basil - *POINTS* value: **4**.) ✓ **Mesclun with Red Grapefruit and Feta, page 114**, 1 serving	**Rustic Skillet Kielbasa and Vegetables over Polenta, page 110**, 1 serving ✓ **spinach salad**, 2 cups ✓ **light Italian dressing**, 2 tablespoons
SNACK	**apple**, 1 medium ✓ **peanut butter**, 1 tablespoon **fat-free milk**, 1 cup ✓	**Red Velvet Cupcakes, page 43**, 1 serving	**strawberry light smoothie**, 1 (7-ounce) container **carrot sticks**, 10 baby ✓	**multigrain rice cakes**, 2 **peanut butter**, 1 tablespoon **fat-free milk**, 1 cup ✓
POINTS VALUE	*POINTS* value for the day: 29	*POINTS* value for the day: 26	*POINTS* value for the day: 27	*POINTS* value for the day: 25

	FRIDAY	SATURDAY	SUNDAY
BREAKFAST	**wheat bran flakes cereal with raisins,** 1 cup **fat-free milk,** 1 cup ✓ **light apple juice,** 1 cup	**instant grits,** 1 packet ✓ **light stick butter,** 2 teaspoons **black cherry light nonfat yogurt,** 1 (6-ounce) carton	**Southwestern Frittata, page 78,** 1 serving **turkey bacon,** 3 slices **blueberry light nonfat yogurt,** 1 (6-ounce) carton
LUNCH	**canned broccoli-cheese soup (made with fat-free milk),** 1 cup **Parmesan-Basil Biscuits, page 29,** 1 serving **pineapple chunks,** 1 cup ✓	**ham and Cheddar hot sandwich,** 1 frozen light pocket **apple,** 1 medium ✓ **carrot sticks,** 10 baby ✓	**Turkey Cobb Salad** (Arrange ½ cup diced turkey breast, ½ cup diced tomato, and 1 chopped hard-cooked egg over 2 cups romaine lettuce. Serve with 2 tablespoons light blue cheese dressing - **POINTS** value: **6.**) **low-fat whole wheat crackers,** 6 **orange,** 1 medium ✓
DINNER	**Burgundy Pot Roast, page 91,** 1 serving **Cauliflower with Green Onions and Parmesan, page 147,** 2 servings **corn bread,** 1 (2-inch) square	**Spicy Chicken-Spinach Pasta Bake, page 100,** 1 serving **romaine lettuce,** 2 cups ✓ **light balsamic vinaigrette,** 2 tablespoons **fat-free milk,** 1 cup ✓	**Sweet-and-Sour Fish Kebabs, page 68,** 1 serving **brown rice,** ½ cup ✓ **steamed broccoli,** 1 cup ✓
SNACK	**Raspberry-Banana Smoothie** (Combine 1 small frozen banana, 1 cup raspberries, and 1 [6-ounce] carton vanilla light nonfat yogurt in a blender; process until smooth - **POINTS** value: **4.**)	**multigrain rice cakes,** 2 **watermelon,** 1 cup cubed ✓ **mozzarella string cheese,** 1	**Chocolate-Filled Brioche, page 34,** 1 serving **fat-free milk,** 1 cup ✓
POINTS VALUE	**POINTS** value for the day: 27	**POINTS** value for the day: 26	**POINTS** value for the day: 26

One day's menu provides at least two servings of dairy and at least five servings of fruits and/or vegetables.

	MONDAY	TUESDAY	WEDNESDAY	THURSDAY
BREAKFAST	**Weight Watchers hearth-baked bagel**, 1 **light cream cheese**, 2 tablespoons **strawberries**, 1½ cups ✓ **light cranberry juice**, 1 cup	**low-fat whole-grain waffles**, 2 **light syrup**, 2 tablespoons **banana**, 1 small ✓ **fat-free milk**, 1 cup ✓	**Pumpkin Streusel Muffins, page 31**, 1 serving **strawberry-banana light smoothie**, 1 (7-ounce) container	**poached egg**, 1 large ✓ **reduced-calorie bread**, 2 slices **light stick butter**, 2 teaspoons **peach light nonfat yogurt**, 1 (6-ounce) carton
LUNCH	**supreme vegetable pizza**, 1 light frozen entrée **blueberry light nonfat yogurt**, 1 (6-ounce) carton **carrot sticks**, 10 baby ✓	**Turkey Chowder, page 160**, 1½ servings **Cheese Toast** (Place 1 [¾-ounce] reduced-fat Cheddar cheese slice on 1 slice reduced-calorie bread. Broil 1 to 2 minutes until melted and bubbly - *POINTS* value: **2**.) **cherries**, 1 cup ✓	**Tortellini Primavera, page 83**, 1 serving over 1 cup **spinach leaves** **honeydew melon**, 1 cup ✓ **fat-free milk**, 1 cup ✓	**Tuna Salad Plate** (Combine ½ cup drained canned tuna in water with 2 tablespoons chopped celery, 1 tablespoon low-fat mayonnaise, 1 teaspoon Dijon mustard, and a dash each of salt and black pepper. Spoon over 1 cup spinach leaves and 4 tomato slices - *POINTS* value: **4**.) **low-fat wheat crackers**, 6 **grapes**, 1 cup ✓
DINNER	**Cilantro-Garlic Shrimp, page 76**, 1 serving ✓ **mixed salad greens**, 1 cup ✓ **reduced-fat olive oil vinaigrette**, 1 tablespoon **french bread**, 1 ounce	**baked pork loin**, 3 ounces cooked and trimmed of fat ✓ **Caramelized Onion Rice, page 153**, 1 serving **steamed broccoli and carrots**, 1 cup ✓ **fat-free milk**, 1 cup ✓	**rotisserie chicken breast**, 4 ounces breast meat with skin removed ✓ **Warm Fingerling Potato Salad, page 115**, 1 serving **steamed asparagus**, 12 spears ✓	**Mexican Skillet Supper, page 87**, 1 serving **Oven-Roasted Zucchini, page 149**, 2 servings ✓
SNACK	**gingersnaps**, 4 cookies **fat-free milk**, 1 cup ✓	**Winter Fruit with Honey-Yogurt Sauce, page 36**, 1 serving	**Chocolate-Berry Sundae** (Top 1 cup chocolate low-fat ice cream with 1 cup sliced strawberries and 2 tablespoons light chocolate syrup - *POINTS* value: **6**.)	**Triple-Layer Mocha Toffee Cake, page 46**, 1 serving **fat-free milk**, 1 cup ✓
POINTS VALUE	*POINTS* value for the day: **26**	*POINTS* value for the day: **26**	*POINTS* value for the day: **27**	*POINTS* value for the day: **28**

	FRIDAY	SATURDAY	SUNDAY
BREAKFAST	**Weight Watchers hearth-baked bagel,** 1 **light cream cheese,** 2 tablespoons **blueberry light nonfat yogurt,** 1 (6-ounce) carton	**Asparagus-Mushroom Omelet, page 78,** 1 serving **honeydew melon,** 1 cup ✓ **light cranberry juice,** 1 cup	**Strawberry Waffles** (Toast 2 low-fat whole-grain waffles; top with 1 cup sliced strawberries, and drizzle with 2 tablespoons light syrup - **POINTS value: 5.**) **fat-free milk,** 1 cup ✓
LUNCH	**Peanut Butter–Banana Sandwich** (Spread 2 tablespoons peanut butter over 1 slice reduced-calorie bread; top with ½ cup banana slices and an additional bread slice - **POINTS value: 6.**) **fat-free milk,** 1 cup ✓	**grilled chicken sandwich,** 1 fast-food with no mayonnaise **fruit cup,** 1 ✓ **fat-free milk,** 1 cup ✓	**Ham and Cheddar Melt** (Top 1 slice of reduced-calorie bread with 2 ounces lean deli ham, 1 [¾-ounce] reduced-fat Cheddar cheese slice, and an additional slice bread. Spread 1 teaspoon light stick butter over each side of sandwich. Cook sandwich in a nonstick skillet over medium heat until browned on both sides and cheese is melted - **POINTS value: 5.**) **Broccoli Slaw Salad, page 112,** 1 serving
DINNER	**Easy Chicken Cacciatore, page 106,** 1 serving **whole wheat pasta,** 1 cup ✓ **mixed salad greens,** 2 cups ✓ **light balsamic vinaigrette,** 2 tablespoons	**Herb-Roasted Fish and Potatoes, page 69,** 1 serving ✓ **steamed green beans,** 1 cup ✓	**Portobello and Flank Steak over Greens, page 120,** 1 serving ✓ **Three-Seed Breadsticks, page 28,** 1 serving
SNACK	**Sweet and Spicy Snack Mix, page 18,** 1 serving **apple,** 1 medium ✓	**raspberry light smoothie,** 1 (7-ounce) container	**gingersnaps,** 4 cookies **banana,** 1 small ✓ **fat-free milk,** 1 cup ✓
POINTS VALUE	*POINTS* value for the day: 28	*POINTS* value for the day: 27	*POINTS* value for the day: 29

One day's menu provides at least two servings of dairy and at least five servings of fruits and/or vegetables.

	MONDAY	TUESDAY	WEDNESDAY	THURSDAY
BREAKFAST	**wheat bran flakes cereal,** 1 cup **fat-free milk,** 1 cup ✓ **blueberries,** 1 cup ✓ **light orange juice,** 1 cup	**Peanut Butter–Banana Oatmeal,** **page 152,** 1 serving **fat-free milk,** 1 cup ✓	**Scrambled Cheese Eggs** (Whisk together 1 large egg, 3 large egg whites, ¼ cup reduced-fat shredded sharp Cheddar cheese, and a dash of salt. Coat skillet with cooking spray; scramble egg mixture in skillet - ***POINTS* value: 5.**) **reduced-calorie toast,** 2 slices	**wheat bran flakes cereal,** 1 cup **fat-free milk,** 1 cup ✓ **banana,** 1 small ✓ **light orange juice,** 1 cup
LUNCH	**Easy Chicken Quesadillas,** **page 98,** 1 serving **orange,** 1 medium ✓	**Greek Salad with Chicken** (Toss together 2 cups romaine lettuce, ½ cup each of shredded cooked chicken breast, diced tomato, and sliced cucumber; 6 large pitted and sliced kalamata olives; ¼ cup crumbled reduced-fat feta cheese; and 2 tablespoons light olive oil vinaigrette - ***POINTS* value: 7.**) **key lime pie light nonfat yogurt,** 1 (6-ounce) carton	**Pesto-Beef Wrap** (Combine 2 teaspoons fat-free mayonnaise with 1 tablespoon pesto; spread over 1 [8-inch] low-fat flour tortilla. Top with 2 ounces lean deli roast beef, ¾ cup lettuce, and ¼ cup diced tomato; roll up tightly - ***POINTS* value: 6.**) **pear,** 1 medium ✓ **fat-free milk,** 1 cup ✓	**grilled vegetable burger,** 1 patty ✓ **light wheat hamburger bun,** 1 **lettuce leaf and tomato slice,** 1 each ✓ **baked potato chips,** 1 ounce **apple,** 1 medium ✓ **peach light nonfat yogurt,** 1 (6-ounce) carton
DINNER	**grilled tilapia (or other white fish),** 6 ounces cooked ✓ **Rustic Mediterranean Salad, page 115,** 1 serving over 1 cup **spinach leaves** **Grilled Rosemary Flatbreads, page 32,** 1 serving	**Beef and Bok Choy, page 88,** 1 serving ✓ **brown rice,** 1 cup ✓ **Orange-Sesame Snow Peas, page 148,** 1 serving	**Mexican Lasagna, page 83,** 1 serving **sautéed summer squash and onions,** 1 cup ✓ **strawberries,** 1½ cups ✓	**baked skinless turkey breast,** 4 ounces cooked ✓ **Baked Butternut Squash Risotto, page 154,** 1 serving **Roasted Garlic Asparagus** (Coat 12 asparagus spears with olive oil–flavored cooking spray; toss with ¼ teaspoon garlic salt. Place on a baking sheet, and bake at 450° for 8 minutes - ***POINTS* value: 0.**) ✓
SNACK	**low-fat graham crackers,** 2 sheets **peanut butter,** 1 tablespoon **fat-free milk,** 1 cup ✓	**caramel fat-free pudding cup,** 1 **pretzels,** 17 small twists	**mixed berry light smoothie,** 1 (7-ounce) container **low-fat graham crackers,** 2 sheets	**Quick Nachos** (Sprinkle ⅓ cup reduced-fat shredded Cheddar cheese over 20 bite-sized baked tortilla chips; broil 2 minutes or just until cheese melts. Serve with 2 tablespoons fat-free sour cream - ***POINTS* value: 6.**)
POINTS VALUE	***POINTS* value for the day: 26**	***POINTS* value for the day: 27**	***POINTS* value for the day: 25**	***POINTS* value for the day: 26**

	FRIDAY	SATURDAY	SUNDAY
BREAKFAST	**oatmeal,** 1 cup cooked ✓ **raisins,** 2 tablespoons **fat-free milk,** 1 cup ✓	**wheat bran flakes cereal,** 1 cup **fat-free milk,** 1 cup ✓ **light orange juice,** 1 cup	**Banana–Macadamia Nut Pancakes, page 28,** 1 serving **light syrup,** 2 tablespoons **fat-free milk,** 1 cup ✓
LUNCH	**spaghetti with meat sauce,** 1 light frozen entrée **spinach leaves,** 2 cups ✓ **light balsamic vinaigrette,** 2 tablespoons **grapes,** 1 cup ✓	**Hummus-Veggie Pizza** (Lightly toast 1 [8-inch] low-fat tortilla; spread ¼ cup hummus evenly over 1 side of tortilla. Toss together ½ cup each shredded lettuce, diced tomato, and chopped cucumber; 3 tablespoons reduced-fat feta cheese; and 2 tablespoons light balsamic vinaigrette. Spoon lettuce mixture on top of hummus - ***POINTS*** **value: 7.**) **orange,** 1 medium ✓	**Ham, Pear, and Arugula Sandwiches, page 124,** 1 serving **grapes,** 1 cup ✓ **carrot sticks,** 10 baby ✓
DINNER	**Spicy Orange-Glazed Salmon, page 70,** 1 serving **Parmesan couscous,** ½ cup **steamed broccoli,** 1 cup ✓	**grilled sirloin steak,** 4 ounces cooked and trimmed of fat ✓ **Bacon-Cheddar Potatoes, page 152,** 1 serving **steamed green beans,** 1 cup ✓	**Curried Chicken Thighs, page 108,** 1 serving **basmati rice,** ½ cup **Zucchini with Pine Nuts and Lemon, page 148,** 2 servings
SNACK	**Chocolate Cream Pie, page 41,** 1 serving **fat-free milk,** 1 cup ✓	**Blueberry-Lemon Dessert** (Spoon ½ of 1 [6-ounce] lemon cream pie light nonfat yogurt carton into a parfait glass; top with ½ cup blueberries and ½ low-fat graham cracker sheet, crumbled. Repeat layers once - ***POINTS*** **value: 4.**)	**strawberry-banana light smoothie,** 1 (7-ounce) container
POINTS VALUE	***POINTS*** **value for the day: 29**	***POINTS*** **value for the day: 28**	***POINTS*** **value for the day: 27**

general recipe index

POINTS® value and Core Plan® index

about our recipes

Each recipe has a complete list of nutrients—including calories (cal), fat, saturated fat (sat), protein (pro), carbohydrates (carb), dietary fiber (fib), cholesterol (chol), iron, sodium (sod), and calcium (calc)—as well as a serving size and the number of servings. This information makes it easy for you to use the recipes in any weight-loss program that you may choose to follow. Measurements are abbreviated g (grams) and mg (milligrams). Nutritional values used in our calculations either come from The Food Processor, Version 7.5 (ESHA Research) or are provided by food manufacturers. Numbers are based on these assumptions:

■ Unless otherwise indicated, meat, poultry, and fish refer to skinned, boned, and cooked servings.

■ When we give a range for an ingredient (3 to 3½ cups flour, for instance), we calculate using the lesser amount.

■ Some alcohol calories evaporate during heating; the analysis reflects this.

■ Only the amount of marinade absorbed by the food is used in calculation.

■ Garnishes and optional ingredients are not included in an analysis.

Safety Note: Cooking spray should never be used near direct heat. Always remove a pan from heat before spraying it with cooking spray.

A Note on Diabetic Exchanges: You may notice that the nutrient analysis for each recipe does not include Diabetic Exchanges. Most dietitians and diabetes educators are now teaching people with diabetes to count total carbohydrates at each meal and snack, rather than counting exchanges.

Almost all of our recipes can be incorporated into a diabetic diet by using the carbohydrate amount in the nutrient analysis and incorporating that into the carbohydrate amount recommended by your physician.

10 SIMPLE CORE PLAN® SIDE DISHES

vegetable	servings	preparation	cooking instructions
Asparagus	3 to 4 per pound	Snap off tough ends. Remove scales, if desired.	To steam: Cook, covered, on a rack above boiling water 2 to 3 minutes. To boil: Cook, covered, in a small amount of boiling water 2 to 3 minutes or until crisp-tender.
Broccoli	3 to 4 per pound	Remove outer leaves and tough ends of lower stalks. Wash; cut into spears.	To steam: Cook, covered, on a rack above boiling water 5 to 7 minutes or until crisp-tender.
Carrots	4 per pound	Scrape; remove ends, and rinse. Leave tiny carrots whole; slice large carrots.	To steam: Cook, covered, on a rack above boiling water 8 to 10 minutes or until crisp-tender. To boil: Cook, covered, in a small amount of boiling water 8 to 10 minutes or until crisp-tender.
Cauliflower	4 per medium head	Remove outer leaves and stalk. Wash. Break into florets.	To steam: Cook, covered, on a rack above boiling water 5 to 7 minutes or until crisp-tender.
Corn	4 per 4 large ears	Remove husks and silks. Leave corn on the cob, or cut off kernels.	Cook, covered, in boiling water to cover 8 to 10 minutes (on cob) or in a small amount of boiling water 4 to 6 minutes (kernels).
Green beans	4 per pound	Wash; trim ends, and remove strings. Cut into 1½-inch pieces.	To steam: Cook, covered, on a rack above boiling water 5 to 7 minutes. To boil: Cook, covered, in a small amount of boiling water 5 to 7 minutes or until crisp-tender.
Potatoes	3 to 4 per pound	Scrub; peel, if desired. Leave whole, slice, or cut into chunks.	To boil: Cook, covered, in boiling water to cover 30 to 40 minutes (whole) or 15 to 20 minutes (slices or chunks). To bake: Bake at 400° for 1 hour or until done.
Snow peas	4 per pound	Wash; trim ends, and remove tough strings.	To steam: Cook, covered, on a rack above boiling water 2 to 3 minutes. Or sauté in cooking spray or 1 teaspoon oil over medium-high heat 3 to 4 minutes or until crisp-tender.
Squash, summer	3 to 4 per pound	Wash; trim ends, and slice or chop.	To steam: Cook, covered, on a rack above boiling water 6 to 8 minutes. To boil: Cook, covered, in a small amount of boiling water 6 to 8 minutes or until crisp-tender.
Squash, winter (including acorn, butternut, and buttercup)	2 per pound	Rinse; cut in half, and remove all seeds. Leave in halves to bake, or peel and cube to boil.	To boil: Cook cubes, covered, in boiling water 20 to 25 minutes. To bake: Place halves, cut sides down, in a shallow baking dish; add ½ inch water. Bake, uncovered, at 375° for 30 minutes. Turn and season, or fill; bake an additional 20 to 30 minutes or until tender.